All Time Belongs to Him

All time is God's time. When the eternal Word assumed human existence at his Incarnation, he also assumed temporality. He drew time into the sphere of eternity. Christ is himself the bridge between time and eternity. At first it seems as if there can be no connection between the 'always' of eternity and the 'flowing away' of time. But now the Eternal One himself has taken time to himself In the Son, time co-exists with eternity. God's eternity is not mere timelessness, the negation of time, but a power over time that is really present with time and in time. In the Word incarnate, who remains man forever, the presence of eternity with time becomes bodily and concrete. All time is God's time.

Joseph Cardinal Ratzinger, *The Spirit of the Liturgy*

All Time Belongs to Him

Seasons and Feasts of the Lord

Hugh Gilbert OSB

GRACEWING

First published in England in 2024
by
Gracewing
2 Southern Avenue
Leominster
Herefordshire HR6 0QF
United Kingdom
www.gracewing.co.uk

No part of this publication may be reproduced, stored in a retrieval system, or transmitted in any form or by any means, electronic, mechanical, photocopying, recording or otherwise, without the written permission of the publisher.

The right of Hugh Gilbert OSB to be identified as the author of this work has been asserted in accordance with the Copyright, Designs and Patents Act 1988.

© 2024 Hugh Gilbert OSB

ISBN 978 085244 992 9

Typeset by Gracewing

Cover design by Bernardita Peña Hurtado
Featuring the new Crucifix in St Mary's Cathedral, Aberdeen by Martin Earle and Jim Blackstone which was awarded the Sr Mary Paula Beierschmitt Grand Prize by the Catholic Art Institute of Chicago.

Contents

Foreword ix

Introduction xv

Advent—The Coming of Christ 1

The Four Sundays of Advent 9

The Immaculate Conception of the Blessed Virgin Mary 21

Christmas Eve 25

Christmas Midnight Mass 33

Christmas Day 37

The Feast of St Stephen 45

The Feast of the Holy Family 49

Mary, Mother of God 53

Epiphany 59

The Baptism of the Lord 71

The Presentation of the Lord 75

Ash Wednesday 83

The Five Sundays of Lent 87

The Solemnity of St Joseph 105

The Annunciation 111

Palm Sunday 117

Maundy Thursday 121

Good Friday 125

The Easter Vigil 129
Easter Sunday 133
The Fifty Days of Easter 137
Behold the Lamb of God 143
The Seven Sundays of Easter 161
The Ascension of the Lord 177
Solemnity of Pentecost 181
Solemnity of the Holy Trinity 189
Solemnity of Corpus Christi 199
Solemnity of the Sacred Heart 211
Solemnity of St John the Baptist 221
Solemnity of Saints Peter and Paul 225
The Feast of St Mary Magdalene 229
The Transfiguration of the Lord 239
Solemnity of the Assumption 245
Nativity of the Blessed Virgin Mary 255
Exaltation of the Cross 259
Saints Michael, Gabriel and Raphael 265
The Guardian Angels 271
All Saints 277
Commemoration of All Souls 281
The Solemnity of St Andrew 285
Christ the Universal King 291

Foreword

All Time Belongs to Him—indeed, an apt title for this book and a phrase that acts as shorthand, meaning to evoke the more ample liturgical text from which the phrase is drawn. It comes from words that a bishop or a priest uses at the solemn beginning of the Paschal Vigil, as he carefully cuts and marks a cross onto the Paschal Candle, saying slowly and deliberately as the cross is cut, 'Christ yesterday and today, the Beginning and the End.' Then he says, 'The Alpha and the Omega', as he traces these letters, titles for Christ, atop the cross and at its bottom. Next he says, 'All time belongs to him', the title for this book. But here we can recall that with these words the bishop or the priest puts the first number of the current year into the left-hand corner of the cross, and continues placing the three other numbers of the year into the other corners, as he says, 'and all the ages. To him be glory and power through every age and for ever.'

Words as simple and eloquent as these, thoughts as deep as these, combined with images and symbols as bold and strong as these—that is what is offered us here in this collection of Bishop Hugh Gilbert's homilies in his cathedral in Aberdeen, Scotland. *All Time Belongs to Him*—the present year, the year in which we are alive, is inserted into the very heart of the Cross on this paschal night in which we remember that the one crucified on that Cross is risen. But this is the radiant centre of the entire liturgical year, and Bishop Hugh's homilies move through the whole year, speaking to his people and teaching them just how Christ crucified and risen is, in the end, the deepest meaning of every season, every feast, every Sunday.

It is fitting and right to present these homilies according to the liturgical year. What emerges from this is that the liturgical year, the mysteries it commemorates and makes present, is clearly the spiritual dimension of whatever might be the pastoral programme of this bishop's diocese. Yes, these homilies could be of help to those who preach in the liturgy—bishops, priests, and deacons—to prepare their own homilies. But I don't think this book is primarily a 'tips for homilies' guide of which there are so many (regrettably?) on the market. Rather, what is presented here is one bishop's way, in the concrete circumstances of his own local church, of feeding his faithful with the riches of the liturgy as these are contained season after season, Sunday after Sunday, feast after feast, throughout the liturgical year. This is sharing that can only awaken in bishops and priests a question of how they might find their own way of doing the same.

That said, the audience of this book ought not be limited to those entrusted through ordination with the responsibility of preaching. This is a book that can also profitably be read by the lay faithful, for it is to these that the words of Bishop Hugh are addressed. One hears said again and again how hungry the lay faithful are for good preaching. Well, here it is. Reading and meditating on these homilies can help them to deepen in the mysteries of the liturgical year, and it may help them to indicate to their pastors the kind of preaching they long to hear, the kind of preaching that can be nourishment for them.

What are its features? What makes this attractive preaching? There are no tricks here, no special techniques. It is basic, solid, traditional teaching. It is like spiritual meat and potatoes, but so good as such that it is exquisite meat and potatoes. 'Exquisite' would not be the average adjective used to describe a satisfying dish of meat and potatoes, but when something so basic tastes especially good and is especially nourishing, then some word like this is perhaps needed.

Sometimes bishops and priests and deacons who sit down to prepare a homily perhaps think, without quite realizing it and with mild anxiety, that they will have to come up with something to say. There is an obvious way in which this is, of course, true, and it can be stressful if one thinks of it that way week after week. And the faithful who come to participate in the liturgy may come wondering what the preacher might say that day, and they may even have their own expectations of what they think he ought to say. Bishop Hugh's homilies do not give the impression of one who has cleverly come up once again with something to say, nor do they seemed shaped by any misplaced conceptions of what others might wish their bishop to say. Instead, here are homilies that indicate that it is the Lord himself, present in the liturgy and in the one preaching, who has come up with something to say. Or better put, here are homilies that indicate that the Lord himself is present and doing something in this very liturgy, and this preacher considers it his role to say clearly for his people what the Lord is doing and saying today.

What we can hear in these homilies is a bishop who has listened carefully to the Word of God as proclaimed on any given day, that is, to the constellation of texts from the Old Testament, the letters of the Apostles, and the Gospel. He has pondered these texts in the context of why the Church's Lectionary would have placed these in this particular season, feast, or Sunday; and from that consideration he opens up the Word for his people. But this preaching bishop has also carefully pondered the liturgical texts that accompany these readings, not infrequently drawing his people's attention to these as well.

Preaching about the Word and paying attention to liturgical texts are not the only things that a successful preacher attends to. Bishop Hugh is also keenly aware of the sacramental presence of the Lord, a presence that the Word announces and prepares for but that is deepened in the sacramental action, especially of Baptism and Eucharist. All of this likewise is present in these homilies, not as something that Bishop Hugh has 'come up with', but that is there already in the Church's liturgy. Bishop Hugh inhabits the Church's liturgy in this way, and one feels that he has long done so. Indeed, he has. His life before he became bishop, as a Benedictine monk and then as abbot, shows itself in this style of preaching. I do not mean to suggest by this that he is preaching to the people of the Church in Aberdeen as if they were monks or that he might be trying to turn them into monks. Instead, this preaching gives evidence something to the effect of 'Well, I've been a monk a long time and abbot a long time. Now I'm the bishop. I suppose I'll have to use what I know from being a monk to be my people's bishop now.'

This is not the first time in the history of the Church that a monk and/or an abbot has become a bishop. A bishop does not need to be a monk to be a good bishop or a good liturgical preacher. But a monk who becomes a bishop is likely to be steeped in the liturgy and its traditions the way Bishop Hugh is. He is also likely to see quickly and naturally the pastoral relevance of insights gained through monastic practices and habits. These habits sink a monk deep into the Scriptures and the liturgy through *lectio divina*, and Bishop Hugh is clearly acquainted with long-established traditional interpretations of the Scriptures. This is why these homilies move so naturally from the proclaimed Scriptures to the sacramental action and from these to the teaching and explanation of fundamental doctrines to his people. This is simply the dictum *lex orandi, lex credendi* in action from the bishop's cathedra. He doesn't use the word 'doctrine' for this task. Some people are afraid of the word or easily misunderstand what it means to express or protect. I mean 'doctrine' here as simply right understanding of the deepest sense of what the Scriptures and sacramental action make present; namely, the Lord Jesus himself, the eternal Son of God, now present to us through a human nature that he assumed for our sake, who through his death and Resurrection reveals God to be Father, Son, and Holy Spirit, inviting us to communion in this divine life. These are not ideas that either the bishop or I myself are floating. This is what happens in the liturgy, and here is a preacher who says so.

In these homilies one senses that this former abbot, now become a bishop, has transposed the key in which he once would have taught his monks and presided at liturgy for them. He plays a similar music in a key transposed for the people of Aberdeen. St Benedict describes the abbot's task, among other things, as being a patient teacher, able to adapt his teaching to a variety of types. Like an abbot might do, in these homilies we hear a bishop patiently and consistently putting before his people the themes they know and have heard before but whose beauty and power we earthlings always need constantly to be reminded of.

Let us turn again to the liturgical text from which the title of this book is taken. I am describing these homilies as steeped in tradition. But the liturgical text proclaims, 'Christ yesterday and today.' That is to say, the Christ of the past is the same Christ present now; and it is now in Aberdeen, this year, that this bishop is preaching. The liturgical text proclaims titles of Christ: 'the Alpha and the Omega.' That is Greek for saying 'from A to Z'. This is what

Christ is, and Bishop Hugh patiently keeps showing his people how Christ is contained in everything and embraces the whole story. 'All time belongs to him,' says the liturgical text and also the title of this book. The 'now' of the bishop's and his people's time is all throughout these homilies—be it in reference to the Covid lockdown, to a tragic train accident near Aberdeen, to a concert in a church, to an unexpected courtesy in the city, to the weather of some given day. 'To him be glory and power through every age and forever,' the liturgical text proclaims. I would not hesitate to say that these words reveal what lies deep in Bishop Hugh's heart and what is behind the careful, thoughtful effort revealed in his preaching.

The decoration or preparation of the paschal candle continues in another text that I have not yet drawn attention to but which I can use to conclude this introduction. The five wounds in the body of the Crucified are marked on the cross with these words: 'By his holy and glorious wounds may Christ guard us and protect us.' From every angle in which the liturgical year does the same, Bishop Hugh draws his people's attention to Christ crucified and risen, and his preaching is a prayer that Christ guard and protect his people.

The last words that a bishop or a priest says in preparing the paschal candle is when the candle is at last lit from the blazing paschal fire. I presume to place those words on Bishop Hugh's lips now as the reader turns the page and hears his homilies. He begins by saying, 'May the light of Christ rising in glory dispel the darkness of our hearts and minds.'

Rt Rev. Jeremy Driscoll, OSB
Abbot of Mount Angel Abbey

Introduction

The Liturgical Year

The liturgical year—with its Sundays and weekdays, Easter and Christmas, Advent and Lent, ferias and feasts—is one of the great givens of the Christian life. We live our lives within it. This is true even when we are not consciously adverting to it. It's a framework, a mould, a supporting rhythm, a background that at some peak times becomes the foreground. It has, too, been one of the great facts of European and Western cultural history. Has anyone done a study on this? We're familiar with the civil year (which comes to us from the Romans), the financial year, the academic year... But there is this other presence too—still hanging on even in semi-pagan Britain—and every revolutionary attempt to conjure it away (1789, 1917) has itself foundered.

Christ died at the time of the Jewish Passover and rose the day after the Jewish Sabbath. The Christian year is the ancient Jewish year, with its cosmic and historical roots, reshaped by the death and resurrection of Christ. The early history of it has been neatly headed 'from Sabbath to Sunday', 'from Passover to Pascha'. That was already accomplished by the second century. By the fourth and fifth centuries, the broad lines of what we are now familiar with were all in place, and St Leo the Great (Pope from 440 to 461) could deliberately preach and publish a series of sermons for the major festivals of the *anni circulum*, the circle and cycle of the year. Christmas, Epiphany, Lent, Easter, Ascension, Pentecost, SS Peter and Paul and the Ember Days are all there. The sixth century witnessed the enrichment of Advent, the seventh century the Western Church's adoption of the major Marian feasts. Almost every century since, and certainly every epoch, has contributed its own additions (Ash Wednesday, Trinity Sunday, Corpus Christi, the Sacred Heart, Christ the King, not to mention the multiplication of the celebrations of saints) Sometimes the original priorities (of Sunday, Easter, the feasts of the Lord) have had to be reaffirmed, and pruning been the order of the day. So it was after the Council of Trent in the sixteenth century, and after Vatican II in the twentieth.

In the Roman rite now, we have a liturgical year both luminously intent on the essentials and rich in its details. 'By means of the yearly cycle,' says the *Calendarium Romanum* of 1969, echoing Vatican II's *Sacrosanctum Concilium*, 'the Church celebrates the whole mystery of Christ, from his Incarnation until the day of Pentecost and the expectation of his coming again.' Central is the Easter Triduum—from the evening Mass of Maundy Thursday to the Compline of Easter Sunday. Out of this flows the Easter season, with its fifty days culminating in Pentecost, and towards it flows the critical season of Lent. Such is the 'Easter cycle'.

Second to it in stature is the 'Christmas cycle', with its similar pattern of a season of celebration, running to the feast of the Lord's Baptism, and a season of preparation, much-cherished Advent. There is the fine Byzantine phrase for all this: 'the winter Pasch'.

Then, as a third cycle—someone has even spoken of the liturgical tricycle!—there are the 33 or 34 Sundays and weeks of 'Ordinary Time', devoted not to a particular event in Christ's life (birth or death or resurrection), but to the mystery of Christ in its simple fullness. This cycle runs from the Monday (or Tuesday) following the close of the Christmas season to Shrove

Introduction

Tuesday, and resumes after Pentecost. It too, therefore, circles around Easter, the shining centre of everything. The final Sunday of Ordinary Time celebrates Christ the King, the One who reigns now in a hidden way and will come in glory. And so we are ready to begin the cycle again with the first Sunday of Advent, itself too focused on the Return of Christ. Interwoven with and subordinate to these major elements come the feasts of Mary, the saints and the angels. It is noticeable that the majority of these 'sanctoral' celebrations fall after Pentecost, in the second period of Ordinary Time.

'Beginning with the Easter Triduum as its source of light,' says the *Catechism of the Catholic Church*,[1] 'the new age of the Resurrection fills the whole liturgical year with its brilliance. Gradually, on either side of this source, the year is transfigured by the liturgy. It really is a "year of the Lord's favour" (Lk 4: 19).' This gives a key to what the liturgical year is about. All Christian liturgy—from the Eucharist to an hour of the Divine Office, from a baptism to a funeral—is about one thing only: the celebration of the Paschal Mystery, Christ's passage from death to new life and ours, incipiently, with him. It recalls Christ's Passover, makes it present, and hastens its full accomplishment. The liturgical year, therefore, in its own way, does the same. It is the celebration of the Paschal Mystery within the cosmic and human framework of the year. It is the risen Christ redeeming and enriching precisely *this time*, this time we call the year, with its weeks, months, and seasons, as in another way he redeems and enriches *the life* of an infant brought to baptism. That is why the Easter Triduum is 'its source of light', its radiant centre. That is why the forty days of Lent and the fifty days of Easter are the most intense period of this year, 'the sacramental season' *par excellence* as Newman said. Both the Christmas cycle, and the cycle of Ordinary Time centred on its succession of Sundays ('the day of the Lord'), are no less essentially 'paschal'. 'In the liturgical year the various aspects of the one Paschal mystery unfold', says the *Catechism*.[2] When we celebrate Mary, we are celebrating the human being closest to Christ, the great initiate and beneficiary of the Paschal Mystery, the icon of humanity redeemed. When we celebrate the other saints, be they local or universal in repute, we are proclaiming the 'illustration' of the Paschal Mystery in a human life, and its completion with their 'birthday' into heaven. Always it is the same point of reference, whether we be focused on the cave at Bethlehem or Jesus tempted in the Judaean desert or the tongues of fire in the Upper Room or Mary assumed into heaven or apostles and martyrs or expectation of the Parousia.

If the Paschal Mystery, then, is what the liturgical year mediates to us, this latter cannot be a negligible thing. If, as Pius XII said in *Mediator Dei*, 'it is Christ himself, living on in his Church, and still pursuing [the] path of boundless mercy ... he began to tread during his life on earth',[3] it is not to be underrated. Is it pedagogical or mystagogical? Is it an annual opportunity for retracing Christ's life on earth, step by step, or a participation in the eternity of his risen life? Both/ands are better here than either/ors. The Church's year is full of instruction, does break us the bread of Christ's earthly life portion by portion, shows us him as *exemplum*, pattern for our living, reads us the appropriate prophecies and Gospels. It makes possible, year after year, a fresh following of

Introduction

Christ. At the same time, 'it is not simply the commemoration of the historical events by which Christ Jesus won our salvation through his death and a calling to mind of the past that instructs and nurtures the faithful ... who meditate on it'; it also 'possesses a distinct sacramental power and efficacy to strengthen Christian life'.[24] In itself, the liturgical year is a 'sacramental', a bearer of Christ's grace by means of the prayer of the Church. The opening prayer of the First Sunday of Lent even talks of 'the sacrament of Lent', and other prayers use the same language of other seasons. But more still: the entire sacramental activity of the Church is shaped by the liturgical year. Advent and Lent bring their penitential services and the opportunity for the sacrament of reconciliation; the Easter Vigil is the prime time for receiving the sacraments of Christian initiation; no liturgy of word or sacrament can be untouched by its 'timing'. The Church's year is always, as it were, the dish on which the sacraments are brought to us. This is most visible in the Eucharistic celebration. It is that, above all, which empowers the liturgical year and its feasts and makes it and them a carrier of the grace and power of the mysteries (*sacramenta*) of Christ's life, and of his saving presence itself.

'The kingdom of God enters our time,' says the Catechism again,[5] speaking of the Christian year. At the very least, this year, with its deep cosmic and historical roots, joins us with so many ancestors, it civilizes and socializes us even now. It is a matrix of our culture. As something shared with different Christian confessions, it has too a great potential for encouraging Christian unity. It is striking, for example, to see how open the Church of Scotland has become to a re-appropriation of Christian seasons and feasts. It is a litmus test for the authenticity of Christian spiritualities. How can a spirituality dissociated from the liturgical year (such do exist!) claim to be truly Catholic? Put positively, how often the readings and rituals and timings of the liturgical year throw light on our personal and communal journey. But the liturgical year is all these things, and more, because through it the kingdom of God enters and transforms the times and seasons of our lives, the Paschal Mystery leavens them, the river of the Holy Spirit flows into them. Sunday after Sunday, Easter after Easter, year after year, the Church and the Christian meet their Lord in this way, and climb the spiral staircase which leads from time to eternity. The liturgical year is not only a given; it gives, and its gift is God himself.

Notes

1. *Catechism of the Catholic Church* (hereafter *CCC*) 1168
2. *CCC* 1171.
3. Pope Pius XII, *Mediator Dei* (1947), 165.
4. Pope St Paul VI, *Mysterii paschalis* (1969).
5. *CCC* 1168.

1

Advent—The Coming of Christ

I

We are about to embark on a new liturgical year, and on Advent. Some thoughts on these. I remember once travelling north on the East Coast route and being struck by the succession of Yorkshire villages we swept through. It was almost like a glimpse of pre-industrial Britain, at least if you didn't look too closely. There was each village, *sibi compacta in idipsum*, 'bound firmly together', like the Jerusalem of the Psalms (Ps 121), a whole, an integrity, a little self-sufficient concentration of human life. Here was geographical space humanized. And in every village was a church, and in every case the church was the building that first caught the eye, that stood out, tall, shapely, the centre (even when it wasn't), the symbol of transcendence. We talk of the liturgical year and the Divine Office as the sanctification of time. Here was physical and human space sanctified, Christianized.

The train sped on to Scotland. Another space. Thinking as a Christian, one might again observe the churches, signs of the Christian sanctification of this space. And as a Catholic one might even think, here is the land of two ecclesiastical provinces and eight dioceses. Not only physical churches but ecclesiastical jurisdictions represent a sanctification of space. And what do we mean by this phrase, sanctification of space? We mean that thanks to the presence of a bishop (and therefore of priests), and thanks to churches, God's holy word and sacraments are present and available in this physical and human space. We mean therefore that those within this space can now be sanctified, and that through them this physical and human space can become, in some sense, God's holy Temple.

Changing what has to be changed, we must mean something similar when we talk of the sanctification of time, even if the latter is a concept less easy to grasp. Time and space are the two dimensions in which we live our lives. When we talk of the sanctification of time, we mean that there are holy things present in our chronological and human time (or times). We mean that, within time, there are special times set apart for God, just as within space, there are special places set apart for God. We mean that time is ordered not only by physical and human criteria (years, seasons, months, weeks, days, hours, minutes etc.) but also by ecclesial criteria (Advent-Christmas, Lent-Easter, Morning Prayer and Evening Prayer etc.), just as physical and human space is also measured by provinces and dioceses and other forms of ecclesiastical territory. We mean therefore that those who live in this time can be sanctified, and all they do and all that happens to them. We mean that Christ, to whom 'all time belongs' is present in this time too.

The liturgical year and the Divine Office are a presence of Christ. And the presence of Christ is transforming. What would our year be like without the liturgical year? What would our day be like without the office? The circuit of the earth around the sun—the solar year—is hallowed by the liturgical year. The earth's turning on its own axis—the day—is filled by the daily celebration, however many times a day, of psalms and hymns, readings and prayers, not to mention the Mass. 'Christ yesterday and today, the beginning and the end, Alpha and Omega, all time belongs to him, and all the ages, to him be glory and power through every age for ever.' So says the celebrant at Easter, proclaiming Christ as the Lord of time, every year and every day belonging to him and coming into being so as to be taken into the 'fullness of time'. Once one has experienced something of this, how empty life feels without this Christianization. The liturgical year, like the daily round of the Office, is a work and a task, it's a road for travelling down as long as we're in time, it's a commitment and a loyalty, but first of all it's a gift, it's a presence, it's something to be grateful for. It's a filling of our emptiness. I just spotted this, this morning, in a book on Augustan Culture: '*Praesens*, the equivalent of the Greek *epiphanes* ... means both "physically present", "alive", and "lending assistance", "propitious", "powerful". That's the Christ of the liturgy.

II

We are about to embark on Advent. Perhaps St Benedict's saying, 'Whatever good work you begin, ask him with most earnest prayer to perfect it' has a place here. We can ask the Lord for help in celebrating these five weeks. May I offer three thoughts.

The first concerns a word. It is possible to take the Epiphany as the climax of Advent and Christmas, and in the same way it's possible to take the word 'Advent'—which is another translation of Epiphany—as describing not just the weeks before Christmas but the time after it as well: the whole Advent-Christmas-Epiphany cycle. The Introit for the Epiphany opens with the words 'Behold, he comes!' It's good to look at it as a whole.

It may help to remember that the liturgy took shape in the period historians call Late Antiquity, let's say from the fourth to the seventh century. Just as the Bible is marked, through and through, by the culture of the ancient Near East, so the Liturgy is permeated by the culture of the later Greco-Roman world. And in that world, the word 'Advent' was a far more resonant one then than now. It belonged to the ancient world's understanding and cult of the ruler. It denoted the Coming of a King, an Emperor to a city, 'Behold, your King comes to you,' says Scripture, and the entry of Christ into Jerusalem bears some of the marks of such an Advent. This is why it was for long a Gospel read on the First Advent Sunday. This 'metaphor', the Ruler's state arrival in a city, fills the Advent and Christmas liturgy. The texts of the prophets about the Messiah or the kingship of Yahweh are amalgamated with the 'Advent' Ceremonial of the Greco-Roman world, just as are the descriptions of the Parousia in the Pauline letters.

Here's an example of an *Adventus*. In the summer of 585, the Merovingian King Guntram 'visited' Orleans. 'A vast crowd of citizens,' says Gregory of Tours,

> came out to meet him, carrying flags and banners, and singing songs in his praise. The speech of the Syrians contrasted sharply with that of those using Gallo-Roman and again with that of the Jews, as they each sang his praises in their own tongue. 'Long live the King!' they all shouted. 'May he continue to reign over his peoples for more years than we can count!' The Jews played a full part in these acclamations. 'Let all peoples continue to worship you and bow the knee before you and submit to your rule!' they kept shouting.[1]

It's also mentioned that the visiting king was invited to banquets in the houses of the townsfolk, was given gifts by his hosts 'and gave them presents in return with lavish generosity'.

When some two hundred years earlier St Athanasius returned to Alexandria after one of his exiles, he was met by the people as if the Emperor. Everyone poured out of the city, a day's journey, all pell-mell with all the usual social distinctions swallowed up. Athanasius himself rode a colt, and people scattered branches, flowers, and clothes on his path, accompanying him back into the city. Everyone was shouting and cheering, perfumed oils were thrown about, the city was ablaze with lights, there were banquets everywhere, and the celebrations went on all night.[22]

Two random, slightly peripheral, examples of an *adventus*. Other features would be a solemn declamation extolling the virtues of the monarch, an amnesty for prisoners, handouts for the people, punishments for any opposition. Interestingly enough, in the sixth century in the West, the ceremony attending the coming of relics to a city was consciously modelled on the imperial 'advent'.

Certainly, there's hardly a feature of the Advent and Christmas liturgy which can't be 'read' against this background. Think, in general, how prevalent the imagery of kingship is in this liturgy, how the themes of redemption (setting-free) and peace and bestowal run through it. King Guntram enters the houses of the citizens and eats with them. 'Behold I stand at the door and knock; if anyone hears my voice and opens the door, I will come in to him and eat with him and he with me' (Apoc 3:20) The Son of David comes to the house of bread to eat with us. His advent comes to a climax in the three Masses of Christmas. Or take, in particular, the Gospels of the Genealogy at Christmas Vigils or of the Prologue of John at the Christmas Day Mass. This is the equivalent of the solemn declamation in the presence of the Emperor. 'And the Word became flesh and dwelt among us, full of grace and truth; we have beheld his glory, glory as of the only Son from the Father' (Jn 1:14). In these two Gospels, the first and last of Christmas Day, our Emperor is hailed as son of Abraham, son of David, son of a virgin, son of God the Father. Again, in Orleans the locals and the Syrians and the Jews go out to meet the King with acclamations: Long live the King! The acclamation, the swift sharp shout, was a great part of court life. 'To him who sits upon the throne and to the Lamb be blessing and honour and glory and might for ever and ever' (Apoc 5:13) is such transposed to the heavenly court. But take the *Gloria*, the Christmas hymn: 'We praise you, we bless you, we adore you, we glorify you ... Lord God, Heavenly King, O God Almighty Father ... For you alone are holy, you alone are Lord, you alone are the Most High Jesus Christ.' These are our acclamations of the Father and the Son.

The *Adventus* then makes one approach to the next five or six weeks. The paradox, of course, is that at the heart of this State Visit is not a deified superman, a *divus Augustus*, but a little boy born in a barn or, if you prefer, a God who hides himself, whose splendour is humility, and who asks us to become children in turn. When Peter Maxwell Davies remarked, 'I always imagine the nativity in a deserted Rackwick house' (that is, on the island of Hoy in the Orkneys), he seems, to us, nearer the heart of things than imperial ceremonial. This coming is a coming-down, and a coming-down which will go on down to a cross and even on down to 'hell'. As the courtier said to Louis XVI, 'This isn't a revolt, Sire, it's a revolution.' It's a very different *imperium* that's coming into being. And yet the Liturgy's sense of regality is precisely what preserves and points the paradox.

Secondly, Advent-Christmas is light rising in darkness. It falls at the darkest time of the year. Christmas is kept on the ancient day celebrating the birth of the unconquered Sun, four days after the winter solstice. 'The people who walked in darkness have seen a great light; those who dwelt in a land of deep darkness, on them has light shined' (Is 9:2). 'Radiant light will shine upon us today.' A great light has come down upon the earth. The Masses of Christmas, midnight, dawn, and day, celebrate the rising of the true Light. 'Through the mystery of the incarnate Word the new light of your glory has shone on the eyes of our mind,' says Christmas Preface I, and at Epiphany the mystery of our salvation is revealed as the light of the nations, the enlightening of the Gentiles. At Easter we celebrate new *Life*, at Pentecost *Love*, at Christmas *Light*.

Thirdly, Advent-Christmas, this Coming of the King, this dawning of the Light, is also a return from Exile. If Lent recalls the Exodus, God's first great deed on behalf of Israel, Advent recalls the end of the Babylonian captivity, the re-gathering of the tribes, the coming home to Jerusalem, God's second great deed on behalf of his people. The Anglican historian of Christian origins, N. T. Wright, situates Jesus' life, ministry, death, and resurrection precisely within this context: that of first century Israel's continuing hope for the definitive return from exile, the final restoration. In the language of the Second Christmas Preface, all things are restored to integrity by way of the Incarnation and man, who was lost, is called back to the heavenly realms. There is a reconciliation of Gentile and Jew and a re-building of Jerusalem, that is, the Church. This explains why the Advent/Christmas liturgy is so full of the second half of *Isaiah*, speaking as it does of this return, this restoration. 'Comfort, comfort my people, says your God. Speak tenderly to Jerusalem and cry to her that her warfare is ended, that her iniquity is pardoned' (Is 40:1–2). This is why Advent-Christmas is always a call to concord, to the reconciliation of the dispersed, to a family life, in home or monastery, centred on Christ and lived in peace.

Notes

1. St Gregory of Tours, *History of the Franks* VIII, 1.
2. Cf St Gregory Nazianzen, *Discourse* XXI, 29.

2

THE FOUR SUNDAYS OF ADVENT

FIRST SUNDAY OF ADVENT

Isaiah 63:16–17, 64:1,3–8; 1 Corinthians 3:3–9; Mark 13:33–37

Today Advent begins. It begins with a shout, with a cry—with Christ crying out: 'Stay awake!' Advent is a wake-up call. Four times in today's Gospel, we hear that phrase 'Stay awake'.

Not long after saying these very words, our Lord found himself in the Garden of Gethsemane, in agony, struggling to accept his Father's will. And Peter, James and John fell asleep. They fell asleep at the very moment Jesus could have done with their comfort. But I don't think our Lord's 'Stay awake' is really about avoiding sleep. He's not calling for all-night vigils (not regularly anyway!) or suggesting we leave our beds on the pavement for the Council to take them away. He's not just talking about literal sleep.

'Stay awake!' What does it mean, then?

In the middle of today's Gospel, there's a mini parable. There's a man, a lord of the manor. He goes away on business. He leaves his servants in charge, each with his own task. But he tells the doorkeeper to stay awake for when he comes back—comes back in the night, at an unknown hour, unexpectedly.

Each of us is a servant of the Lord. Each of us is a member of society and of the household of the faith. Each of us has a task to do. And we're meant to do it. It's part of our obedience. But while we do it, while we're in the kitchen or the office or the grounds, there must be a part of us that's doorkeeper too, part of us with our nose pressed against the window watching for lights on the road, or, if you like, with a mobile in our pocket waiting for the call. So we do our allotted work, we do it the best we can, we do it for the Lord and not for men, we try to put our hearts into it. But we don't let ourselves be completely identified with it, be all-absorbed by it. There's something in us which keeps detached, aloof, inwardly free, a little bit apart, turned elsewhere. God has given us two eyes: one for this world, but another for heaven, for the Lord.

'The world is too much with us,' said William Wordsworth. It certainly is. The world seems never more worldly than at this time of year. And it's so easy to let it absorb us. Advent says, 'Stay awake!' Do what you have to do but keep the door as well. Advent says, 'Stay awake!' Advent says, 'Pray!' Stand a little more at the window of prayer, even only three more minutes a day. At the very least, it helps us keep sane while the world goes mad. Yes, Advent prays. Let's pray with her.

> Oh, that you would tear the heavens open and come down.
> God of hosts bring us back; let your face shine on us and we shall be saved. Amen.

Second Sunday of Advent

Isaiah 11:1–10; Romans 15:4–9; Matthew 3:1–12

Four weeks of Advent (one gone already), four weeks of waiting. Mary had nine months of it. But she and we are in this together, however separated by the centuries. She was waiting to take the child she was carrying into her arms and see his Face. We are waiting to renew that birth in our Christmas liturgies. We are waiting for him to come in glory. We are waiting, one by one, to see him face to face when we die, and, please God, be wrapped in the welcome of his merciful arms.

There's a growing, building momentum, as it were. A great collective waiting.

Icon painters talk of 'writing' an icon. And, in today's readings, that is what Isaiah, the Psalmist, St Paul, and, in the Gospel, John the Baptist, are all doing. They are, literally, writing the icon of the coming Christ. They are outlining, sketching his Face. He is beyond any description, he's always greater than our imaginings and representations. And yet, if they're Scriptural, they're not false and can kindle our desire. 'It is your face, O Lord, that I seek. Hide not your face from me.'

Let's focus on the Gospel, on John the Baptist and his portrait of Jesus. 'Repent, for the kingdom of heaven is close at hand.' 'Repent', here, means 'turn round.' Something tremendous is on its way. We are in our back garden fiddling away in a flower bed, and meanwhile the King is coming up our front drive, is about to knock at the door. 'Turn round, stop looking in the wrong direction, look here.' And then, as it were, John starts to sketch. It's not a Christmas-card like, pretty picture we're asked to look at.

Its lines are stark, strong, scary. It has something of a desert landscape to it. 'The kingdom of heaven is close at hand'. 'Kingdom of heaven' is code for Jesus himself. It's he who is near. And he comes with an axe to fell dead trees. He comes with a winnowing fan to blow away chaff. He's the One 'behind' John, looming over his shoulder. He's the 'stronger one', John says. He's the real Baptizer, and he comes to immerse us in the Holy Spirit and a torrent of fire.

This is hardly 'gentle Jesus, meek and mild' or the sweet Child in the manger. It's a Jesus on fire, we could say. And yet it is the one, same Jesus. He is more one than we ever are, and yet he combines such amazing opposites. He's beautiful and terrifying all at once.

Who is he, then, the Jesus of John? He's Someone coming to remake the world, to create a new one, to make all things new. That's why John proclaims him in the desert. It was in the desert that Israel was formed. It was after forty days in the desert that Jesus would begin his mission. It was out of waste and void, out of nothingness, that God created in the beginning. Jesus is a second Genesis. He's a new beginning. So, first he has to end the old, sinful world: not just in the Pharisees and Sadducees, but in all of us. And if we cling to that old world, then he's an axe or a winnowing fan or a bushfire. But if we let go, if we turn round to look at him, run to meet him, then out of our stony hearts children of God will be raised up. Our desert will bloom. In the water of his baptizing, we'll become fruit-bearing trees. We'll be grain gathered into his barns, and his wholesome fire will bake us into nourishing bread for the life of the world.

The fiery Christ of John the Baptist re-fashions, re-creates. He brings something better and new to birth. We see it in healthy monasteries, in communities, in a parish where what St Paul says goes, where the Eucharist is really the centre, and we are united in mind and voice, welcoming one another as Christ has welcomed us. We see it in households and families where Christ is acknowledged. We see it in holy individuals, in the saints. These are all the living icons of the Jesus John the Baptist saw coming. They're the outline of his Face, here below. Always limited, imperfect, written in tears sometimes, waiting for completion, but real.

It's a beautiful Advent custom to set up a crib in the home. Homes can be mad houses as we all know. But the crib is quietly there. Or think of the actual birth of Jesus and the manger in the cave: the animal smell, the rowdy pub next door, imperial politics pushing people around. And in the midst of all that, the sign of the new beginning: Jesus, Mary and Joseph, angels and shepherds, adoration and prayer and unexpected joy. So, let's try and paint our own living icons of the coming Christ. Let's be places Christ has changed from desert into garden. In our own hearts and together. Let's try and make our homes and parishes and friendships proofs and presences of Christ, glimpses of grace, Bethlehem and Nazareth, places where, whatever our failures, we can start again. That's Christmas.

Third Sunday of Advent

Isaiah 61:1–2, 10–11; 1 Thessalonians 5:16–24; John 1:6–8, 19–28

This is the Third Sunday of Advent, Gaudete Sunday. 'Rejoice in the Lord always, again I say rejoice.' The Entrance Antiphon quotes St Paul. He repeats himself in today's second reading: 'Rejoice at all times.' In the first reading, from Isaiah, even poor old Jerusalem, so often bashed and bruised, says, 'I exult for joy in the Lord, my soul rejoices in my God.' In the Psalm we hear the voice of Mary: 'My soul magnifies the Lord and my spirit rejoices in God my Saviour.' There's a sense of a choir coming together here. Even our vestments lighten up, and purple turns pink.

The trouble is: you can't command an emotion. I can tell myself to get out of a chair, but not to feel about something, at least not to immediate effect. We learn too that it's not wise to say to someone who is seriously miserable, 'Cheer up, old girl!'

We're being summoned today to a joy that's more than an emotion inside us; rather, it's a joy with a reason. We're being invited to look outwards. This is an objective, out-there joy, founded on a reality. 'Rejoice because the Lord is near.' This is a real, tangible, down to earth joy. It's a child. And not just any child, but the Child, God's eternal Child now become a Child for us. Children can run us through every emotion in the book, positive or negative. But still, surely a child is a joy. And should we want to contest that, well, surely this one is. This one isn't one too many. This one doesn't bring grief.

Gaudete: this Child is almost there. But we can go further.

The Collect begins, 'O God, who see how your people faithfully await the feast of the Lord's Nativity.'

'O God, who see...' God here is God the Father, and he sees us. The Father is looking at us, gazing at us. He loves us so much he can't take his eyes off us. The Latin word translated 'see' here—*conspicere*—is not any kind of seeing or looking, certainly no blank stare. It is an attentive, appreciative, and caring looking. So, God is looking at his faithful, believing people, looking at us as we prepare to keep the birth of his Son. He knows how preoccupied we are, how much there is to distract us, but he sees beyond that. He sees how, as Advent moves on, we do try to focus. In our clumsy way, we are heading for Bethlehem. And the Lord sees that. He loves it. And by looking at us in his attentive, appreciative, caring way, he carries us with him. He 'enables' us, says the Prayer, to get there, to 'arrive' (*pervenire*). This is a beautiful, joy-giving thought. God's looking does the job. Collects always emphasize the action of God.

When we come to Bethlehem and the Crib and Christmas night, we come to Jesus, Mary and Joseph, to the angels and shepherds and animals. Somewhere on the horizon are the wise men with their camels and gifts. Even an Emperor and a Roman governor are unwittingly involved. But there's Someone else as well: 'O God, who see...' Over the whole scene, framing it, holding everything together, like the stable roof, like the night sky, is God the Father. We can think of him looking at his Son and in his Son at us, looking attentively, appreciatively, caringly. Mary and Joseph, the angels and the shepherds, are looking too in the same direction, looking with the Father at his beloved Son and the world reborn in him.

We are all united, all one, one in the Son, one with each other, linked by the Father's look.

'May you all be kept safe and blameless, spirit, soul and body, for the coming of our Lord Jesus Christ,' says St Paul. 'God has called you and he will not fail you.' Here are we, people of faith, sometimes stronger, sometimes weaker, pilgriming to Bethlehem in spirit, soul and body, with the Father's attentive, appreciative, caring eyes upon us. And it's not just to a memory we're travelling. It's to a fullness. It's to what Bethlehem points to. It's to that we pray to reach (*pervenire*). This is where we hope to end, to be complete as human beings. We are called to a great unity of creation and humanity and our whole selves in Christ. To his glorified mystical body, the heavenly city, the kingdom of God, where we will see everything as the Father sees, and joy will overtake us like a flood.

God has called us, says St Paul. And he is faithful. He looks at us, body, soul and spirit. He 'will not fail' us. What Paul actually says is, 'he will do it' (*ipse faciet*)—the action of God. We will get there because he will get us there: to Bethlehem and beyond. It might be an idea to worry less and trust more.

Fourth Sunday of Advent

Isaiah 7:10–14; Romans 1:1–7; Matthew 1:18–24

Today we are on the brink of Christmas. On 25 March each year, we celebrate the Annunciation: 'the Angel of the Lord declared unto Mary, and she conceived by the Holy Spirit.' This Sunday we do too. It's March in December. It's a dramatic foreshortening, not nine months before Christmas, but seven days. It's spring in winter. And this Year, Year A, we hear not St Luke's account of the Annunciation to Mary, but St Matthew's account of the Annunciation to St Joseph. 'Joseph, son of David, do not be afraid to take Mary home as your wife, because she has conceived what is in her by the Holy Spirit.' Like Mary, Joseph puts fear aside. Like Mary, he gives the 'obedience of faith' to what he hears.

The Incarnation is the ultimate free download, and to access it, to agree to its terms and conditions, all that's needed is that click of faith. 'You are now connected.'

Think of today's Sunday as an Annunciation to us. Think of the liturgy as an angel announcing the birth of Jesus, asking for our faith.

'The Lord himself will give you a sign,' Isaiah says to King Ahaz. Ahaz does not respond with faith: 'I will not put the Lord to the test,' he says. This is sophistry. But the sign will still be given, and it is: 'the maiden is with child and will soon give birth to a son whom she will call Emmanuel.' The Hebrew word here translated 'maiden' refers to a young woman of marriageable age. It implies virginity, rather than affirming it. But in the ancient Greek translation of Isaiah, and in our Greek New Testament, a word was used making the virginity more explicit. So we have 'a virgin shall conceive.' A hidden depth in the text has been brought to light; it's a prophecy of Mary's virginal conception of Jesus. This is what the New Testament affirms, and the Church believes: 'he was conceived by the Holy Spirit and born of the Virgin Mary.' This is a basic and non-negotiable article of faith.

'The Lord himself will give you a sign.' This is it. Jesus had a human mother, but no human father. Mary's conception came from above, from the Holy Spirit. That he had a mother shows his humanity, that his mother was a virgin signifies his divinity. And so: 'Emmanuel, God is with us.' He is with us in a new, unprecedented and, oh! so gracious and courteous a way. The Old Testament is full of stories of infertile women unexpectedly conceiving, beginning with Sarah. The New Testament itself begins with one in the person of Elizabeth. These conceptions were always a sign of God drawing close to his people. They were a sign of his mercy and creative power. When Israel was down and out, these unexpected conceptions revived their hope. They meant new life, a new beginning. But in a virginal conception, God is drawing still closer. There's a quantum leap. God is respecting the dynamics of his own creation, respecting the power to reproduce he has given living things, but he is entering into it more intimately. He's raising generativity to a higher power. He's introducing a new charge of divine energy into it. A woman becomes 'Mother of God': the mother of God made man. A virgin conceiving is a sign of God coming. There's a new creation, a new beginning, a second genesis. In Genesis, the Spirit of God is seen moving over the primal waters. He makes them life-giving, and out of them springs the ordered, beautiful world, with man and woman as its crown, made in the image and likeness of God. Now the Holy Spirit moves over the virginal waters of Mary, and she conceives and gives birth to the only begotten Son of God himself, God from God, the eternal image and likeness of the life-giving Father. And so everything can begin again, everything be regenerated. We too, we most of all. God is with us in a quite new way: in the person of Jesus, the God-man, fruit of the Father's heart and Mary's womb, one of the Trinity and one of us.

Christmas and Easter go together. At Christmas, the baby God-man comes from a virginal womb. At Easter, the crucified God-man rises from a tomb 'where no one had yet been laid'. At Christmas, we see the Son of God in weakness. At Easter, we see him proclaimed Son of God in power through his resurrection from the dead. The Christmas sign of the Virgin Birth points to the Easter sign of the Resurrection. And both say the same. They signify God is with us, God is close. They mean a new beginning, new life, a new world. And this isn't outside us. It's interactive, as it were. It's only the 'click' of faith away. Ahaz stood outside it because he wouldn't believe, but Mary and Joseph did believe, and they entered in. When we're baptized the Spirit of God moves over the waters of our mortal life and we're reborn as children of God. It's the one same pattern, unfolding in stages. It embraces us. And it's always spring in winter, life from death, the new in the midst of the old.

'The Lord himself will give you a sign.' And here's the final wonder. In the obedience of faith, Joseph takes Mary home as his wife. Together they become a sign of the Christ in their midst. St Paul, a Jew, proclaims the Resurrection to the Gentiles, and by the preaching of the Apostles, the Church is born as a sign of reconciled diversity, a miracle of unity. We are here now, thanks to the Eucharist. We're laity and clergy—baptized, married, ordained—with a diversity of vocations but one in faith.

We're a sign of a new beginning, an alternative future. We sense the closeness of God, our Emmanuel, and we can communicate it. What an empty, glitzy Christmas the world puts on! How full it is of empty signs, signifying little or nothing. How like Ahaz it is, not wanting what God offers. But 'The Lord himself will give you a sign', nonetheless. And if we give this sign, this presence, the obedience of faith, we become it ourselves. It's interactive, and we're part of the story. We can signify the newness and closeness of God. We can feel it ourselves and sign it to others. And Christmas can become very real.

3

THE IMMACULATE CONCEPTION OF THE BLESSED VIRGIN MARY

Genesis 3:9–15, 20; Ephesians 1:3–6, 11–12; Luke 1:26–38

Today we celebrate the Immaculate Conception of the Blessed Virgin Mary. This is not the virginal conception of Jesus by Mary, but the conception of Mary herself. It's not Jesus' beginning we're marking today, but Mary's. And we mark it, not because there was anything biologically unusual about her conception, but because of who she was from that moment on, in the sight of God: a human being untouched by original sin, graced. There is an Old Testament Psalm with the line, 'Glorious things are spoken of you, O city of God' (Ps 87:3). The 'city of God' was Jerusalem, and the prophets did have 'glorious things' to say about her. The same line is often applied to Mary too. Our faith says many 'glorious things' of Mary, and one of them is what it says today. Our faith says that, from the very beginning of her human life, from her mother's womb, she was freed from all stain of original sin and therefore 'graced', 'redeemed', 'adopted', a delight to the heart of God, all that human beings are meant to be.

'Where are you?' the Lord God asks Adam immediately after the first sin. It was a question that should never have needed asking. But Adam, as we know, had sinned, felt shame, and was hiding, like a naughty child, in the bushes. He was off-line; he had lost the connection. He was not where he was meant to be: with God in every part of his being; at home; in the presence. But Mary was. Mary, this first century Jew, a village girl, a Galilean peasant woman, was always 'in the presence', always. And why? Because 'before the world was made', she was predestined to be the mother of the Saviour, God incarnate, the One who would restore the connection all of us had lost in Adam. She was the city who was to open her gates to the king. She was, pardon the image, the landing strip on which the divine plane, the Son of God, was to land. She was Israel now ready to welcome her God. She was the one fitted to utter the 'yes' on behalf of us all and so allow the Incarnation to occur. And she was the one who would do for Jesus—God made man, the Holy One—everything a mother does for her son. So, from the beginning, she was prepared and equipped for her mission: properly dressed for the occasion, as it were, 'highly favoured', 'full of grace'. The angel did not have to go looking for her; she was 'there'. By the Spirit of the Son who redeems us all, she was already 'connected', 'online'. She had oil in her lamp. She was awake and watching. She was the Advent that, on the human side, made Christmas possible. 'Glorious things are spoken of you, O city of God.'

Another Psalm line can help us too: 'Sing a new song to the Lord.' We have just been singing it. Sing with your lips, sing with your lives, says St Augustine somewhere. And here's another metaphor. God, says an old tradition, sang creation into being. Creation is itself a song and we are to sing it. But we have lost the note, lost our sense of pitch. Or, if there is a musical score for us to perform, the instrument we are is out of tune. Mary's ear, though, or the instrument she is, was always perfectly attuned. And so, through her, God's music can enter the world. When we are baptized, we in turn are re-tuned, as it were. We become capable of hearing and catching and taking up the Lord's new song. The Church is the choir of us all, and we are called to join to it the voice of our own unique life. Mary was the first to join the choir, the 'beginning of the Church',[1] just as Miriam was the first to take up the Song of Moses as the people of Israel crossed the Red Sea. And so, with her, all humanity and the whole universe becomes an Oratorio for God, an Ode to Joy. 'Before the world was made, he chose us, chose us in Christ, to be holy and spotless'—to be in tune—'and to live through love in his presence', singing the song of the Lord, making music to his Name.

When we bishops of Scotland met Pope Francis at the end of September, one of us asked what holiness is. 'Closeness', said the Pope: closeness to God in prayer, closeness to each other and our clergy as brothers and fathers, closeness to our people as shepherds. It's a challenge! I mention it because Mary's holiness might seem to distance her from us. We're shy of perfection. But, as the Pope said, 'holiness is closeness'. Sin, by contrast, is selfishness. And selfishness means such a focus on ourselves that we are 'closed' to others and to God. Sin is being closed; holiness is being close. A holy person is a sensitive person. So Mary 'most holy' is the human being closest to Christ, closest to us. She's our sister, our fellow-traveller, our mother. If we open our hand, she will take it, and lead us to Jesus. She's not lost in herself; she's turned to us. She's 'online'. She always responds, however unexpectedly, to the 'emails' of our prayers.

How easily the serpent slips into things and spoils them! But isn't it a beautiful thought and a great comfort that, some two thousand years ago, hidden in Israel, hidden even from herself, there was this child, this girl, this woman who was pure openness, giving such joy to

God? And isn't it a beautiful thought and a very great comfort that this woman, now 'hidden with Christ in God', is close to us, 'connected' to us, an 'advocate of grace and a model of holiness',[2] coaxing us on, bringing us ever closer to the Father, the Son and the Holy Spirit. Amen.

Notes

1. Preface of the Mass of the Immaculate Conception.
2. *Ibid.*

4

Christmas Eve

'Hasten! Don't delay, Lord Jesus! Let those who trust in your love, be relieved by the consolations of Your coming!' What a prayer this is! One of the very few Collects of the year directly addressed to Jesus himself. Expressing the Church's longing—hunger and ache, holy impatience—for the coming of Christ.

With certainty too. Christ *is* coming... And in the coming Christmas season, we will hear about him in words; we will see him, his image in the Crib, his image in the Host; we will touch him and taste him. He comes to our spiritual senses, opening them to himself. And because he comes so powerfully, at this time, in word and image and sacrament, because he is truly born for us by way of the rites we celebrate, then our whole time becomes sanctified time, and so we know he will come to us too in our personal reading and prayer, in the movement of our hearts, in the 'good cheer' we have together, in all the kindnesses that people lavish on us at this time of year. All of this is Christ's birth too. It is an anomaly that the word 'Advent' has slipped into denoting the time of preparation. Today, more rigorously, as the Collect implies, is *Advent* Eve, the Eve of his Coming. When we enter the Church for the Mass of the Epiphany, we will be singing the imperial Introit, *Behold, the Lord has come.* If we have, like citizens of an ancient city, run out to meet our Emperor, well, the meeting is now. And our

Emperor, scattering his bounty, is leading us back into the city. And who, as St Athanasius remarks, would dare attack a city which the Emperor is visiting? Even, we can add, if this Emperor is a child.

So, Christ is coming. And he is coming to us. He is coming to each of us, to me. Coming with consolations. And what do we expect? What do I expect? What consolations do we look for? Beyond the tension and temper of the season, beyond the element of weariness and 'heard it all before', what do we expect? What would it be culpable sloth and sadness not to expect? I offer as an answer something familiar, something true. 'And now faith, hope and love abide, these three; and the greatest of these is love' (1 Cor 13:13). This is the balm Christ brings to ravaged souls. We can expect, each of us can expect—through the celebration of Christ's *Adventus*—a revival of our faith and our hope and our love.

Our faith, first of all. Historically, the Christmas liturgy is deeply linked to the great Christological debates of the fourth and fifth centuries, and their resolution in the first ecumenical Councils. As the Byzantine churches instituted a feast of Orthodoxy (the First Sunday of Great Lent in 843) to hail the defeat of the iconoclasts in the eighth–ninth centuries, so the whole Church was already celebrating Christmas as a proclamation of the full divinity and humanity of Christ, in repudiation of all false doctrine. 'An amazing mystery is proclaimed today: natures are changed: God has become a man: he remains what he was, and he has assumed what he was not: suffering neither mingling nor confusion.' That Benedictus antiphon of the octave day of Christmas only explicates a spirit that runs throughout: a spirit of certain and joyful proclamation. 'To you is born this day in the city of David a Saviour, who is the Messiah, the Lord' (Lk 2:11). What the angel announces, 'evangelizes', at the Mass of midnight, first the Prologue of the Letter to the Hebrews and then the Prologue to the Gospel of St John bring to sonorous climax at the day Mass: 'But in these last days, he has spoken to us by a Son, whom he appointed heir of all things, through whom he also created the worlds. He is the reflection of God's glory and the exact imprint of God's very being' (Heb 1:2–3); 'and the Word became flesh and dwelt among us' (Jn 1:14). It is this newborn child, sleeping or snuffling in the manger, this child who on the eighth day will be called Jesus, who is all these, and other, astonishing things. It's hard not to cry out as the liturgy does at a baptism: 'This is our faith. This is the faith of the Church. We are proud to profess it.'

And so our own faith can be reborn, revitalized, refreshed; our own appreciation of Jesus; our own realization of Jesus. Faith, in this sense, is seeing what the Father sees. Faith is a participation in the mind, in the vision of the Father. That is why Christian faith is so centred on Jesus: because the Father is centred on his Son, eternally and infinitely. Christmas begins with the Father addressing the Son, or, strictly, with the Son repeating the word the Father has spoken. Christmas opens with the Father gazing at the baby in the crib and proclaiming him—as He will at the Jordan and on Tabor and at Easter—His beloved Son, begotten now as man as well as God. All true knowledge of the Son comes from heaven, comes from the Father of lights, and our believing will be refreshed and rekindled as we allow the eyes of the Father to look Christ-ward through us. Faith is seeing what the Father sees. So can faith see anything other than the Son? Take ourselves. When the Father looks at us, what does He see? He sees us many and one in Christ. 'This is my Son [too] the Beloved; my favour rests on him.' No one on earth, nothing in history, nothing in contemporary events, nothing in the story of my life isn't under this gaze of the Father, isn't therefore full of Christ, even if it's Christ rejected or Christ wrapped in the stone-cold tomb waiting the touch of the Father. Christmas shows us Christ. Christmas revives our faith.

Christmas revives our hope. Every newborn child has that power; this Child uniquely. He revives the hope of a better world here and now, of a change for the good. His birth coincides with the lengthening days. It gives fresh energy in the doing of good: ordinary, daily, mundane good. It sends us out to battle once again. Our sense of it all being somehow worth it finds itself strangely rekindled by that Mother and Child.

> For all that loveliness, that warmth, that light,
> Blessed Madonna, I go back to fight,[1]

These words were penned by a great British general in 1943. He revives the hope, looking higher, of the Kingdom to come. He's already a fulfilment, by way of cross and resurrection, of the hopes of the Chosen People: those hopes of God reigning and idols toppling, of a new covenant, of a gathered people and Gentiles converted, of a new Presence, of a new purity and inward renewal, of the forgiveness of sins, of the Messianic king. All these promises have a first, unfinished but real, fulfilment in the Church and in her saints. Seeing this much, as St Augustine says, our hope is revived in the ultimate happy ending. He revives our hope, thirdly, for heaven. In the Collect for Christmas night, we pray to 'enjoy in heaven the joys of him whose luminous mysteries we celebrate on earth'. The best is yet to come, for each of us.

There is a key. It's to be deeply, inwardly convinced of being personally loved by the Lord. This is what withers fear and stirs up hope. The Holy Spirit will show each one of us how to decipher the script of our life in the light of Christ's love. My baptism, my being or becoming a Catholic, the Eucharist, my vocation, my ordination if such, the work I've been given, the people I know—even my infirmities—these are all of them the words of Christ's love in my life. And the last and best of the words, the word to illuminate everything, completing the sentence in unimaginable fullness and joy, is still to come. It's the word of my final salvation, the word of eternal life, the word: 'Your sins are forgiven'; the word: 'Well done, good and faithful servant, enter into the joy of your Lord'. And strange though it may seem, it is the hope of that word that this Child brings. It's the hope of birth into bliss. Christmas revives our hope.

Christmas revives our love. According to the doctrine of what is called the hypostatic union, Christ's human nature—which is completely like ours, sin excepted (and sin is not a part of nature)—belongs as his own to the divine person of the Son of God, who assumed it. In other words, one of the Trinity has made a human nature part of himself. This is love, quite overwhelming, mind-blowing, heart-ravishing love. This is love, than which no greater can be conceived. There is a being, God, who is completely, infinitely, eternally, unassailably happy, blessed, joyful, in his own Trinitarian life. And yet—and this itself is amazing—this being decides to create other, finite beings outside itself, in order to share its happiness with them, and centrally man. And when it does this, it does it to the maximum conceivable, even though or maybe even because, the creature man has refused the love. One of the Trinity, in order to connect to each and every human being, takes to himself an individual human nature in a marriage than which no closer, no more intimate can be conceived. Humanity is part of the Trinity: indissolubly and forever. Really, a clatter of genuflections at the *Et incarnatus est* ('and became man') hardly rises to the occasion! I'm only giving what astonishes me. There's the child, the teacher, the Eucharist, the Cross, the Resurrection. They all speak the same love. And the Incarnation too. This is the Christmas love. And it's as universal as the Easter love, the outstretched arms. By taking a human nature to himself, the Son of God has united himself in a certain way to every human being. Christ is part of every man's humanity, more me than I am. The only possible knock-on effect—though heaven knows how many Christmases it takes to come to it—is St Benedict's 'enlarged heart'. The heart of the Trinity is large enough for all humanity. And Christmas it is that conveys this.

'Hasten! Don't delay, Lord Jesus! Let those who trust in your love be relieved by the consolations of your coming.' 'Faith, hope and love; these three abide.' Cold comfort? Yes, in a sense. Anything but, in a truer sense. Faith, hope and love: they are the balm; they are the sustenance; they are the consolation. They bind us to God and they bind us to one another. They complete the incarnation. They bring us to the childhood which is salvation. They keep us going till He comes.

'Let us think of this night,' said St Aelred, 'as the night of his birth. Let us keep our vigil as if beside his crib. Let us embrace his sweet childhood with intimate love. Let our voices be fervent, our hearts tranquil, our minds in light, our desire full of love—and so we shall see the joy that comes to us from Christ's birth.[2]

Notes

1. A. P. Wavell, 'Madonna of the Cherries' in *Other Men's Flowers* (London: Pimlico 1992).
2. St Aelred of Rievaulx, Sermo XLVIII *In Vigilie Nativitatis* Domini (author's translation).

5

Christmas Midnight Mass

Isaiah 9:1–6; Titus 2:11–14; Luke 2:1–14

Christmas works. Every year we have the same prayers, same readings, same rituals; we hear the same story; we see the same decorations. But it doesn't pall. It's always fresh. We can always be touched. As we get older, that's a great comfort. I'm not so jaded that I can't still be moved. 'For there is a child born to us, a son given to us'—tonight, once again, as if for the first time. 'And here is a sign for you: you will find a baby wrapped in swaddling clothes and lying in a manger.' The Roman Emperor issues his decree, his officials busy about, people take to the roads to be registered, a young couple among them. They come to the noisy, overcrowded village, the pubs and B&Bs are all full. There's just a steading, and there it happens. 'A child is born to us, a son given to us.' And we turn aside, and there he is.

Here he is.

I know a gynaecologist. She has no children herself, but she has helped many come into the world. And she'll always say, it is the most beautiful thing imaginable. Through the door of effort and pain, into the world comes this tiny, perfect being. As a new father said to me once, 'you can't watch this and be an atheist.' God is with us, we say. It's as if God wanted to live this himself, from the inside, as a human being, as one of us. God sees creation. He sees it, Genesis says, as good. He sees how, like a thoughtless child, we've scribbled over the page, spoiled the gift, or covered it with dirt. But like an archaeologist, God gets down on his knees, patiently scrapes away the debris and reveals the hidden treasure. He comes into our life, rescues the buried good that we are and gives it back to us. And he begins from the beginning, from conception, from birth. The Second Person of the Trinity, the Son of the Father, took on our humanity in a woman's womb.

Here's an image for Christmas. It's a marriage, a marriage between God and us in the person of Christ. It's the primal marriage, which any others are called to reflect. It's indissoluble. There'll never be a separation or divorce. The angel proposed on behalf of God and Mary said 'yes' on behalf of humanity. At Christmas it was announced and celebrated. 'The Bridegroom comes forth from his chamber' and the wedding is held. On the Cross, the union was consummated when the Son made the ultimate act of love. Now it's seated at the right hand of the Father, fruitful in history. It's wherever Jesus is, God and man in one. It's in the manger tonight. It's every day on the altar. God with us. 'Yes, like a forsaken wife, distressed in spirit, the Lord calls you back. Does a man cast off the wife of his youth? says your God … I did forsake you for a brief moment, but with great love I will take you back … for the mountains may depart, the hills be shaken, but my love for you will never leave you' (Is 54:6, 10). So, the angels chivvy the shepherds down the hillside to the reception in the stable. And to this wedding we are all invited. In fact, it's ours.

Things can catch the eye sometimes. Celebrating Mass recently, I noticed kneeling side by side a university professor and a primary school girl. They weren't connected, they were together by chance, occupying empty places. And I thought: what a sign of what Christ does! 'Wide is his dominion', says Isaiah, 'in a peace that knows no end.' We're all invited to the marriage feast: woman and man, young and old, wealthy and poor, simple and educated. Of course, a great personality can attract opposites, or love of a country can, or any of the great world religions. But Jesus does it more widely, more lastingly, at another level. This marriage creates a family. It creates the unity we call the Church. It joins the beginning and end, time and eternity, heaven and earth, angels and animals, Gentile and Jew, the visible and the invisible, the lion and the lamb, the child and the professor. 'Let the heavens rejoice and earth be glad, let the sea and all within it thunder praise, let the land and all it bears rejoice, all the trees of the wood shout for joy.' In the collection of the Metropolitan Museum of Art in New York, there's a Flemish painting dated 1515, *Adoration of the Christ Child*, set at night. It has been pointed out that one angel and one shepherd have the faces of those with Down Syndrome, one of the earliest evidences of this condition, so often nowadays ended in the womb. Both are adoring. 'Wide is his dominion.' No one is excluded.

All this is already hidden in tonight, 'waiting in hope', waiting to be unwrapped like a gift, waiting like a hidden explosion, waiting to grow.

'For there is a child born for us, a son given to us.' Here, tonight. What do we do with a baby? We take it in our arms. Mary offers him to us. The Church offers him. So here's a spiritual exercise for tonight—for any time before the Crib; for the moment of Holy Communion, if we're receiving him; for our hearts, whether we are or are not. Faith is enough. Imagine Mary offering you Jesus to hold and Joseph looking kindly on. You can hold him to your breast, you can kiss him, cuddle him, rock him, tickle him, or just look at him. Here's the thing. If we were in Aleppo, we could do this. If we've just lost someone close to us, if we've just lost a job, if we've just mucked up in some way, we can still take the child in our arms. He's greater than anything wrong. 'Dominion is laid on his shoulders.' And he is given to us, and we can hold him. So, everything is changed. Everything is reframed. The context is different now. Everything can always begin again. We're holding hope, we're holding a future. We're holding the marriage of God and us. We're holding joy. And why? Because he's Emmanuel, God with us, and he is holding us. Listen to the angel: 'Today in the town of David, a saviour has been born to you: he is Christ the Lord.' Let us open the arms of our heart and hold him close. Amen.

> There is fallen on earth for a token
> A god too great for the sky.
> He has burst out of all things and broken
> The bounds of eternity.
> Into time and the terminal land
> He has strayed like a thief or a lover.
>
> ... unmeasured of plummet and rod,
> Too deep for [our] sight to scan,
> Outrushing the fall of man
> Is the height of the fall of God.[1]

Notes

1. G. K. Chesterton, 'Gloria in Profundis' in *Collected Poems* (London: Methuen 1933).

6

Christmas Day

Isaiah 52:7–10; Hebrew 1:1–6; John 1:1–18

Every Sunday Mass, every feast day, has its own set of prayers and readings. Christmas, being a great feast, the second after Easter, has four. It has a Vigil Mass, a Night Mass, a Dawn Mass and this Mass, the Day Mass. The Vigil Mass one might compare to a star, the Night Mass to the moon and the Dawn Mass to the dawn. At this Mass, it's as if the sun has fully risen and fills the sky. Recently, there has been a solitary violinist playing in Union Street. He could have been a guest in the stable. This Day Mass, though, is like passing from a solo or trio or quartet to a full choir and orchestra. It's less the magic of the child in the manger and the eagerness of the shepherds that prevail. It's more the sense of the huge reality this child conceals.

'The Lord bares his holy arm in the sight of all the nations, and all the ends of the earth shall see the salvation of our God,' says Isaiah This child is not just a local boy. He's the Saviour of the world.

> Welcome, all wonders in one sight!
> Eternity shut in a span;
> Summer in winter; day in night;
> Heaven in earth, and God in man.
> Great little one, whose all-embracing birth
> Lifts earth to heaven, stoops heav'n to earth.[1]

'We saw his glory.' Let's ask Mary and Joseph to see it, ask the angels, ask the apostles. 'To all who did accept him, he gave power to become the children of God.' We are not the children of God by nature, but we are by adoption. We are sons in the Son. The Son of God became the son of man so that the sons and daughters of man may become the sons and daughters of God. The Collect says the same in other words. The sun is high in the sky.

If we deny the divinity of Christ, the light goes out of our humanity.

The glory of Christmas runs through to us. It is all for us. 'The Lord bares his holy arm in the sight of all nations.'

If God has become man, we have been affirmed in a way that goes beyond our own devising. We have been endorsed. We have been recognized. We have been told we are wanted, that we count. Every one of us. We're all contained in that child. Our freedom is the chance of accepting that: of endorsing God's endorsement by trying to live like Christ. We don't have to puff ourselves up. We don't have to make a god of our self. We don't have to do better than others or suck them into the vortex of our frantic search for self-esteem. We can be what we are: this strange mixture of weakness and strength, selfhood and dependence. Our dignity is there, safe in the hands of the child. Absolutely sure. Our humanity, our individuality are safe now. Our life is safe, whatever comes. If we give it over, it is filled. The Magi offered gifts—good for them. But the shepherds just brought themselves and went away glorifying God. They had seen the glory.

'No one has ever seen God; it is the only Son, who is nearest to the Father's heart, who has made him known.'

There are so many Christmases, aren't there? It's tempting to catalogue them. There's the retail Christmas. There's the paganized Christmas of 'winter festivals' and 'season's greetings'. There's the Christmas of politicians with messages of good will and peace on earth. There's the culinary Christmas, of good food and drink. 'Bring me flesh and bring me wine', says Good King Wenceslas. Why not? 'The Word was made flesh.' There's the family Christmas. The historians say that the Victorians invented this. The cynics say that the number of files for divorce rises after it. But surely, it's a holy and wholesome thing. There's the Christmas of charity, of helping the unfortunate. King Wenceslas' 'flesh and wine' were for a poor man, not just himself. We all know: there are cold and lonely Christmases, Christmases in war zones, Christmases ill in bed.

And isn't there also the *Christmas of faith*? That's what brought us here. It's what's in this liturgy. It can help us sift and sort out the many Christmases on the market, as it were. It leaves some aside, and others it quietly enriches from inside. This Christmas of faith is surely head of the list.

We've come to Bethlehem. We've heard the words of the angels: 'Glory to God in the highest.' We've come down from the hills and found the cave in the rock where the animals are stabled. We've seen the child. We've felt the grace. I'm talking of us and all the believers throughout the world who've kept and are keeping this Christmas and have been at least to the Vigil Mass or the Night Mass or the Dawn Mass or have kept what they could as they can. And we know that there are eight days of Christmas before us, the Christmas Octave, or Twelve Days, or all the days to the Epiphany and the feast of the Lord's Baptism, or that in some churches the Christmas trees will be there till 2 February.

Each of the Masses I've mentioned, each of the feasts of the Christmas season, have their own prayers and readings. It's dish after dish, none of them quite the same. But this Mass, the Mass of Christmas Day, is the most reflective of all. It's as though we have been spending time at the Crib and then have gone outside and walked under the stars, thinking what it is we've been shown, what we've seen. The shepherds have gone back to their sheep, the angels have returned to heaven. Mary has a moment to ponder. And in the space opened up, there are thoughts to be had. We hear the opening of the Letter to the Hebrews: 'At various times and in various different ways, God spoke to our ancestors through the prophets; but in our own time, the last days, he has spoken to us through his Son, the Son that he has appointed to inherit everything and through whom he made everything there is. He is the radiant light of God's glory and the perfect copy of his nature, sustaining the universe.' These are solemn, mysterious words. If only we had time to linger on them! Extraordinary words to hear beside a newborn baby's cradle! Then the evangelist John begins to speak, words we know well: 'In the beginning was the Word: the Word was with God and the Word was God. He was with God in the beginning.' And this Word has become flesh and lived among us. He began his life among us in the arms of a Jewish girl. And we have seen this unexpected glory: this God who humbles and hides himself. In our pride, we can miss him. But to all who accept him, says John, is given the power to become children of God.

What difference does this Child make? There's a sense in which he changes nothing. There were Herods then and there are Herods now. People died in those days, and we die now. People then felt overworked and underpaid, and we do too. Nothing has changed but everything is changed. Imagine a darkened room, and a light going on. Nothing moves in the room, but everything in the room is changed. 'Today,' says the liturgy, 'a great light has shone upon the earth.' Everything is different.

And what is this light? It's Jesus himself. He is the difference. 'Grace and truth have come through Jesus Christ,' says St John. He is God's free download of Christmas. He is the Light from Light, and he brings light: the light of knowing we are loved. 'Henceforth and for ever,' Pope Francis has said, 'the infinite and eternal God is God with us. He is not far off. We need not search for him in the heavens or in mystical notions. He is close at hand. He became man and he will never withdraw from our humanity, which he has made his own.'[2] Can there be any greater endorsement of our humanity, our life than this? God has made us part of himself. Any greater 'yes' to who and what we are? In the person of his Son God has taken us on, body and soul, taken us into himself. This affects everyone of us, everyone we pass in the street. Every child in the womb, every baby, every youngster, every father, every mother, everyone able, everyone disabled, everyone healthy, everyone dying. Everyone for ever. The heavenly Father wants us. He cherishes our human-ness. Love is affirmation, and affirmation is saying 'yes'. What greater affirmation could there be than what we call the Incarnation? It's a yes to our common humanity, to our unique individuality, to our hands and our feet, to our neurophysiology and our spiritual capacities, to our youth and our age.

What difference does Jesus make? Never again need we say, I'm worthless. Never again, no-one loves me.

Never again, what's the point? We needn't justify our existence, prove ourselves better, do others down to reassure ourselves, fluff out our feathers. We will do and say those things, of course. We all fall into our own holes or sit on our own little thrones. And life can be short and brutish. But a light has gone on. Nothing has changed and everything is different.

Brothers and Sisters, why has he done this? Why has God become a human being? Why has the Word become flesh and lived among us? Why has the radiant light of God's glory and the perfect copy of his nature put his light under the bushel of human flesh, human nature? Why has the Son of the Father become the child of a woman called Mary, a baby with brittle fingers and tiny toes, something to warm and feed, to tickle and cuddle, to look at and smile at? Why have we been given God as our baby brother? This is Christmas. It's a wonder. It's meant to wow us. Every child we care about takes us out of ourselves. Every baby rescues us from selfishness. Every birth is astonishing. And this One still more.

Think of carols. They're everywhere too. Where there's Christmas, there are carols. They open our lungs and our mouths. They go to the heart. They're homely and sublime. They often have a story behind them. Take 'O little town of Bethlehem ...' It was written in 1867 by a six-foot-seven American Episcopalian priest, Philip Brooks, after a Christmas visit to the actual town. He just wrote it for the children back home and asked a friend to set it to music. He didn't expect it to be remembered. 'How silently, how silently, the wondrous gift is given. And God imparts to human hearts, the blessings of his heaven.' Again, carols too bring Christmas close and us to it.

We can think of all the poetry, the music, the song, the sculpture, the paintings, the films Christmas has engendered. So much art shared over the centuries, so much still burgeoning today. The Word became flesh and lived among us. The Word has become paint and wood and stone and sound and lives among us. He lives in our eyes and ears and our hands. Some twelve hundred years ago (in 787) the bishops of the Church held a great Council (Nicaea II) in what's now Turkey—the Seventh Ecumenical Council. Cutting a long story short, they said that this translation of the Word made flesh into art is good. It brings the Gospel home to us. It extends the enfleshment of Christ into the matter and flesh of the world, and so into our lives.

'The Word became flesh and lived among us.' There is Christmas in a sentence. And hidden in that sentence is an answer to the why of the wonder. The Word who was in the beginning, is with God, is God; the Word that created; the Word that shines through creation; the Word that offers its light to every human being; the Word that cast its brightness on God's chosen people, has at last entered the sphere of humanity, has become flesh, has taken on our human stuff. And he has 'lived' among us. 'Lived' is one possible translation of the word St John used. We can also say: He pitched his tent among us, set up his tabernacle among us, has dwelt among us, made his home among us. And why has he done this? Why has this happened? So we can make our home with him. We are close now. Ever since Adam and Eve left the garden, ever since Cain became a wanderer on the face of the earth, ever since the human race was scattered after the Tower of Babel fell, ever since Abraham left Ur and Haran for a land the Lord would show him, we have been on the road. We may or we may not have good homes, warm houses, close family—it's a blessing if we do—but at the level of the heart we are all exiles, refugees, migrants, vagrants, wandering Jews, displaced persons, of no fixed abode, homeless. We all tend to evict each other too, unable to be under the same roof. We are all scattered and all in search of home. That is why Christmas happened. It is why God was born in a ramshackle, make-do place on the edge of a village. It's why the Word became flesh and made his home among us. So we at last have a home.

The Child who was born in a shed came to build us a house and call us home. Here's the why: a place of communion with God and unity among ourselves, his risen Body, God's Church, our common home. We find it in faith. We enter it when we pray. We live in it when we love. It's where we learn to house each other, be homes to each other. Then the Word has really become flesh and lives among us.

Notes

1. Richard Crashaw, 'In the Holy Nativity of Our Lord God', in *English Poems* (London: Methuen & Co 1901).
2. Pope Francis, *Homily at the Mass on Christmas Eve*, 24 December 2016.

7

The Feast of St Stephen

Had any of us been asked what to celebrate the day after Christmas, it's unlikely we'd have suggested St Stephen. Suddenly we pass from the serenity of the stable to a furious theological argument that ends in someone being stoned and to a Gospel that tells us everyone will hate us. It seems a far cry from Bethlehem.

Yet throughout almost all of Christian history St Stephen has been celebrated precisely here: in the Eastern churches on the 27th of December and among us today, the 26th. And this strange juxtaposition has proved to be full of meaning.

Who was Stephen, first of all? Let's attempt his personal profile. He was a leading figure in the Jewish-Christian community in Jerusalem in the years immediately after our Lord's death, resurrection, and ascension. He's the first-named of the seven men proposed by the community and ordained by the apostles to distribute food to the needy—the seven men seen by Tradition as the first deacons. He was clearly an exceptional and Spirit-filled personality. 'Full of faith and of the Holy Spirit,' says St Luke, 'full of grace and power.' And he embarked on his mission with energy and success. He was a worker of 'great wonders and signs', a gifted speaker: no one could resist 'the wisdom and the Spirit with which he spoke'. He was a man on whom the power of Pentecost had come to rest. And such are not usually left in peace. The Christians in Jerusalem were a new, growing group. And as they grew so did tension with the Jewish authorities and their Council, the Sanhedrin. In the story of Stephen, it reaches a climax. Previously the apostles had been *warned* against preaching that Jesus was the Christ. Then they had been *flogged* for doing so. And now Stephen is arrested, accused, brought before the Council, and finally sent out of the city and *stoned*. 'And that day a bitter persecution started against the church in Jerusalem', with Saul, who had approved Stephen's killing, a prime mover. But what is the upshot? The persecution compels the Christians to go elsewhere, and with them goes their message. The risen Christ changes Saul into Paul and sends him, not only to Jews, but to the Gentiles. The word of God passes beyond Jerusalem, out into the great wide Gentile, pagan, Greek and Roman world. Stephen's life and death was the turning-point that made all this possible, a bridge from the Church's Jewish beginnings to its Gentile future. In him, the protomartyr, the famous words first came true, 'The blood of martyrs is the seed of Christians.'

But to return to his arrest and trial and death. In the course of it, he's transfigured—something that has happened to others too. 'His face was like the face of an angel,' says St Luke. Against the garbled accusations thrown at him, he lays out the Christian position with considerable power, provocatively even. Anger rises against him. Proper judicial procedure seems to be set aside. But he 'full of the Holy Spirit, gazed into heaven and saw the glory of God, with Jesus standing at the right hand of God.' His passion has the form of Christ's. Like Christ, he's a subject of false accusations, undergoes a trial, stands firm. And he dies praying, praying to Jesus, and praying like Jesus: 'Lord Jesus, receive my spirit', 'Lord, do not hold this sin against them.' We catch the Gospel echoes. And out of this Christ-like passion comes the resurrection of the wider mission, the growth of the

Church, the salvation of Saul. In the end, Stephen's profile is that of a disciple shaped to his Master.

And so back to Christmas. The question is, what does this divine Child bring? St Stephen is an answer. It isn't the so-called Gospel of prosperity. It isn't an easy life. It isn't universal popularity. Today's Gospel could hardly be starker: 'You will be hated by all men on account of my name.' 'You are well aware, then,' wrote Paul to Timothy, 'that anybody who tries to live in devotion to Christ is certain to be attacked.' Persecution is woven into the history of the Church. It's a bitter part of the Church's present. The German bishops, for one, ask their faithful on St Stephen's day to remember the many Christians suffering for their faith now—in China, in India, in some Muslim countries and elsewhere. So it's something other than a comfortable life this Child has in his hand. It is something other and better. It's striking how often Luke uses the word 'full' of Stephen. This is it: Jesus brings a fullness. In him all the fullness of God dwelt bodily, says St Paul, and of his fullness we have all received, says St John. Stephen is full of faith, says Luke. He's full of grace and power. He's full of wisdom. He's full of the Holy Spirit. These are charged New Testament words. They are different aspects of the fullness Jesus brings. They are namings of the grace of Pentecost, the fire Jesus came to cast on earth.

St Stephen is a sign, a 'witness' (martyr), to this fullness.

And so we go back to his martyrdom. Thanks to this fullness he sees heaven opened and Jesus standing at the right hand of God. He sees the new closeness with God that Jesus brings. He sees his victory over death. And this turns the day of his death into a day of victory, a birthday into true and everlasting life.

And out of this fullness he can even pray, 'Lord, do not hold this sin against them.' Here is more victory. We won't all be martyred, but we do all get hurt, and hurt each other. Our natural instinct is to hug that hurt, and let it fill us, till we're full of resentment. Resentment is a cancer of the spirit. It's not what we're made for. No, it's not a comfortable life Jesus brings us. It's something other and better. It's the capacity to forgive and even ultimately forget. Saul and Stephen are friends now. It's the impossible the Christ Child brings, the unthinkable, a fullness that can even forgive the hurt. This is a gift so precious, so unique to Jesus, so quintessentially his, so at the very heart of the redemption he brings, that the day after his birth we celebrate someone who welcomed this gift to the full.

So we pray with Stephen, 'Lord Jesus, receive my spirit.' Receive it and fill it—not with me, but with your Spirit. Fill it with faith and power and wisdom and grace. Amen.

8

THE FEAST OF THE HOLY FAMILY

We're in Christmas time. Our Lord has entered our world as a human being, and everything he touches, takes on, involves himself with, he heals, restores, fills with new energy and goodness and lifts to a new level. He takes our flesh. He eats and drinks, sleeps and feels. He thinks and decides, talks and argues. He lives our life and shares our death. And the resurrection is the sign of the difference he makes, and its power is at work already.

The Bible is full of families. It begins with a couple, and mentions three of their children: Cain, Abel and Seth. The story of the people of Israel begins with Abraham and Sarah and their children. Genesis is all family histories. The Gospel of St Matthew begins with Jesus' family tree. The Gospel of St Luke begins with an elderly couple, Elizabeth and Zechariah, and their child John. The whole New Testament story begins with Jesus, Mary and Joseph.

The Bible is full of genealogies, family trees. There are some twenty-five in the Old Testament and two in the New. Three of the Ten Commandments have to do with marriage and family life: 'Honour your father and mother; you shall not commit adultery; you shall not covet your neighbour's wife.'

What's true in the Bible is true of our own experience. Our own lives are full of family. How often do you dream of family members? Each of us here is a son or a daughter. Many here husbands or wives, mothers or fathers. Most of us are brothers or sisters. Much as we sometimes wish we could, we can't get away from it!

First of all, I suppose, this Feast and its first two readings encourage us to reflect, to examine our conscience. What kind of son or daughter, husband or wife, mother or father, brother or sister or cousin, have I been, am I now? Have I done all that 'the law of the Lord requires'? We all have ground to make up here. We all have to keep the kettle on and the tea warm, as it were. One of the lessons of family life, certainly, is the long view: to wait for things to come right or be all they could be. But there is usually some step we can take here and now. This year this Feast falls on the last day of the year. Perhaps, there is a resolution about our family relationships we could make?

Our Lord took on family life not because it's always lovely, but, as he took on our whole humanity: to right it from within, to heal it, redeem it, inject it with saving grace, to turn the water into wine. Even Mary and Joseph were left puzzled and anguished at times. Even more his wider family who, at the beginning anyway, were set against him. And what he did in his earthly life, he does in his risen life: through the Sacrament of Matrimony, through the prompting of the Holy Spirit, he injects saving grace into marriage, into family life. Grace can undermine the difficulties, turn them into opportunities. So today, a second thing could be to remember this grace, realize our need, ask for God's help. Invite him into the family circle. Stir up the gift. God gives us our baptism every day. We can say too: God gives me my marriage every day, God gives us our family every day. The Incarnation is now. Jesus, Mary and Joseph are now. I've mentioned before a dramatic Italian lady who, when war broke out in the kitchen, would fling out her arms and cry, 'Veni, Santo Spirito!' Family life needs a constant *epiclesis*.[1] So, let's remember grace.

So we can think of the Holy Family of Jesus, Mary and Joseph as the centre and core of something larger, and as a kind of holy leaven. They were doing then what the Liturgy prays the example of the Holy Family will do now. They were a source of grace.

There's a message of today, for married Christians, for Christian or half-Christian families, for all of us: not to despair of the grace of God. It is at work. St Paul speaks of husbands and wives, children and parents. The family is the place where we overcome the tendency to 'me, myself and I', and realize we're relational beings. We have to give way. We have to think of others. We learn to say 'sorry', 'please' and 'thank you'. We move from being 'me' to 'us'. And this is the opening to grace, to the Trinity. It strikes me too that when we do see Jesus, Mary and Joseph by themselves, without the wider network, it's in times of trouble: having to seek asylum in Egypt, or when Mary and Joseph go back to Jerusalem looking for Jesus. This is so often when the family proves its worth, shows its mettle. When one member is having a hard time, the family can be the place of comfort and a new start. The family is the first hospital, the Pope has said. There are wonderful stories of separated husbands and wives, or parents and children, hanging on against all the odds, staying loyal and finding their way back together. This is the power of love. And grace is in it.

Jesus became human, and now our humanity can radiate him. He belonged to a family, and now our families can be full of him. Let's not underestimate the radiant beauty and saving power of a family with Christ at its heart. Christ has made family life a way to God.

> Jesus, Mary and Joseph,
> Graciously hear our prayer. Amen.

Notes

1. The *epiclesis* (Latin *invocatio*) is the name of a prayer that occurs in all Eastern liturgies (and originally in Western liturgies also) after the words of Institution, in which the celebrant prays that God may send down his Holy Spirit to change this bread and wine into the Body and Blood of his Son.

9

Mary, Mother of God

Numbers 6:22–27; Galatians 4:4–7; Luke 2:16–21

> *When the appointed time came, God sent his Son, born of a woman...*

Today, it's this 'born of a woman' that shines out. Today is the octave day of Christmas, the start of another year, and the solemnity of Mary, Mother of God. 'Hail, holy Mother', says the Entrance Antiphon, 'who gave birth to the King who rules heaven and earth forever.'

So let's follow the grain of the Liturgy and look at Mary.

'As for Mary', the Gospel says, 'she treasured all these things and pondered them in her heart.' Christmas was something Mary took inside herself and thought about. It engaged her memory: 'she treasured all these things / all these words.' She kept them, remembered them, didn't forget them. And they didn't just sit there, at the back of her mind, as it were. She 'pondered them in her heart.' Literally, 'she threw them around', turned them over, mulled them over. She looked at them from different angles. She was trying with God's help to understand their meaning. She had a child in her arms and the words of angels and shepherds in her mind. And she wanted to put all this together. She wanted to make sense of it.

'As for Mary, she treasured all these things and pondered them in her heart.' When I was a boy, these words intrigued me. And now what strikes me is just what an experience the first Christmas must have been for Mary. That's why she had to think about it. We don't know what she thought; it's her secret. But we can try and guess something of what she went through, something of what happened to her. I think St Luke, in the way he presents her, wants us to do this. And what strikes me again is how, moment by moment, scene by scene, everything in Mary is, so to speak, brought out by Christ, how her whole being rises up and becomes focused and energized by him. It's the earth opening up in the face of heaven coming close.

Think back nine months to the Annunciation. Here she is, a simple Jewish girl from an obscure village, going about her daily work. And suddenly she's greeted, fulsomely, by an angel. 'Deeply disturbed,' says St Luke, 'she asked herself what this greeting might mean.' She's already affected. He delivers his extraordinary message: she'll be the mother of the Messiah himself. Now her common sense asserts itself: 'How is this possible if I'm a virgin?' He explains that a man won't be the cause but the Spirit of God—more extraordinary still. He assures her 'nothing is impossible with God'. And now the hidden grace in her speaks up. She gives her full consent to God's bewildering project and her own part in it. And she does indeed conceive by the Holy Spirit and become the Mother of God.

Think of this as an experience. Here's a human being, Mary, meeting the divine, and everything in her is involved, engaged, brought into play. Her femininity, the intimate parts of her body, all her chemistry, her emotions, her reason, her will, the hopes she shared with her people, her marriage-to-be with Joseph—it's all affected, touched, sparked. All of it wells up to meet the coming Christ.

Then go on through the Gospel. She visits Elizabeth. She wants to share her experience. She wants to help someone else caught up in the same story. And here still more emerges. When Elizabeth praises her, she bursts out in praise of God. Her joy overflows. She sings the Magnificat. It's more of the human! Then she has her baby. She cuddles him, breast-feeds him, keeps him warm and dry, tickles him, rubs noses with him, makes funny noises back at him. She sings to him. There's a lovely carol *I heard an Infant weeping*. It has Mary singing a lullaby:

> My Lamb, from God forth-faring,
> My Life, my guiding Star,
> Fair Lily, of my bearing,
> Than jewel rarer far:
> Babe Jesu, lullaby!

Whatever, she was the real mother of a real baby. Then the shepherds come, and there are more strange angelic words to take on board.

These are just glimpses, flashes of what the Incarnation, the coming of Christ, meant for one human being, his mother. Enough of a flash I think to see that *everything* in her was affected. Every violin-string of her nature plucked and called upon to play. All her threefold potential—as a human being, a woman, a unique individual, as body, soul and spirit—elicited. And in time, not least, her capacity to suffer. She'd meet Simeon and Anna, hear that her son would be a sign of contradiction, and a sword pierce her heart. And indeed, she'd have a three-day agony losing her boy in Jerusalem, she'd have the ultimate horror of watching him die on a cross. What was left of herself then? There's nothing in Mary, no corner of her, no aspect of her humanness, that wasn't taken up by Christ, emptied out and filled with Christ, given to Christ and the things of Christ. There was nothing in her outside her mission to be the Mother of God, and the Mother of the Church, the mystical Body of her Son. And there's nothing in her now, assumed as she is body and soul into heaven, outside his joy. It floods her. 'My soul glorifies the Lord, and my spirit rejoices in God my saviour.' 'My Lamb, my Life, my Guiding Star, fair Lily of my bearing!' My pearl of great price. My treasure hidden in the field. My Jesus.

And Mary's song, Mary's discovery, Mary's experience has the potential to be ours as well. Her son, God and man, is the one for whom the humanity of each and all of us has been waiting and in whom it is brought to birth. He is the One who makes us human, whom we were made and designed from all eternity to know, love, serve and be happy with forever.

I might object: such passionate intensity is beyond me. Mary after all had a direct contact with Jesus, whereas my life, my body and soul, my emotions and thoughts and desires are all tied up, yes, in part with church and religion, but with other things as well: with family, with work, with friends, with worries over health and money and all the rest. But say that and we've missed the point. The point is, there is only one divine plan and it's for all of us. It's to bring together everything and everyone into Christ. This beloved baby body Mary holds in her hands is growing day by day into the mystical Body of the one same Christ. And all the people with whom our lives and emotions and thoughts are tied up are, potentially or actually, part of this body. So it is the same for us. Christ is everywhere and in everyone. He meets us in everyone and everything. And our whole life too, like Mary's, every nook and cranny of it, can, through the grace of the Eucharist and the power of the Spirit, be turned to him, engaged by him, taken hold of by him—through others for the most part. Our humanity too, as we live with and for each other, can be born and suffer and die and rise. Through him, with him, in him, it can realize its capacity for love. And this is what living really is.

When a Benedictine makes profession, he or she sings a Psalm-verse: 'Receive me, Lord, according to your word, and I shall live. And you will not disappoint me of my hope.' 'Receive me. Lord, according to your word, and I shall live.' Today's Collect calls Mary's son the Author of Life, its well-spring, its source. Let us, as this year begins, ask him to receive us—everything we have and are. Then we will live, as Mary did, as Mary does.

10

Epiphany

Isaiah 60:1–6; Ephesians 3:2–3a, 5–6; Matthew 2:1–12

Epiphany means 'manifestation'. But that's a heavy word. An 'epiphany' is an outburst, an explosion, of light and of a light falling on us, lighting us.

This is a beautiful feast, and in the Church's mind a great one.

'After Jesus had been born at Bethlehem in Judaea during the reign of King Herod, some wise men came from the east.' So, after keeping Jesus' birth at Christmas, we remember these wise men at Epiphany.

They have always fascinated the Christian imagination, and they can fascinate ours. Probably they were astrologers and astronomers (the two things were not differentiated then). In our terms, a mixture of scientist and philosopher and religious inquirer. Probably they were from Babylon, in what is now southern Iraq, and was a centre for study of the stars. Perhaps the star they saw was an unusual conjunction of the planets Jupiter and Saturn in the constellation of Pisces which took place in the years 7–6 BC, now thought to have been the time that Jesus was born. And here's an interesting detail: the planet Jupiter was associated with the chief Babylonian god, Marduk, and the planet Saturn with the Jews. So if the two came together this would have been charged with significance. Certainly, many non-Jewish people of the time knew the Jews were expecting a Messiah. There were still Jews in Babylon too. Perhaps the wise men were in conversation with them. Perhaps they heard of the prophecy of the Gentile Balaam in the book of Numbers: 'I see him, but not now; I behold him, but not nigh: a star shall come forth out of Jacob and a sceptre shall rise out of Jerusalem.' These are all real possibilities.

Whatever, these intrepid, pure-hearted magi 'saw' and 'went'. They followed the star. They read the runes, as it were. They picked up the clues. They followed the trail and came with their gifts to worship the new-born King. In the Rule of St Benedict when a young person wants to enter the monastery, the first question he or she is asked is, 'Are you really seeking God?' These men were. And they are patterns for us. They had a star in the sky. We have the star of faith. Their goal was Bethlehem. Ours is heaven.

Today is an explosion of light. Christ has both depth and breadth. His depth is his divinity, his eternity, his union with the Father. His breadth is his humanity. It's his relevance, his connection to every one of us, all the way to the furthest away. 'He shall rule from sea to sea, / from the Great River to earth's bounds', says the Psalm. 'He shall save the poor when they cry / and the needy who are helpless.' And today it's this universality—Jesus' catholicity—which begins to rise, like a star, over the world's horizon. Isaiah had already foreseen the return of scattered Israel, the diaspora Jews, to Jerusalem: 'Lift up your eyes and look around: all are assembling and coming towards you', your sons and daughters. But then his vision seems to expand. It's not just Jews who come to

Jerusalem, but the abandoned Gentiles too: 'the riches of the sea will flow to you; the wealth of the nations come to you ... everyone in Sheba will come, bringing gold and incense, and singing the praise of the Lord.' And in the strange gift-bearing men from the east who make their way to Jesus, this hope begins to be fulfilled. They're the pioneers, the forerunners. Even 'though night still covers the earth', even though a Herod is king, prophecy is being fulfilled, and the star of faith guides the questing magi to their goal, these 'people of inner unrest'.[1] And what began with them explodes again in the mission of the Church after Pentecost. Jesus is the Jew for all men, and Paul the Jew, who grasped this with his whole being, proclaims the pagans, the Gentiles—us!—as co-inheritors of heaven, co-members of the body of Christ, co-beneficiaries of the promises of God.

We take the decorations down now. But the grace of Christmas, please God, will have been to remind us of our star, and allow it to shine afresh. Follow your star! If we feel it's gone missing, then let's ask God to let us glimpse it again. There are myriad possible stars, enough to confuse us. Also, we're told that some stars, while we still see their light, have long since died. So, there are false stars, glitter without substance. But still, God gives each of us a true star. How do we know if it's true? By where it takes us. The magi were non-Jews, Gentiles, outside God's revelation to Israel. But they were men on a quest, scientific and religious, moral and intellectual. They were truly seeking God and looking for something better. They followed the star, and it took them, first, to Jerusalem, to the Jewish Scriptures, the message of the prophets. Then, on to Bethlehem, where 'it halted over the place where the child was.' And they went into the house. And 'they saw—not the star anymore—but the child with his mother Mary, and falling to their knees, they did him homage (worshipped him). Then, opening their treasures, they offered him gifts of gold and frankincense and myrrh.' If, with a pure heart, we follow the star God gives us, the lesser lights of our conscience as it were, we will come to the greater light: the Star of Judah, the bright Morning Star that never sets because he has risen from the dead. A good star, a true star will lead us where it led the magi: to revealed truth and into the house where Mary shows us Jesus. That house in Bethlehem—the 'house of bread'—is the Church, which Mary-like offers us Jesus, the Living Bread come down from heaven. There we learn to worship and to offer gifts. We learn to pray and to serve, to love God and our neighbour. We begin to arrive. We begin to be human beings. This is the gift of the Church.

Did the magi have cricked, strained necks for watching the star for so many miles? But when they enter the house, they have to look down at a little child, they go down on their knees. We too, perhaps, have to go down to see Jesus.

Epiphany is to Christmas rather what Pentecost is to Easter. At Pentecost, the message of Christ's death and resurrection goes global. People from 'every nation under heaven' heard what Peter had to say in their own languages. The Church universal, catholic, was born. And today it's the same dynamic. To be precise, it's the *sign* that it is going to happen. These wise men—searching scientists, religious seekers—were a beginning, the firstfruits of the vast non-Jewish world. 'All nations shall fall prostrate before you, O Lord,' promises the Psalm. 'The nations come to your light and kings to your dawning brightness,' says Isaiah. These and other ancient prophecies had their first realization in today's heroes. If they came from modern-day Iran, it's almost a thousand miles from Tehran to Jerusalem, and a good deal further by road. It was a long journey they and their camels had of it. But on they went, gradually unlearning their idolatries, following the star of their search and their conscience, fuelled by inner hope. Pioneers of all who, from Pentecost on, would make the journey to faith, to Bethlehem, to Jesus, us included. 'This mystery means,' says St Paul, 'that pagans now share the same inheritance, that they are parts of the same body, and that the same promise has been made to them, in Jesus Christ, through the gospel.' So, Epiphany too is the birthday of the Church universal. It begins the regathering of the Father's scattered, straying humanity around the person of Jesus. The prodigal Gentiles are coming home. Christianity is global. It's for every human being and the whole of our humanity. Jesus isn't someone to be imposed, but proposed. He doesn't come to crush or diminish us, but to heal us, call out our beauty, make us whole, reconnect us. How much further Christmas, the Incarnation, has to go in each of us and in the world! How not think of China? That great land to our east...

'We have come to do him homage.' Here's a second thing. This was their simple goal from the beginning: to worship, to adore. And they reach it, not in Herod's magnificent Temple, but in a tiny, rented house in an insignificant village. 'And going into the house they saw the child with his mother Mary, and falling to their knees they did him homage.' There's no more mention of the star. The Star was now in his mother's arms. It's a beautiful moment. It's a moment of freedom. When these men fall down, all the idols and false gods, all the misguided worship of the pagan world falls with them and turns to dust—and all the treasures of that world can become gifts. We are made to worship, to yield to what is greater and prior to ourselves. Our hearts are that large. Our tragedy is worshipping what, however honourable, doesn't deserve our whole self. We prefer the created to the Creator, as St Paul neatly puts it. Possessions, pleasure, power, or just our dear old egos. And so we lose our freedom. What the wise men did, Mary was already doing in her heart. It's what we do in our liturgy, in Eucharistic adoration. It's where Mother Church is always leading us: to the freedom of the children of God.

In the second reading St Paul speaks of a mystery 'unknown to the people of past generations' now being 'revealed'. And the magi, the pagans, the Gentiles respond. A star shone in the night sky and drew them from the East, a physical light led them to the spiritual light, a lesser light to the greater light, 'the true light that enlightens all men'. And faith responds.

How taken aback Mary and Joseph must have been when these strange figures drew aside the curtain and came in, and fell to their knees, and offered the Child their sumptuous gifts.

This feast proclaims just how attractive Jesus is. He draws us. The Christmas Gospels show this. Think how from the Annunciation onwards, Mary must have been drawn to the son she conceived by the Holy Spirit. Drawn in mind and will through her engagement with the angel; drawn in joy as the child took root inside her; drawn in soul and spirit when she sang the Magnificat; drawn in her heart where she pondered every word about him. How glued to him she must have felt when she had him in her arms! Joseph too, surely, was drawn surely, by his Annunciation: 'do not fear to take Mary as your wife, for that which is conceived In her is of the Holy Spirit.' 'And he did as the angel commanded him.' I'm sure! Think of John the Baptist giving a leap in Elizabeth's womb at the sound of Mary's voice. Think of the shepherds after their annunciation: 'Let's go over to Bethlehem ... and they went with haste.' Forty days later, 'inspired by the Holy Spirit', the old man Simeon 'comes to the Temple' and sweeps Mary's child up into his arms, and Anna 'comes up at that very hour'. T. S. Eliot speaks of the 'drawing of this love and the voice of this calling'.[2] Christ draws and calls and attracts. All these felt it. And with the Magi from the east, the screen widens, the reach extends. 'We have seen his star', they say: it was Christ appearing, appealing to their eyes. 'And we have come': Christ drawing their feet, despite 'a wearisome, irksome, troublesome, dangerous, unseasonable journey'.[3] 'Where is he?' they ask in Jerusalem; Christ is already honey in their mouth, someone they loved to speak about. And when they reach Bethlehem, the sight of the Child gently pulls them to their knees and opens their hands as they spill out their gifts. Their whole selves, their whole anatomy, their body, soul and spirit have been drawn to the Infant King on his mother's lap. They are captivated, worshipping men. The shepherds had already been enthralled—local guys, rough, working men, poor Jews like Jesus. Now it is sophisticated astronomers, scientists, sages, and not Jews, but Gentiles. 'The riches of the sea, the wealth of the nations.' No wonder that legends, good legends, have multiplied. One wise man was young, another middle-aged, the third elderly: Christ draws at any age. One was from India, another from Africa, another from Europe: from every known continent of the time. 'The drawing of this love and the voice of this calling.'

And all this is just a beginning, a morning-star, when Jesus is merely a child, a first, very modest epiphany. There was so much more 'epiphany' to come. The other epiphany of his baptism and the third of water blushing into wine; or the bread multiplied by the lake or the haemorrhaging woman touching his hem or Lazarus raised. The Beatitudes spoken, the Lord's Prayer handed over, the parables of the Good Samaritan and the Prodigal Son told. 'I am the Vine and you are the branches', and this bread is my Body and this cup holds my Blood. And so 'he stretched out his hands in the Passion to break the bonds of death and manifest the Resurrection.' This is the Epiphany rolled out, as it were, in his public life and Paschal mystery, to be rolled out through time as the Gospel goes forth and the Eucharist gathers. After the Magi so many more, year after year, will feel the attraction: 'the riches of the sea and the wealth of nations.' People will believe and follow. 'And I, when I am lifted up, will draw all people, all things to myself.' 'The pagans now share the same inheritance, they are parts of the same body, and the same promise has been made to them.' The Psalm is fulfilled.

> For he shall save the poor when they cry
> and the needy who are helpless.
> He will have pity on the weak
> and save the lives of the poor (Ps 72:12–13).

It is the poor who feel the pull of this poor man who is God. And he can draw from anywhere, any hole, any mess, any sin.

Epiphany happens when something previously hidden shines out. What shines out today is the power of Christ the Light to attract. He shines in the darkness and the darkness cannot overcome it. The Glory may strike unexpectedly and interrupt lives, or steal up imperceptibly. 'It will flame out, like shining from shook foil'[4] or burn, steadily growing, through a lifetime. It may seem to flicker but then rekindle. 'Kindly light', it can lead out of any darkness.

Christ the Uniquely Loveable, Christ the Attractive, Christ the Star who draws. Jew and Gentile, great and small, young and old, woman and man. This is the message of this feast. And it looks to the great Epiphany of his Coming again when this will be fully unleashed and fully received, 'a great crowd which no one could count, from every nation, from all tribes and peoples and tongues, standing before the throne and before the Lamb ... and crying out, Victory!'

So, people of inner unrest, I hope, not quite satisfied with anything here below, we come. We come drawn by the star of faith, despite ourselves at times. Our hearts set on the heavenly beauty, Sunday after Sunday, we come, every Sunday a stretch nearer. We come with the gold of our love, the incense of prayer, the myrrh of our sadness and losses and sufferings. And Christ, and our mother the Church, accept them. We can come from any place, at any age—it's never too late to convert!—and be welcomed into this house. Jesus receives the gifts of any person, any culture, any age.

So, first of all, let's give thanks: for the star of faith that God has set in the sky of our lives. Let's give thanks for the catholicity of the Church, something we experience, Sunday after Sunday. And lastly let's think of the magi: how they must have been changed by their meeting with Mary and Jesus. 'They returned to their country by a different way'—not just to avoid Herod, but because they were different men. And the star disappears. It disappears because now it's in them. They'd discovered the joy of the Gospel—*Evangelii Gaudium*. They'd seen the light and, without knowing it perhaps, they'd become light. Night still covered the earth, and Herod was still on his throne, and so it is, more or less, still today. But now there were people with a star of faith and hope and love in their hearts. And now there's us too. 'In the midst of a crooked and perverse generation,' says St Paul '… shine like stars … holding fast to the word of life' (Phil 2:15–16). Let's be like the magi, when we return home as well as coming here. Let's not be ashamed of our faith. Let it shine out of us in what we do and say. And, as one last fancy—not a fancy at all—let's pray, with the poet George Herbert, to this star:

> Take a … lodging in my heart
> …
> First with thy fire-work burn to dust
> Folly, and worse than folly, lust:
> Then with thy light refine,
> And make it shine.[5]

And make it shine!

Notes

1. Pope Benedict XVI, *Homily on the Epiphany*, 6 January 2012.
2. T. S. Eliot, 'Little Gidding' in *The Four Quartets* (London: Faber & Faber 1959).
3. Bishop Lancelot Andrewes, Sermon on Christmas Day 1622: Project Canterbury anglicanhistory.org/lact//v1/sermon15.html
4. G. M. Hopkins, 'Gods Grandeur', *The Poems of GMH* ed. WH Gardner & NH Mackenzie (Oxford: OUP 1970).
5. G. Herbert, 'The Starre' in *The Temple* (London: Methuen 1905).

11

The Baptism of the Lord

Isaiah 42:1–4, 6–7; Acts 10:34–38; Matthew 3:13–17

Today, as it were, we fast forward. The child in the manger is suddenly an adult by the river. Instead of the arms of his mother, there's the voice of the Father: 'This is my Son, the Beloved; my favour rests on him.' Instead of a birth, a baptism. Today John the Baptist's mission comes to its climax and conclusion, and the prophetic baton, as it were, is passed to Jesus. He is anointed by the Holy Spirit and goes out to his life's work, 'doing good and curing all who had fallen into the power of the devil'.

All four Gospels, in their different ways, have Jesus' public life begin with him receiving a baptism in the Jordan from the hands of John. John is baffled by Jesus' request. So were the early Christians. Why did the Sinless One undergo a ritual meant for sinners?

Yes, why did 'righteousness—God's will—demand' this? Why did he go down into the water?

Let's take a step back. As our Creed says so magnificently, Jesus is the Son of God. He exists from all eternity, God from God, Light from Light, true God from true God, and 'for us, and for our salvation, he came down from heaven and was made man'. He *came down, descendit de caelis*. This isn't space travel or astrophysics; it's metaphor for the divine humility. There's a lover in search of his beloved, approaching us step by step. 'Come down' means come close. First, he's 'conceived by the

Holy Spirit and born of the Virgin Mary'. The Son of God becomes a son of man. With a body and a psyche like ours. With a mother, with a family, with a people. Child of a particular place and time, like us. Having to learn, having to work. And now at his baptism, he takes a second step down. He goes under the water, submarine. It's divine humility again, the Lover in search of his beloved. The Fisherman fishing. Coming closer. It's the same dynamic.

But why water? Water, water, it's such a thing. It's everywhere in the Bible. It means so many things. Water is at the beginning of creation, of the life of our planet. Genesis opens with the Spirit of God moving over the waters. So, Jesus goes into water to say something new is beginning. Again, water—take Noah's flood—means cleansing; it's to wash away sin. So Jesus enters the waters to put himself beside everyone longing to be clean, forgiven, yearning to start again. He joins the queue of John's penitents, and grubby humanity suddenly has the Sinless One in its midst. Again, in the Psalms and Prophets, water means trials, life's difficulties, the things that overwhelm us and can wash us away. 'Save me, O God,' cries a psalmist, 'for the waters have risen to my neck' (Ps 68:1). Water a flood, water suggesting personal misfortune, others' negativity, foreign invasion, events turning against us; humanity 'not waving but drowning'. There's an ancient human instinct that, in deep water, lurks a dragon or a monster. When Jesus goes into the water, it means he will go into this darkness, share the experience with us. His baptism is a symbolic rehearsal of his Passion and death: 'I have a baptism to undergo,' he'll say. That will be divine humility going further still, a third step completing the second. 'He was humbler yet, and became obedient even unto death, death on a cross.' He would let himself be drowned under human hostility, washed, as it were, downstream. The Lover in search of his drowned beloved, his Ophelia.

He comes to the water. Perhaps there's another aspect too. Five hundred years before Jesus, a Greek philosopher—Heraclitus—famously said, 'No one steps twice into the same river.' Why not? Because if I go into the river one minute and then again three minutes later, the water is not the same. And from that he inferred, 'everything flows', everything is in flux. So Jesus, on the brink of his public ministry, about to become an actor in history, goes down into the flowing river. He enters our experience of time, of everything passing, of change and transience. 'I have sunk into the mud of the deep and there is no foothold' (Ps 68:2), says the Psalmist again. Life and society today have been called 'liquid'.[1] So many solid things being washed away. So many uncertainties and unclarities. Marriage and family, my trade or my profession no longer guarantee stability or identity in the ways they might have fifty years ago. Nor can my own country: how many have to migrate. How many of us can be sure where we'll be or what be doing this time next year? 'Everything flows', everything is in flux.

Down from the hill town of Nazareth, down to the valley of the Jordan comes the Lord. Down under the waters, the 'immensity of waters', goes the Lord. Into the creativity of water, into its cleansing power, into its liquidity, into its destructive potential, he goes. He enters into all it is and symbolizes, all it stands for in our life for good and ill.

What is going on? 'As soon as Jesus was baptized, he came up from the waters.' He *came up*. The heavens open—communication restored. The Dove descends—the Flood recedes. The Voice 'resounds on the waters'—

the one born, baptized and crucified is declared Son of God. As the going down looks to his Passion, so the coming up looks to his resurrection. After the three steps down—birth, baptism, death—come the three steps up: resurrection, ascension, the sitting at the Father's right hand, 'the Lord ... enthroned over the flood'. Now we know that, if we are in Christ, there is a new creation. We know there is a baptism in the Holy Spirit to forgive our sins. We know there's something in us no flood of circumstances can drown. We know the satanic monster has been crushed. Nor need we be deterred by any instability, any flux. He is close. 'All time belongs to him, and all the ages.' Divine humility has conquered. The marriage holds, made indissoluble on the Cross. The divine fisherman has us in his net.

Let the Lord speak through Isaiah, one last time this Christmas season: 'When you pass through the waters I will be with you; and through the rivers they shall not overwhelm you' (Is 43:2). We can go forward. We have a future.

Notes

1. Z. Nauman, *Liquid Life* (Cambridge: Wiley & Sons 2007).

12

The Presentation of the Lord

Malachi 3: 1–4; Luke 2: 22–40

'Behold, he comes to his holy temple, our Lord and Master: rejoice and be glad, Sion, running to meet your God.' This is the Invitatory Antiphon for the feast of the Presentation of the Lord.

Forty days after his birth, in the arms of his mother, the Lord comes to his temple, fulfilling the prophecy of Malachi, and other prophecies besides. He comes to his temple to build the true Temple, the temple not made with hands, unless it be the hands outstretched on the Cross. 'Behold ... he shall build the temple of the Lord' (Zech 6:12–13). This is what our Lord, King and Priest, has done. 'Destroy this temple and in three days I will raise it up' (Jn 2:19). 'Do you not know that you are God's temple and that God's Spirit dwells in you? If anyone destroys God's temple, God will destroy him. For God's temple is holy, and that temple you are' (1 Cor 3:16–17). The feast of the Presentation, like that of the Epiphany in a different way, is about the Church. The Lord reveals himself, and the issue is the Church. The Lord comes and opens up this new, broad place, no longer of restricted access, like the Jerusalem Temple, but open to all who have faith in Christ. Suddenly, there is *Lebensraum*, Catholicism.

And in this new Temple, this new space, the new worship comes into being. This too is the fulfilment of the prophecy of Malachi: 'For he is like a refiner's fire and like fuller's soap; he will sit as refiner and purifier of silver, and he will purify the sons of Levi and refine them like gold and silver, till they present right offerings to the Lord. Then the offering of Judah and Jerusalem will be pleasing to the Lord as in the days of old and as in former years' (Mal 3:2–4). This new, pleasing worship is adumbrated in Mary and Joseph. They bring the offering of the poor, 'a pair of turtledoves or two young pigeons' (Lk 2:24). Essentially, they bring their poverty of spirit: their openness to the word of God that the Holy Spirit will speak through Simeon and Anna. They bring their willingness to learn more about the child they are carrying, and to enter into his paschal mystery. Liturgy of the Word, liturgy of the Eucharist. For 'this child is set for the fall and rising of many in Israel, and for a sign that is spoken against (and a sword will pierce your own soul also)' (Lk 2:34–35). This is the new worship which Paul will solemnly intone, as it were, at the beginning of Romans 12. 'I appeal to you, therefore, brethren, by the mercies of God, to present your bodies as a living sacrifice, holy and acceptable to God, which is your reasonable worship' (Rom 12:1). Joseph Ratzinger/Pope Benedict makes this text the Invitatory Antiphon, so to speak, of Christian worship as such. It is striking that Mary and Joseph come to Jerusalem to 'present' their child to the Lord, and St Paul bids the Romans to 'present' their bodies (same verb). And Mary and Joseph come—the second thing Luke mentions—'to offer a sacrifice', and St Paul says, 'present your bodies as a living sacrifice'. The gestures of Mary and Joseph, still within the parameters of the old Law, anticipate remarkably the worship of the new.

The Presentation of the Lord

The Lord comes to his temple, Herod's temple, that deeply ambivalent place, and there, tiny and silent, he begins to build the new Temple and initiate the new worship, which is his, his paschal Mystery.

In this feast, there's a movement, a double movement. On the one hand, the Lord comes. On the other hand, Sion, Simeon and Anna, the Church, run to meet him. There's the approach of the Lord, his Advent, and there is our going forth to meet him. The second movement answering the first.

Our whole life is lived within this. And the liturgy especially. God comes close to us every day, and we approach him. 'What was visible in our Redeemer has passed over into the mysteries,' said St Leo.[1] The Lord, risen and ascended, still comes to us. He comes to us in 'the mysteries', the sacramental life of the Church. And so, we can say with St Ambrose, 'I find you in your mysteries.'[2] They enter into us and we into them. These sacramental mysteries include Holy Scripture, the Sacraments in the strict sense, the Divine Office, icons and images, churches and their furnishings, and, not least, the 'sacramental' we call the liturgical year. In all of these, in differing ways, the one transforming mystery of Christ's death and resurrection comes to us and we can run forth to meet it. What a joy it is when children run to meet you, when they throw themselves at you. Isn't this a joy we could give the Lord? He is our Father and we are his children. He comes in his mysteries, and we can't hold back. We rush to him. But what draws us is the presence in the Mysteries.

And again, carrying the thought on into our own life, as we meet the Lord: 'In the mystery of worship the Holy Spirit acts like a Mother, a maternal Spirit bringing us rebirth in Christ and in turn bringing Christ to birth in us.'[3] And so Christ is born for us and in us at Christmas.

At Epiphany he is made manifest and we are illumined. At his Baptism and the changing of the water into wine, he lets his glory be seen, and we like his first disciples can believe in him. At the Presentation he comes to his Temple and we become his Temple.

Through the Eucharist, each day of our life becomes a 'place', a 'time', a Temple, in which Christ celebrates his advent, his death and resurrection, his sending of the Spirit, and even, in anticipation, his return in glory. Through the grace of Sunday, each week becomes this.

In the Presentation, the Lord enters his Temple and we run to meet him. It's the double movement which for faith is the deepest rhythm of life. It's in the liturgy to be in our lives. 'What is visible in the Redeemer has passed over into the mysteries', and it is there we run to find him. And so the mysteries of Christ become ours, we are transformed into the likeness of Christ, and the Church comes to be, 'which is his body, the fullness of him who fills all in all' (Eph 1:23).

And this leads to another, brief thought. 'All things are twofold, one opposite the other, and he has made nothing incomplete. One confirms the good things of the other, and who can have enough of beholding his glory?' (Sir 42:24–25) God's glory is beheld in the Temple, this Temple, the building of which is the innermost meaning of history, the Church. And God's glory becomes visible there in the twofoldness of things, one opposite the other, each confirming the good things of the other. This is precisely what we see in the Gospel account. An old man holds a young child in his arms. Joseph and Mary are young, Simeon and Anna are old. There are two men, two women. Christ is declared 'the light of revelation to the Gentiles and glory to your people Israel'. The Church, the monastery, the praying, Catholic heart is not only a place where God meets man and man God, but, because of that, a place where young and old, male and female, Jew and Gentile meet each other, and confirm the good things of each other. And so God's glory is seen.

The devil loves to infiltrate, his smoke entering the Temple, as Pope Paul VI said.[4] He loves to set brother against brother. He loves to point out to us each other's little faults, he loves to create false impressions, sow distrust, misgivings, fear. He prowls around. We have to guard our hearts, to keep them ecclesial, Catholic. Whenever we close ourselves to a brother or sister, we close down part of ourselves, and therefore part of our hearts to God. His glory can no longer dwell there. The 'Advent' is less than it could have been.

> Pray, then, come and join this choir, every one of you; let there be a whole symphony of minds in concert; take the tone altogether from God, and sing aloud to the Father with one voice through Jesus Christ, so that He may hear you and know by your good works that you are indeed members of His Son's Body. A completely united front will help to keep you in constant communion with God.[5]

At the heart of the Gospel today, there's an unexpected moment of physical contact: 'Simeon took him into his arms' (Lk 2:28), 'him' being, of course, the Child Jesus. It's a moment often caught in art. I'd like to reflect a little on it.

Firstly, this gesture is not necessary to the story. We have been told that the Holy Spirit had revealed to Simeon 'that he should not see death until he had set eyes on the Christ of the Lord' (2:26). We would therefore expect the text to read: 'and when Simeon saw him, he blessed God and said ...' This would also lead nicely into the *Nunc Dimittis*, 'for my eyes have seen your salvation'. Instead, at the moment of encounter, there is no mention of 'seeing'. Rather, Simeon takes the Child in his arms. It's an outbreak of physical contact and emotional warmth. To me, it suggests the Eucharist.

The Greek may be better rendered by 'he took him up' or even 'received' him 'into his arms'. The Greek verb is *dechomai* and in the Latin translations *accipere*. When people are its object, *dechomai* can mean 'to receive kindly, hospitably; to entertain'. A beautiful title subsequently given Simeon is *theodochos*, 'the one who receives God'. This can suggest a further thought: if he 'took up' or 'received' the Child, it was because he was offered, handed over, passed to him. It is natural to think that this was the doing of Mary. And as Simeon's holding of the Child is worth pondering, so is Mary's gift of him. Perhaps not every mother would have relinquished her son in such circumstances. Mary, however, shows her courage, trust, and generosity. She knows that her Son is not her private property. He is, as Simeon will shortly declare, light and glory for Gentile and Jew, destined for the falling and rising of many. Mary therefore does not cling to him. She does not recoil; she is not frightened. She hands him over to this perhaps frail, flushed old man. She is 'apostolic'. Every parent, surely, lives through these moments of letting go: to let their child take its first steps alone, leave it at the school gate, allow for the mistakes of adolescence and all the rest.

The candle transmits light by being burned up. It is actually, for parents, the often painful path to a fuller parenthood, for only if the child is allowed to leave father and mother and cleave in time to a spouse will the parents see 'their children's children'. Mary here is anticipating her final letting go under the Cross, which will be the moment and means of her motherhood expanding to embrace all her son's brothers and sisters. At the Presentation, Jesus is the 'first-born' (cf. Lk 2:23). St Paul will later clarify that he is the first born of many brothers and sisters (cf. Rom 8:29), who are by implication Mary's children. Twice, in what he goes on to say, Simeon too will speak of 'the many'. We may think of 'the many' for whom Christ will shed his blood (cf. Mt 26:28). It has been said that Simeon's words to Mary are a 'second annunciation': that is, of the Paschal mystery, of her part in it, and of its universal scope. All that is embodied in that simple, presumed action of Mary entrusting her child to Simeon. Mary here is Israel handing over the Messiah, not keeping him simply for herself. Mary is the Church, not self-referential, but missionary, handing on her Jesus in proclamation and celebration.

May we be Simeons too. He came to the Temple to 'see', but when he saw Joseph, Mary and the Child, something more than his eyes lit up. He must have thrown out his arms in delight. He did not just believe. He felt a rush of love. Mary saw this and responded. And what might have been just faith became communion, eucharist, blessing: a heart unlocked and consoled.

May this feast of the Presentation, then, do its work in us. May we be grateful for this new space the Lord has opened for us and live in it always. And allow each other space as well.

Notes

1. Pope St Leo the Great, *Sermon* 74.2 (*CCL* 138A:459–61).
2. St Ambrose, *On the mysteries*.
3. G. Collins OSB, *Meeting Christ in His Mysteries* (Dublin: Columba 2010), p.110.
4. Pope St Paul VI, *Homily* (29 June 1972).
5. St Ignatius of Antioch, *Ephesians* 4.

13

Ash Wednesday

Joel 2:12–18 and 2 Cor 5:20–6:2; Matthew 6:1–6, 16–18

When I became bishop, I found in the house chapel a casket. Inside the casket were relics of several saints. Some of these were actually bones, one or two a few inches long. They claimed to be the bones of saints of many centuries ago. Recently, I thought it would be good to take these out of the dried paper in which they were wrapped and wrap them instead in cloth. Someone helped me to do this. You had to handle the bones carefully. They were dry and brittle, even crumbly. You had to be careful that they did not turn to dust. And my helper remarked, how true it is that we are dust and unto dust we shall return.

I wonder how many millions all over the world are having their foreheads marked with ash today, and are hearing the words, 'Remember you are dust and unto dust you will return': words of God to man after the first sin.

'There is a time to be born and a time to die,' says the book of Ecclesiastes (3:2), and again speaking of the other animals as well as ourselves: 'all go to one place; all are from the dust and all turn to dust again' (3:20). So it is. 'I repent in dust and ashes' (Job 42:6) are Job's last words. Today's ashes are a sign of our smallness, the shortness of our life. A sign of our desire to repent, to come right with God. 'Now is the acceptable time.'

But let's take this on. You may remember how a couple of years ago a Westminster MP had been to Mass on Ash Wednesday and received the ashes on her forehead. Then she went straight to a Committee Meeting in the House of Commons, still with the ashes very visible. Someone took a photo, a journalist saw it, there were comments and so on.

Something struck me here. The ashes are a reminder—'Remember,' says the one giving the ashes—a reminder to ourselves and to others when they see them. But also, I think, to God, whether the ashes have stayed on our skin or not. The ashes are a prayer, first and foremost a prayer. They say to the Lord, 'Look, I am dust.'

And that is glorious. What is dust? The smallest visible particle of creation. Something we walk on, something that's scattered, that's blown about in the wind. Something insignificant. 'Remember, Lord, that I am dust.' But, God loves his creation, even this tiniest part of it. God does not love pride, human arrogance, when we put all our tanks on parade or launch our fly-pasts into the air. He loves dust. He loves the small and overlooked, the blown-about and the trampled on. And he remembers. 'As a father has compassion on his sons, the Lord has pity on those who fear him, for he knows of what we are made, he remembers that we are dust' (Ps 102:13–14). He sees the dust, he remembers the dust, feels for the dust, bends down to the dust, can do marvellous things with it. In the beginning, according to Genesis, he scooped up the dust of the earth and made humanity of it. Hannah, the childless woman who becomes unexpectedly pregnant, sings in her song: 'He raises up the poor from the dust; he lifts the needy from the ash-heap, to make them sit with princes and inherit a seat of honour' (1 Sam 2:8). And a Psalmist echoes her: 'Who is like the Lord, our God …

who stoops from the heights to look down, to look down upon heaven and earth? From the dust he lifts up the lowly, from the dung heap he raises the poor' (Ps 112:5–7). And, says Daniel, 'many of those who sleep in the dust of the earth shall awake' (Dan 12:2).

Israel in the Old Testament was forever finding herself in the dust: in the dust of slavery in Egypt, in the dust of exile in Babylon, her beautiful Jerusalem reduced to dust by her enemies. But dust is a good thing to be. God doesn't it find it yucky or repellent; he doesn't ignore it or trample on it. He's like William Blake; he sees 'the world in a grain of sand'.[1] He finds it irresistible. God loves what he makes, dust included. Usually we don't notice dust; sometimes we treat each other like dirt. But God remembers it. God sees it. God bends down to it, takes it up, wakens it, shapes it, does wonderful things with it. It is all gold-dust or stardust to him. It's good to be dust. God even became dust, became flesh. He came into 'the land of dust'. And in the Psalm Christ prayed on the Cross, 'My God, my God, why have you forsaken me?' were the words, 'they lay me in the dust of death' (Ps 21:16). He went even there.

Lent is a journey. It reproduces the journey of the people of Israel from Egypt to the Promised Land. In a way, it reproduces every human journey. It begins in the dust and it ends with an empty tomb. It begins with the first man, Adam, the 'man of dust' St Paul calls him: us, and it ends with the second man, the 'man of heaven', the risen man, Christ. We bear 'the image of the man of dust', says Paul, and are destined to 'bear the image of the man of heaven' (1 Cor 15: 49). Lent and Easter, death and resurrection, dust and glory.

'Remember, Lord, that I am dust'. It's a prayer. If we pray it from the heart, not ashamed to be dust, if we stop treating others like dirt, we can be sure of an unforgettable grace. God will find us irresistible. God will do to us what he did to his Son who went down, with us, into the dust of death, and now lives and reigns forever and ever. Those old, crumbly bones in the casket: he can transform them. My going down to the dust: it's there he'll find me.

Notes

1. W. Blake, 'Auguries of Innocence' in *Collected Works* (London: OUP 1966), p.531.

14

The Five Sundays of Lent

First Sunday of Lent

Genesis 2:7–9, 3:1–7; Romans 5:12–19; Matthew 4:1–11

Since time immemorial the 1st Sunday of Lent has focused on the temptations of Jesus. Hence the Gospel, and the Preface of today's Mass. If we then add the first reading from Genesis on the Creation and Fall of man—if we add the second reading, St Paul on the two Adams, on the drama of sin and grace in human history—if we add the Responsorial Psalm, which presupposes the spectacular sin of David—then here too we meet serious stuff. Indeed, it's almost a summary of basic Christian doctrine.

Let's just focus, though, on the theme of temptation.

In the first Reading we hear of the fashioning of man/Adam. Adam is man in general; he's humanity collectively; he's an individual man. And he is given himself by God: in-breathed dust, Pascal's 'thinking reed'. He is given his humanity. He is given the woman, equal and complementary. He is given a garden and its trees. He is given authority to name the animals. He is given the closeness of God.

And immediately the snake of temptation appears. Adam is gifted, privileged, empowered. And immediately he is tempted. And he sins. There has been much analysis of that temptation and sin, of what it means to 'be like gods, knowing good and evil'. Put simply, the sin was this: they took what they were given (their humanity) and took it away from the Giver. They disconnected it from the Source, took it to themselves and saw it as their own. One word used in this context is autonomy—being a law unto oneself.

It was the setting of a pattern.

Take the Psalm (50/51). It presupposes David, chosen by God, a man after God's own heart, anointed by the prophet Samuel, king over all Israel. He sees a beautiful woman washing and he's tempted to take her as his own. He has the power to have her. He's a man. He's the king. Inconveniently, she has a husband. But David has the power to eliminate him. And he does. He gets her.

Here is the pattern again. And here is each of us with our humanity, our sexuality, our knowledge, relationships, position, power. Here is each of us at each new stage of our life, when a new potential is unfurled, or a new identity taken on and new responsibilities assumed. Here is each period in history even, with its own gift and power. Here is our age with its technological prowess. And immediately it is followed—we are shadowed—by temptation, by the lure of abusing the gift. Taking it away from the Giver and taking it to ourselves.

So we come to the Gospel. Just before the story of Jesus' temptation comes that of his baptism by John in the River Jordan. A voice from heaven has just declared him the Father's beloved Son. The Holy Spirit has just been seen resting on him. He has been invested with the mission of the Messiah. And immediately he's tempted. Immediately the Tempter says to him, 'If you are the Son of God...'. Once again, there has been much fascinating analysis of the burden of each of the three temptations. Putting it simply though, Jesus the Messiah is being solicited to write his own script. He overcomes that temptation by referring to his Father's script found in Scripture. He does not separate the gift of his mission from the Giver. Instead, he makes it the ground of the gift of himself, the gift completed on the Cross and accepted in the Resurrection, the gift of himself to the Father for us, the gift before us in the Eucharist.

But here's one last thought about temptation. Why are we tempt-able? Because we are not self-sufficient, because we are a work in progress, incomplete. We talk of 'giving in' to temptation, of 'yielding' to it. And we also talk, as I just have, of 'giving ourselves'. But to give ourselves means consenting to be taken. Everything around us and in us is, in a sense, asking for us, wanting to take us, stretching out its arms to us, begging us to yield. The question is to what, to whom, and how we yield. Yield, though, we must. We are made to be taken. Jesus did not yield an inch to Satan. Nor must we. 'Be off, Satan!' Let it be 'no' to our passions, 'no' to evil influences from outside, 'no' to fads and fashions. But Jesus did freely yield his whole self to his mission, to the will of God revealed in Scripture and the inner influence of the Holy Spirit. He let himself be taken—all the way to the Cross. The answer to temptation, therefore, is prayer. The prayer of self-surrender.

Second Sunday of Lent

Genesis 12:1–4a; 2 Timothy 1:8b–10; Matthew 17:1–9

> *There in their presence he was transfigured: his face shone like the sun and his clothes became as white as light.*

Why do we have this Gospel this Second Sunday? We always do; it's a fixture. Last Sunday's Gospel makes good Lenten sense: Jesus goes into the desert for forty days. So do the long Gospels we'll hear the next three Sundays: the meeting with the Samaritan woman, the cure of the Man born blind, the raising of Lazarus. Their resonances and connections are clear. But, left to ourselves, would we ever have chosen today's? Yet, it has been there for at least 1500 years. It was there long before a feast of the Transfiguration appeared on 6 August.

So, why? What does it offer?

What did it give Peter, James and John? Why did Jesus take them up a high mountain where they could be alone? That he did so, that something extraordinary happened on that mountain, that they experienced what's called a theophany—like Moses by the burning bush or Moses and Elijah on Mt Sinai—seems certain enough. The episode is embedded in early Christian tradition, occurs in three of the four Gospels, and comes again in the 2nd Letter of St Peter. It is credible.

So again, why? Why then—the three disciples? Why now—us?

Here's a first thought. Just six days before Jesus had asked his disciples who people said he was, who they thought he was. And Simon Peter 'spoke up': 'You are the Christ, the Son of the living God.' We might think: Well done, Peter; you got the right answer; you've passed your theory test. No. More was happening here. Peter, like Abraham leaving his own world in the 1st reading, was taking a great step. Peter the fisherman was throwing himself into the sea of faith, with courage, insight, trust. And six days later, Jesus takes him and his two fellow fishermen up a mountain, another different place, and was transfigured before them. Jesus unveils his Christhood and his divine Sonship. Yes, Peter, I am who you say. I am the Christ. I am the fulfilment of the Law (Moses) and the Prophets (Elijah). And the voice from the cloud, the voice of the Father, comes like an echo: Yes, Peter, 'This is my Son, the Beloved; he enjoys my favour. Listen to him!' Here's the heavenly endorsement of the earthly profession. So, why this Gospel? Perhaps here's a first answer: to confirm from above Peter and his friends' faith, to confirm our faith. Faith comes by 'hearing', but sometimes it turns to 'seeing', like here. And we can sense its truth.

Here's another thought. 'You are the Christ,' said Peter. And then, the Gospel continues: 'Jesus began to show his disciples that he must go to Jerusalem and suffer many things from the elders and chief priests and scribes, and be killed, and on the third day be raised.' We remember Peter's reaction. Peter, says the Gospel, 'took' Jesus and began to put him right. Ah! The wrong way round. Jesus, in turn, lets him have it: 'Get behind me, Satan.' Then he tells his disciples that if they are to follow him, they must deny themselves and take up their cross. They must in some sense lose their lives. Peter must have been in bits by this point. He didn't seem to hear the other things Jesus was saying: 'I will be raised on the third day ... here is how you save your life ... the Son of man will come in his glory.' This passed Peter by. The human psyche is far better at finding reasons for fear than reasons for hope. We are more naturally purveyors of bad news than good news. The unknown kingdom in our lives isn't sadness; it's joy. So, six days later, Jesus 'takes' Peter and friends—the right way round—and gives them a preview of the beauty of the Resurrection and the Coming in glory. 'And he was transfigured before them, and his face shone like the sun, and his garments became white as light.' Jesus is the face of the Father and his clothes—says a long tradition—are us, his Church, the people who cling to his body and will be glorified too; indeed, already are. So, here's perhaps a second answer: this Gospel is here for our hope. In each of us, there's a dark inner gravity which pulls us back down to nothingness. Jesus takes them and us up a mountain, upwards not downwards. To a place where they could be alone, away from the constant low noise of human negativity, a place where they could see beyond the immediate, a further horizon. It's akin to the vision at the end of the Book of Revelation when John is carried away in the Spirit to a great, high mountain, and shown the holy city Jerusalem coming down out of heaven from God, radiant with his glory (cf. Rev. 21:10–11).

Hope doesn't cancel the Cross. It takes it up knowing it is the way to Resurrection. Hope integrates, accepts life's suffering, but looks beyond it. Despite the Transfiguration, Peter did stumble at the scandal of the Cross and deny his Master. But he wept when the Face turned towards him and three days later gathered up his tunic and ran with John to an empty tomb. Is that why this Gospel is here? 'Don't be afraid,' Jesus tells his disciples as things return to normal. It's the meaning of that whole episode.

'There in their presence he was transfigured: his face shone like the sun and his clothes became as white as light.' This face, this humanity therefore, born of Mary, first formed in her womb, now transfigured. These clothes perhaps woven for him by her, now bright with the glory of God. Humanity not burned up by divinity. Receiving a God who's not out to thwart us, not in competition, a God who fulfils and doesn't abolish, a Lover of beauty longing to beautify us. So, looking for reasons, can't we add love to faith and hope?

Third Sunday of Lent

Exodus 17:3–7; Romans 5:1–2, 5–8; John 4:5–42

> *Jacob's well is there and Jesus, tired by the journey,*
> *sat down by the well.*

This week we meet the Samaritan woman. She is an unusual one. She's feisty, argumentative, with a checkered past and present (she's on man number six). She comes to the well with not just a pitcher, but a number of disadvantages. She's a woman, a second-class citizen in her world. She clearly had men-problems. And why does she come to the well by herself at the hottest time of the day when everyone else will be resting indoors: was she something of an outcast? From a Jewish point of view, as a Samaritan, she certainly was. There she is, member of a minority with a long resentment towards her Jewish neighbours, a heretic in their mind, worshipping stubbornly at the 'wrong' place, Mount Gerizim, her mind perhaps narrowed and heart hardened by the accumulated centuries of theological controversy and incidents of violence. These things scar the soul. 'What? You are a Jew and you ask me, a Samaritan, for a drink?' 'Are you out to cause trouble?'

But Jesus, 'tired by his journey', sits down by the well. And this remarkable conversation begins.

Here a man and a woman meet, just the two of them, under the midday sun. A setting for romance, but that's transmuted into something more. We're beyond the erotic here. We're on another level and the story expands as it unfolds. Here's a man and a woman, a Jew and a Samaritan. But the connections build between them. Jesus becomes more and more in the woman's eyes: first

Sir, then a prophet, then the Messiah. And more and more of herself comes out. She's real and symbolic all at once. 'Let us recognize ourselves in her,' says St Augustine.[1] She's each and all of us. Yes, this woman now on her sixth man and with her mixed-up religion. Looking for life here and then there and then somewhere else again, looking for more than any other person can give, hewing out cisterns for herself, broken cisterns that can hold no water (cf Jer 2:13), worshipping what she doesn't know, seeking God but in the wrong places. Don't we recognize her? Doesn't our heart go out to her?

And what does Jesus see in her? Her thirst, her many-layered thirst, an aching near-eastern thirst for water, another thirst as well for love, for real relationship, the thirst she had tried to quench with her many men. Jesus shows himself as Jacob's Well, the one who opens the aquifer of the Holy Spirit: 'the water that I shall give will turn into a spring, welling up to eternal life'. In the presence of this unconventional Jew who shouldn't have been talking to her, she feels more and more known. 'Go and bring your husband.' Her whole steamy life story is already read by him and thus already in process of being sorted. Perhaps she feels she is being given back to herself, body and soul. The conversation is taking a personal turn. She has to cause a diversion by trying to start an argument about Temple-worship. But for Jesus, the great Evangelist, this is just another occasion to lead her on. 'The hour will come—in fact is here already—when true worshippers will worship the Father in spirit and truth.' After the real water comes the real worship; after the infusion of the Holy Spirit comes worship of the Father in spirit and truth. She is being led out of her cultural and ethnic confines into a good and broad land, into a new kind of freedom, a larger space, where her whole life can become one act of praise. What is happening in her is what St Paul would later advocate: 'I appeal to you therefore, brethren, to present your bodies as a living sacrifice, holy and acceptable to God, which is your spiritual worship. Do not be *conformed* to this world but be *transformed* by the renewal of your mind' (Rom 12:1–2). No wonder St Augustine again calls her the '*form* of the Church'; this is what's coming out in her. He is leading her into the Trinity too. He has disclosed the Holy Spirit to her, and then the Father; we could say too Baptism (Confirmation) and the Eucharist. And all the while the Man before her grows and grows before the eyes of her mind: the Jew becomes a prophet and the prophet the Messiah. 'I who am speaking to you,' said Jesus, 'I am he.' She's on the brink of the Trinity. She has travelled so far, so fast.

She leaves her water by the well—a point to note—and back she goes to her people, thirsting to tell. Like Mary Magdalene on Easter morning, the evangelized one is now an evangelist herself, a missionary disciple. 'This man knows me. Is he it, do you think?' And her fellow-townsfolk catch the flame from her, and go to Jesus. Then, in their turn, they are persuaded too. 'We have heard him ourselves and we know that he really is the Saviour of the world.'

What a piece of storytelling it is! What a journey, hers and ours! The whole of our Lent and Easter is traversed by this woman. Through the whole process of Christian initiation she goes, purified, scrutinized, exorcized, enlightened, transformed. Through the whole process of Christian life. At the end of the story, she in a sense disappears. She has accomplished her mission. She has led her townsfolk to Jesus, and now it's he, not her reportage, that leads them to believe. But in another sense, of course, she doesn't disappear. She lives in the Gospel. She remains a guide for every generation. And

Tradition has added a telling detail, has given her a name: *Photina*, the 'luminous one', the one full of light. That is the real upshot of her encounter with Christ. She has become a light. 'Recognize yourself in her,' says St Augustine.

Fourth Sunday of Lent

*1 Samuel 16:1b, 6–7, 10–13a; Ephesians 5:8–14;
John 9:1–41*

'If I should walk in the valley of darkness, no evil would I fear. You are there.' Familiar, famous words. 'The Lord is my shepherd': today's Responsorial Psalm.

In all of today's readings, with the man born blind in the forefront, there is a movement from darkness to light. Samuel passes from seeing as man sees to seeing as God sees, recognizing Israel's future king, the great David, in the most unlikely of Jesse's sons. 'You were darkness once, but now you are light in the Lord,' St Paul says to his new Christians. He is talking of the light of faith that is lit at baptism. In the Gospel, thanks to the touch of Jesus and the water of the Pool of Siloam, the man born blind moves from physical darkness to recovered sight, and then further still to the recognition of Jesus. '"Do you believe in the Son of man?" asks Jesus. "Sir" the man replied, "tell me who he is so that I may believe in him." Jesus said, "You are looking at him…" The man said, "Lord, I believe", and worshipped him.' Meanwhile, the Pharisees become ever more entrenched in their own darkness.

'If I should walk in the valley of darkness, no evil would I fear. For you are there.'

The light into which these readings take us is what St Benedict calls the 'deifying light'.[2] It is the light lit in us at baptism, the light of faith, the light that helps us see things not as man sees but as God sees. It is the light of the risen Christ. Everything we are passing through at the moment can be a passage out of darkness into this light.

'Those who believe, see,' said Pope Francis in his first Encyclical; 'they see with a light that illumines their entire journey; for it comes from the risen Christ, the morning star which never sets.'[3] It is 'not a light,' he explains, 'which scatters all our darkness, but a lamp which guides our steps in the night and suffices for our journey.'[4]

Does this Psalm have anything specific in mind when it speaks of the 'valley of darkness'? There may be an answer in one of the darkest episodes of Israel's history: the seventy-year exile in Babylon in the sixth century before Christ. Jerusalem their hilltop city had been devastated, the Temple that crowned it destroyed, the people led away—led away to the river valleys of Mesopotamia. All gone into the dark. The Temple, with its Presence and its worship, was the light of their eyes, and that light went dark.

But then in that historical dark ravine, Israel made its discovery: 'no evil will I fear, for you are there.' The seventy years of Exile, of forced isolation, of distancing from what they held dear was perhaps the most creative of Israel's history. The prophet Ezekiel taught them that the divine Presence had gone into Exile with them: 'You are there.' It was a time of repentance, of examination of what had been done and left undone; a time of conversion; a time when Israel began to realize who she really was in the sight of God and in her darkness was being mysteriously prepared for the coming of Christ, the light of the world.

Psalm 23 speaks of water and oil, a banquet and a cup, of the sacraments that make the Church and make us Christians. This is a moment for their truth and grace, their power and reality, to pass, at last, into the fibre, the hard drive, of our lives. The grace of the liturgy lives beyond the liturgy. This can be the moment for that truth to be felt. And then he, the shepherd and host of the Psalm, will truly Easter in us.

> If I should walk in the valley of darkness,
> no evil would I fear. You are there.

Fifth Sunday of Lent

Ezekiel 37:12–14; Romans 8:8–11; John 11:1–45

Jesus cried out in a loud voice, 'Lazarus, here! Come out.'

The Gospels tell us that Jesus loved Martha, Mary and Lazarus. They were friends. It's a beautiful glimpse of how really human Jesus was. He loved them. And his love made them holy: the Church recognizes all three as saints.

It's possible to see how Martha and Mary were saints. But Lazarus? All he did was fall ill, die and smell. Yet he's a saint—hope for us all! But surely a saint has to do something, be active? Well, on closer inspection, he was. 'Lazarus, come out!' 'The dead man came out.' Lazarus responded to Christ's command. He obeyed. A most bewildering obedience it must have been, but he did it. He left the world of the dead. He came back to the world of the living. This is not resurrection in the full Christian sense: he was not transported to a new kind of life; he would die again. But he was raised. That was his obedience. So, here's a first thought: every obedience in our life, every response to the clear call of the Lord, whatever form it may take, is a resurrection. And so it has always been. Lazarus did what the whole world did in the beginning and does every moment: coming out, coming forth from nothingness. God says, 'Let there be...' 'And there is.' Lazarus did what Abraham did: who went as the Lord told him. He did what the people of Israel did at the Exodus. He did what they did after the seventy years of exile, when they left Babylon and returned to their own land, raised from their graves, as Ezekiel put it. Lazarus did what Mary did: 'let what you have said be done to me.' He did what Joseph did after the angel told him to take Mary as his wife and assume responsibility for her child. 'He rose from sleep and did what the angel said.' He does what the prodigal son does in the parable, when he ways: 'I will arise and go to my Father.' He did what Jesus would do when he was raised by the Father before the dawn that Sunday. 'My heart is ready, O God, my heart is ready', says the Psalmist. 'I will sing, I will sing your praise. Awake my soul, awake lyre and harp, I will awake the dawn' (Ps 56: 8–9). What are we about? What are we made for? What's our first and last vocation? To be raised from the dead! Lazarus fulfilled that. He heard the word of the Lord—that basic biblical 'thing'—and he responded, body and soul. And that word spelt 'resurrection'. There is the core of holiness.

There's no 'any old Gospel'. But if there were, it certainly wouldn't be this one. It is the greatest of Jesus' signs. It's what precipitates his death. It has a sense of majestic movement. He waits in Galilee. Then he goes towards Bethany. Then he meets Martha outside the village, then Mary. Then he comes to the tomb. It builds to a climax. Then, again, these wonderful lines: 'Jesus loved Martha, and her sister, and Lazarus.' 'I am the Resurrection and the Life.' 'Jesus wept.' 'Lazarus, here, come out!' 'Unbind him, and let him go free!'

But let's just stick with this one. 'Lazarus, here, come out.' In Greek, *'Lazare, deuro, exo'*. In Latin, *Lazare, veni foras*! In English, 'Lazarus, come forth!' 'Lazarus, come out.' 'Come out, Lazarus, to my side!' That last is a very suggestive one. A literal translation would be: 'Lazarus, here! Out!' It's imperious. It's 'cried out with a great voice'. It's curt. It's like someone bringing a dog to heel. It's almost angry: not at Lazarus, but at the enemy death.

This scene is charged with all the anger and sorrow of God at the destruction of humanity, with the passion that drove Jesus to the sacrifice of himself for us. This is the inner passion that turned the outer passion into a prayer for our resurrection.

'Come out! Come here! Come out, beside me!' Let's take that to ourselves. In spring, the whole of nature is responding to that divine voice, to the word that holds it in being and gives it life. Lent and Easter are the same great voice, crying out to us, calling us forth. Let's do a Lazarus! Leave our inner illnesses, leave our deadness, leave whatever is smelly in our life, let the bandages be taken off. Leave our anger and resentments, leave our obsessions and anxieties. Leave perhaps even our most cherished thoughts and desires. Lazarus appears once more in the Gospel. He appears at table with Jesus. We leave what leads to death, so as to live with Christ. Those who'll be baptized and / or received at Easter are doing a Lazarus. They are leaving themselves, in a sense. They are entering into the communal life of the Church, to have their sins forgiven, share her faith, her sacraments, her love, her mission: to be beside Christ, to take their seat at his table. May all of us have this sense of God's will as resurrecting us. May we all hear this voice. Maybe we have to wait for it: there's the mystery of Lazarus' four days in the tomb and the silence of Holy Saturday. But these are moments when the Lord, as it were, is simply breathing in before he cries out: 'Come here, come out, come to my side! Don't die! Live!

Notes

1. St Augustine, *Treatise on the Gospel of John*.
2. *Rule of St Benedict*, Prologue 9.
3. Pope Francis, *Lumen Fidei* (2013), 1.
4. *Ibid.* 25.

15

THE SOLEMNITY OF ST JOSEPH

Joseph, son of David, do not be afraid to take Mary home as your wife.

Isn't it good, isn't it poignant, that our last public Mass for whatever length of time it proves to be coincides with the feast of St Joseph?[1] And should have that call 'not to be afraid' at its heart?

Joseph, son of David, was given by God, by the Father, to Mary and Jesus. He was given to be a sacrament, an efficacious sign, of the Father's own care for the Virgin Mother, and her son, the Word made flesh. Catholic instinct then takes the further step: as Mary and Jesus were entrusted to Joseph, so is the Church throughout her history. 'Just as St Joseph took loving care of Mary and gladly dedicated himself to Jesus Christ's upbringing, he likewise watches over and protects Christ's Mystical Body, of which the Virgin Mary is the exemplar and model.'[2]

Devotion to Joseph is ancient. It must have begun in the hearts of Mary and Jesus, when she as wife and he as child, recognized what a gift of God was theirs. St Matthew's Gospel clearly cherished him. The stream has flowed on, surfacing in fourth century Egyptian Christians and the Desert Fathers, emerging again in the West among the Franciscans and the Carmelites, in saints like Bernardine of Siena, Teresa of Avila, Francis de Sales. In 1870, Pope St Pius IX declared him Patron of the Universal Church. In 1962, Pope St John XXIII added his name to the Roman Canon and in 2013 Pope Francis had his name included in the other main Eucharistic Prayers. And the same Pope chose this feast—seven years ago today—to begin his ministry as the Successor of St Peter.

Thinking of this living tradition, embodied in prayers and dedications and devotion, it's as if St Joseph has been drawing every closer over time. It's as if the Lord wants us to feel his—the Lord's—protection through this good, just, honourable Jewish man, descendant of David, the worker, the carpenter, the provider, the husband and father, the man of faith and obedience, who has left us no words of his own, but who 'did' what the angel of the Lord told him to do.

This is Joseph. As the mystery of the Incarnation unfolded, as his beloved became a mother, as her child grew in wisdom and grace, there he is—entrusted with them. There he is, now at home in God, entrusted with the Church which is Mary and its life which is Christ. And here he is too, surely, in this unexpected, difficult moment, entrusted afresh with us, with Mary the Church, and with the life of Jesus in us, with everyone who is, as it were, Jesus in waiting.

It's a great human and divine thing St Joseph brings with him: the protection, the watchful care of God. 'He who dwells in the shelter of the Most High and abides in the shade of the Almighty says to the Lord: "My refuge, my stronghold, my God in whom I trust."' This divine sheltering and nurturing never abandons either nature or human history. And it calls, again and again, for replication in us. In Genesis chapter 1, we are told we are created in the image and likeness of God. In Genesis chapter 2, the man is placed in a garden to till it and keep it. Here's our echo, our imitation of the divine: to *till*, develop, cultivate the land, the garden, the tree that each of us and human life is—by culture, by nurture if you like, and then to *keep* it, watch over it, care for it, protect it from harm. Adam was called to take care of the garden; Abraham, Isaac and Jacob took care of their families and servants, their herds and flocks; David was taken from care of the sheep to be the shepherd of the people of Israel, the priests and Levites had care of the Temple and its sacred vessels and the sacrifices that happened there, just as the priests of the New Testament now have care of the holy Eucharist and the holy oils and of the souls entrusted to them. So much of life is or can or should be this kind of taking care, this imitation of God, who neither slumbers nor sleeps, but watches over his people and his whole creation night and day.

This is our vocation, our Joseph-ite vocation, as it were. Pope Francis said this of it seven years ago today: 'The vocation of being a 'protector' ... means protecting all creation, the beauty of the created world, as the Book of Genesis tells us and as St Francis of Assisi showed us. It means respecting each of God's creatures and respecting the environment in which we live. It means protecting people, showing loving concern for each and every person, especially children, the elderly, those in need, who are often the last we think about. It means caring for one another in our families: husbands and wives first protect one another, and then, as parents, they care for their children, and children themselves, in time, protect their parents. It means building sincere friendships in which we protect one another in trust, respect, and goodness. In the end, everything has been entrusted to our protection, and all of us are responsible for it. Be protectors of God's gifts!'[3] Haven't there been many Josephs in our own lives: fathers, grandfathers, elder brothers, teachers, mentors, tutors, protectors? And not simply men!

So it is a beautiful coincidence that, as we sadly abstain—a kind of Lent—from public liturgies, St Joseph is there. We do this to protect each other, in fact, from illness. This is a good thing to do. It is more than compliance with civil authority; it is a keeping of the fifth commandment. We might think of the Holy Family here. To protect their lives from the human virus of Herod, Joseph took Mary and Jesus away from the Holy Land, away from its Temple and its glorious Liturgy. It must have been a sad exile for them in that respect. But they had two things. They had, first, the great Jewish traditions of family prayer, grace at table, blessing of food, the Psalms, the Hebrew Bible. Let's seize this unexpected moment to enhance our personal prayer life, to give ourselves a daily discipline: to read the readings of the day, for example, to commit ourselves afresh to the Rosary. On Sundays, let's try to access Mass on TV or the internet. It would be so good for every home to become a domestic church. Secondly, the Holy Family had each other. Already surely a united family, but after this experience still more so! This is a time for caring for each other in new ways: by prayer, by messages, by phone calls. A Councillor told me the other day how generously a call for volunteers had been answered. The phrase is used: the New Normal. Would it not be wonderful if these things became that? In our parishes too.

Yes, like Adam, we are on this earth to till and to keep the garden. In Bethlehem, Egypt and Nazareth, Joseph, son of David, fulfilled this vocation supremely. He cared for Mary and her divine Child. May he care for us! And may we, with him, protect the life of Mary and of Jesus in ourselves and in each other. Amen.

Notes

1. 19 March 2020. This was just before 'lockdown' for the Covid19 pandemic.
2. Pope St John Paul II, *Redemptoris Custos* 1.
3. Pope Francis, *Homily on the Solemnity of St Joseph,* 19 March 2013.

16

The Annunciation

It's always good to keep this feast, but better still to do so now.

Today's calendar date, 25 March, has proved magnetic to more than the Annunciation. It falls, consciously of course, nine months before Christmas. In other measuring systems of time, it has been New Year's Day, or the day of the vernal equinox, even the first day of creation. It has been thought to be the day of Christ's Crucifixion or Resurrection, of Easter Day. Tolkien, unsurprisingly, could not resist it. In the long calendar of his epic sub-creation, it is the day the loathsome Ring of Power falls back into nothingness, Sauron is defeated and a wholesome human life begins again. It's true that in the Gospel we've just heard there are many continuities, snatches of familiar Old Testament melodies: a visiting angel, an unexpected conception, a sign, talk of the favour of God, of a son of David and a throne of Jacob. History is flowing here, but as it rises to its climax, it mutates, it leaps to a new level: St Paul's 'fullness of time'. There is something quite new: a virgin conceives by the power of the Holy Spirit, will give birth as a virgin, and remain a virgin. Still more, the Child, who is biologically, embryonically hers, is personally the Word of God, now flesh in her womb. The Incarnation occurs. From today, God is with us, not just eternally but in time; not just universally, but concretely, historically; not just divinely, but humanly; not just spiritually, but physically. And the truth of this is sealed by Mary's new title of *Theotokos*, the God-bearer, the Mother of God. From today, there is something different, something new in the world, something capable of changing everything and making everything right. From within, outwards from a womb, from a fertilized earth, pushing up like the spring that's so around us.

No wonder Luke's description of the angel's visit to Mary has for centuries entranced believers, and not only believers. Frescoes, icons, paintings, sculpture have blossomed round it like spring flowers by the base of trees. How did this event unfold, we wonder? What was she doing when the angel came? Was she indoors or outdoors? Working or resting? Drawing water, or weaving, or reading? In one ancient tale this young Nazarene girl has just been co-commissioned to weave a new veil for the Holy of Holies in Jerusalem's Temple. She's allotted the weaving of the cords of purple and scarlet. One day she goes to the well to draw water, and hears the words, 'Hail, full of grace, the Lord is with you.' Thoroughly alarmed, she returns home with the pitcher, and to calm herself resumes her weaving. The angel appears and the rest of the conversation follows. In Nazareth, today you find a shrine built over a well, and another over a house. The purple and scarlet of this tale look to the Passion of Christ, the cloak and the blood. Mary herself becomes the Holy of Holies veiling the Presence in her womb and for nine months inwardly weaving the human body of God's Son. There is something that so holds us here: 'The angel and the girl are met,' says Edwin Muir.[1]

> Outside the window footsteps fall
> Into the ordinary day
> And with the sun along the wall
> Pursue their unreturning way...
> But through the endless afternoon
> These neither speak nor movement make,

> But stare into their deepening trance
> As if their gaze would never break.

'My message to the British people,' said the Prime Minister the other evening, 'is, stay at home.' It was when she was at home that Mary met the word of God. The decisive turning points of history, Edith Stein once pointed out, are determined out of the public eye: in reflection and resolutions, in secret annunciations. Couldn't this be happening in our own home-bound days? New beginnings, again.

In the Greek Church, this feast is called the Evangelization of Mary. Gabriel is an evangelist, bringing the Gospel to Mary, what we call the *kerygma*, the primary Christian proclamation, but focused on her, her Jewish hope, her womanhood, her youth. Her response is actually an exclamation of joy, with the nuance, 'Oh, yes, let this happen!' The angel is a catechist too, unfolding successively the grace of the Father, the coming of the Son and the power of the Holy Spirit. And Mary is the first to listen, to question and consent, a thoughtful student of the ways of God. She is the prime, archetypal, pioneer believer, of faith seeking understanding. She stands at the threshold of the new Covenant. And over that threshold, which is her groundedness, through the open door of her free will, the Saviour comes. The Annunciation is the mystery, says St Thomas Aquinas, of the Lord's *ingressus*, his entry into the world. 'You have prepared a body for me ... God, here I am! I come to do your will.' The dialogue of Mary and the angel is the Entrance Antiphon of the liturgy of redemption. It will continue with the preaching of the adult Jesus, the liturgy of his word. It will be consummated in his sacrifice on the Cross and issue in our communion with his risen body. And the rubric holding this liturgy is obedience. 'I am coming to obey your will.' 'Let it be done to me according to your word.' So the knot of the primal disobedience of Adam and Eve is untied by Mary and Jesus. His obedience begets hers, but hers too will be the matrix of his. He 'learned obedience' from his mother, as well as from his suffering. There are two voices singing here, distinct, and yet entwined. It is a new song in a fallen world.

How much new obeying is being asked of us currently, civilly, socially! On its high plane, Mary's obedience was literally life-giving, giving human life to the Author of life. May ours protect life too! Let's try to live it with that responsibility in mind.

Again, how often nature and history seem visited by dark angels. How many cruel visitations this 2020 has endured already: bushfires, storms, floods, not to mention global warming. And now this. It's hard not to hear the hoof beats of apocalyptic horsemen. But today's feast can reassure us that there are other, gentler angels abroad. 'Gabriel' means the 'strength of God', gentle strength. He comes, in Muir's phrase, 'feathered through time'. He comes to Mary and gently disconcerts her with another and better future. Even though Covid–19 is yet to hit us with its full force, and will alas sometimes be tragically lethal, people are imagining new beginnings, better worlds:

> Because the Holy Ghost over the bent
> World broods with warm breast and with ah!
> Bright wings.[2]

The Annunciation reminds us that the overshadowing of the Holy Spirit and a human will given to God form an irresistible combination, create irreversible new beginnings, are always the genesis of better things. And whatever happens here and now, or sooner or later, what happened in Nazareth can never be taken away, in time or eternity. 'The angel and the girl are met', God and us. It only needs our yes. Why not, this 25 March? 'Thy will be done.'

The last word from Mary, courtesy of another poet:[3]

> It was and it wasn't a choice.
> Though I didn't know why—
> and how even less—
> how could I, in the face
> of such great gentleness,
> not say 'Yes'?

Notes

1. E. Muir, 'The Annunciation' in *Complete Poems* (Aberdeen: Association for Scottish Literary Studies 1991).
2. G. M. Hopkins, 'God's Grandeur' in *Collected Poems* (Oxford: OUP 1967).
3. Sr L. Johns, 'Mary Reflects' (Stanbrook Abbey, England).

17

Palm Sunday

Today we enter on Holy Week and Christ enters Jerusalem and enters into his Passion. What is it all about?

Essentially, it's a simple story. He enters into what is ours so that we can enter into what is his. Today would normally be the Solemnity of the Annunciation: the feast of the day the Word became flesh and entered our humanity, taking on the form of a servant. As today's second reading has it, he was humbler yet, even to death, death on a cross. He enters human life, suffering and death. It's the mystery of the Cross. All so that we can enter his divine life. It's the mystery of the Resurrection. It's what Mr Trump would call a 'deal', a good deal. It's what the Fathers of the Church more elegantly call a 'wonderful exchange'. He drinks the cup of human experience, so we can drink new wine in the kingdom. He enters our 'distance' from God and one another, so that we can access his closeness. He 'becomes sin', so we can become righteousness. He shares our sadness so we can have joy. He experiences dis-grace so we can be graced. He's stripped so we can be clothed. He's mocked so we can be praised. He's wounded so we can be healed. He thirsts so we can drink. This is how the New Testament and early Christians express it. He is put to death 'in the flesh' so we can receive the Spirit. The Incarnation leads to the Cross, the Cross to the Resurrection, the Resurrection to Pentecost. By faith and the sacraments we're enrolled in the new world Jesus' sufferings have opened up for us, a world that will flower in its fullness when everything is achieved and our hearts are purified.

So, one spring afternoon before the Passover, Jesus makes the two-hour walk with his disciples from the village of Bethany to the Mount of Olives overlooking Jerusalem, joining the crowds on their way to the feast. He mounts a young donkey, goes down the winding road over the valley of the Wadi Kidron, and then up again to the walls of Jerusalem, passing through the Valley Gate and so to the Temple. Then a few days later, beginning in the Upper Room, he enters on the sequence of events we have just heard from the Gospel of Mark and will hear again on Friday from the Gospel of John.

It's the beginning of a wonderful exchange. And what else can we say?

In the Eastern (Byzantine) liturgy, on Palm Sunday Eve, the service begins with a particular icon being carried into the church. The icon of Christ the Bridegroom. And it remains in the church for the first days of Holy Week. It's another clue to what is happening. A Bridegroom is coming! But this Bridegroom isn't wearing a kilt or a white suit. He's dressed in the purple robe the soldiers mock him with. He wears the crown of thorns and he's holding the reed they strike him with. He's a joke, apparently. But, in fact, he's the Bridegroom. He has come to win the heart of his Bride, who is us, his Body, the Church. He'll give everything for her. He will be raised to embrace her. And at Easter the Church becomes a mother birthing child after child, generation after generation, from the womb of the baptismal font.

Holy Week is a wonderful exchange. Holy Week's a marriage.

What is it all about? Let's ask a third time. I live now opposite St Machar's Cathedral, our city's first Cathedral (now a Church of Scotland church). I was coming back past it last night. Lights were on. I thought I would look in and ask the prayers of the medieval bishops buried there. Then I realized other people were entering the Cathedral. Something was on. I went in. There was someone I know. 'What's on tonight?' I asked her. A concert by the Con Anima Chamber Choir. Yes, marking the start of Holy Week, called 'Hosanna to the Son of David'. 'Would you like a free ticket?' So there I was, caught. And the concert's centrepiece was Bach's 11-part Chorale, *Jesu meine Freude*, Jesus my Joy. It struck me I was living a parable. The generous lady with her free ticket to joy was a symbol of the inviting Church, a symbol of grace, introducing me to Christ's death and resurrection. And Bach, the Evangelist, was setting to music words like these: 'Jesus, my joy, the field of my heart. Jesus, my jewel … Lamb of God, my Bridegroom, nothing on earth will be dearer to me than you … Surrender, spirits of grief, for Jesus, my Joymaster, enters in … Though I suffer here, even in my sorrow, Jesus, you remain, my joy.'

What is Holy Week about? It begins with children full of joy and will end with the joy of Mary Magdalene and her friends. It is Christ—Christ the New Deal, Christ the Bridegroom, Christ the Master / the Bringer of Joy—Christ who went through all of this to do one thing: become our Joy.

18

Maundy Thursday

Aberdeen in Lockdown, 9 April 2020

Isn't it strange to be keeping the Last Supper like this? Here we are, very like the Israelites, locked down in our households and houses as the destroying angel of a plague passes us by—hopefully.

Here we are recalling the familiar gestures and words of our Lord over the bread and the cup. Here he is, saying to his disciples, take this all of you and eat of it, take this chalice and drink from it. And yet only a few of us can. And so it seems to be over great tracts of the world. A great Eucharistic fast. It is extraordinary. The whole current experience is extraordinary. More than extraordinary, it's mysterious. But if it's mysterious—with the hand of God over it—there must be a goodness here.

Perhaps we've needed this distance, this discipline. Perhaps we have under-appreciated. Perhaps we have not, as St Paul says, 'discerned the Body' (1 Cor 11:29). Perhaps we have seen Holy Communion as something of a token or badge, or an endorsement of whatever we choose to be. Perhaps we have forgotten that Christ is in the host so that he can be in our hearts, and that he comes to our hearts to fill our lives. Perhaps we have forgotten St Augustine's phrase that it's we ourselves who are on the altar: that the bread becomes the Body so that we become the Body.[1] Perhaps we have forgotten to wash each other's feet.

Now, in a strange way, it is as if the world's pause button has been pressed, and the Church's too.

I like to imagine we've been given this different fast and abstinence in order that a new hunger will come awake in us. When we can return to normal sacramental life, it could be like making a new First Communion, a new beginning. There will be postponed Baptisms to celebrate, Confirmations to catch up with—personal Pentecosts. I suspect there will be confessions coming from a new depth. I think priests will feel reborn when they see a flesh and blood congregation in front of them. Can't we dream of a new birth, new beginning for all of us? So, perhaps our houses and households are like wombs. Perhaps they are what their houses were for the Israelites that night of the full moon in Egypt: the beginning of an exodus to a better place, to a fresh freedom. The night Jesus was betrayed, the night they came together in someone's upstairs room in Jerusalem, was a night of new things. Jesus made the Jewish Passover something new by replacing the Passover Lamb with himself, by becoming the Sacrifice, and by making himself the Bread and Wine, the food and drink for the journey. The old yields to something new, as St Thomas said: *novo cedat ritui*.

A surprising ancient name for the Lord's Supper was 'the birthday of the chalice'. 'The cup of salvation I will raise; I will call on the Lord's name' goes tonight's Psalm. The birthday of the chalice means the birthday of the Church's Eucharist. There is a new presence of God in the world. And with that birthday coincides the birthday of the ministerial priesthood. Jesus included the apostles in his own future when he offered himself and told them to do what he had done. So he made them priests of the New Covenant. This is another novelty. It's another paradoxical form of Christ's presence in the world. Then, there's the new commandment: 'love one another as I

Maundy Thursday

have loved you.' A new mindset, a new ethic, a new way of human living springs forth from the water Jesus used to wash the disciples' feet. Humble love is being born; Dostoevsky called it the most powerful thing of all. It is the truest sign of Christ.

Somehow these things come together: Israel's Passover on the eve of the Exodus, the Upper Room, the strange world we're in at the moment.

The blood on the lintels, the destroying angel, the silence around closed airports and the waning of pollution, the numbers dying, the spirit of service, Judas like a virus going about his murky background business, sealing Jesus' fate, all of us variously confined. Will it all go back to business as usual afterwards? Not impossible. But wouldn't that be worse than sad? And what about us Christians? Can we change? Can we be reborn?

The Anglo-Saxons called these days of the Triduum the 'still days'—still because the Lord was going down into the silence, into the dust of death: an end of all things. But they knew that in those still days something else was happening, something was shifting in the womb, something stirring in a tomb, the cosmic egg was hatching Easter. They knew—we know—that in this quiet time something else rises up before us. It rises up in the Upper Room and towers over everything: nature and history, sin and death, life and the world, and each one of us. 'Jesus knew that the Father had put everything into his hands', and into those hands, he, the God-man, takes the bread of creation and humanity and lifts the human cup of sorrow and joy. This is the ultimate newness and the beginning of everything. This is what rose and rises tonight, in the long night of human history. It is the humble love of Christ: his body given for us, his blood poured out, the gift of his divine-human life. It is his 'love to the end'. This is what holds the world in being and the Church and our families and ourselves. It is before and within and beyond all words, all sacraments. It is greater than everything. It is always there. 'Take and eat.'

Notes

1. See St Augustine, *Sermon 227*: 'It was by means of these things that the Lord Christ wished to present us with his body and blood, which he shed for our sake for the forgiveness of sins. If you receive them well, you are yourselves what you receive.'

19

Good Friday

Three times in the Gospel of John, Jesus said he would be lifted up (Jn 3:14; 8:28; 12:32). He was talking of his death. And that Friday in Jerusalem two thousand years ago he was. And today in our liturgy he is again lifted up. Today the Cross is lifted up over us, over all believers, over the whole world. And why is the crucified Christ lifted up? I offer three reasons: to be seen by us, to shelter us, and to flower in us.

Think of how many standards, banners, emblems, symbols, flags have been lifted up over us humans throughout history. Think of the hammer and sickle, the swastika, the rising sun, the imperial eagles—all promising shelter and security, unity, and victory. And how often they are simply lies and abuse of power! How often they just march us to death! But the Son of Man is lifted up so 'that whoever believes in him may have eternal life' (Jn 3:15). And for the Gospel of John, believing means seeing.

It isn't easy to look at the Cross. It shows a horrible thing: an excruciating death, the killing of an innocent man. The early Christians were ridiculed for preaching a crucified God. In AD 79, the Italian city of Pompeii was destroyed by an eruption of Mount Vesuvius. When centuries later the ruins were excavated, there drawn on a wall was an anti-Christian cartoon: a crucified donkey. Then again, at times, Christians themselves have used the Cross to legitimate crude aggression and oppression. It isn't always easy to look at the Cross. St Paul speaks of it as a scandal, a stumbling-block, as craziness.

'Behold the wood of the Cross', though, says the Liturgy. Don't just look, but 'behold', see with the eyes of faith, with inner eyes opened by the Holy Spirit. It's a matter, let's say, of seeing salvation.

For the year 2000, Neil MacGregor, then the director of the National Gallery in London, decided to put on an exhibition called precisely that: 'Seeing Salvation'. It featured paintings of Christ, many of them, naturally, crucifixions. He was told by the chattering classes and intelligentsia that it was a waste of time, if not offensive. None of the Gallery's potential commercial sponsors would touch it. In the end it proved by far the most popular exhibition in Britain with 5000 visitors a day and the fourth most popular in the world.

There's a story about three Jewish boys in France. I have to say clearly, it's not an anti-Jewish story, but there is a point in the boys being Jews. As a prank, they decided to go to confession, and to make up extravagant, lurid sins. So the first one went in and came out, laughing at what a fool he had made of the priest. The same with the second. In went the third. The priest now realized what was happening. The boy told his fantastic tales. So the priest said, 'For your penance go and stand beneath the crucifix in the church, look steadily at Christ's face and say three times: "You did all this for me and I don't give a damn."' The boy was surprised. He went. He looked at the figure. And he said the words twice. He couldn't bring himself to say them a third time. He left the church changed. Years later, he was the Cardinal Archbishop of Paris.

Christ is lifted up to be seen.

Christ is lifted up to shelter us. 'I will draw all people to myself.' Christ is lifted up today and we will go to him and kiss the Cross and put ourselves under the shelter of its grace. Think of the millions doing that today! I think of a man I once saw at the sanctuary of Chimayo in New Mexico, distressed, on his knees before the image of Christ on the Cross, arms outstretched, shouting for mercy. We think of the three Marys beside the Cross: Mary, the mother of Jesus, Mary the wife of Clopas and Mary Magdalene. We think of the beloved disciple. We think of the 'many women' who had come from Galilee whom St Mark mentions. Jesus' 'acquaintances' St Luke speaks of. The centurion who says, 'Truly, this man was Son of God.' These people were the beginning of the Church: the first of a crowd that will grow and grow. And over us the Cross is like a benign eagle, overshadowing us with its wings. The Cross stretches out its arms to gather us. It embraces east and west, north and south, Jew and Gentile, male and female. The Cross is like a great tree bending over us. On the Cross there is ultimate goodness hidden under the evil of others. Strength underneath weakness. Grace beneath apparent disgrace. Gathering despite the marginalisation. Hospitality overcoming hostility. Space beyond the constriction. Life defeating death. And on the cross, like a throne, reigns the King, not just of the Jews but of the whole world. A suffering king doing good in return for evil, dispensing bounty, favours, good things, giving shelter: 'Father, forgive them for they know not what they do.' 'Today you will be with me in paradise.' Bequeathing a seamless tunic, symbol of a new unbroken unity, of the Church gathered together. Saying, 'woman, behold your son' and, to the disciple, 'behold, your mother': a new family created. Gift upon gift. 'He bowed his head and gave up his spirit': the Holy Spirit, the divine Breath. Blood and water from the broken side: blood / forgiveness; water / life; water / baptism; blood / the Eucharist. Grace upon grace. The power of Satan broken, evil exhausted, shelter and protection. So, let's go to the Cross, let's kiss the Cross, let's put ourselves under its wings, let's take the fruit from its branches.

Lastly, Christ, and his Cross, is lifted up to flower in us. To be planted in our hearts and grow its flowers and fruits in our bodies and lives. On Good Friday, something new was born in the world. All the negatives are still here, but now they're stamped with an expiry date. Now there is something else and greater among them. Now there are flowers in the wilderness. There is a springtime. It was illustrated just the other day, when the French Gendarme, Arnaud Beltrame, took the place of a woman hostage in the French supermarket siege by an Islamist terrorist, and paid the price of his life. Such sacrifices, the French President said, 'honour and elevate us', lift us up. Indeed they do. They lift up the Cross too. They flower from the Cross. Arnaud Beltrame was a practising Catholic, converted in 2008. He had been preparing for the last two years, under the guidance of Fr Jean-Baptiste, for his sacramental marriage to Marielle. What a loss for her, but what pride she can carry in her heart forever for having loved such a man, who did such a Christ-like thing! She and the priest were with him when he died in hospital in Carcassonne. And another woman lives too. And we have all been lifted up.

May the Cross flower in us as well!

Let St John have the last word: 'In this is love, not that we loved God but that he loved us and sent his Son to be the atoning sacrifice for our sins. Beloved, since God loved us so much, we also ought to love one another' (1 Jn 4:10–11).

20

The Easter Vigil

Brothers and Sisters, this is the night when our Lord Jesus Christ passed from death to life. It's the night he passed from the dark confinement of a tomb on the edge of Jerusalem into the radiant expanse of an unfettered and glorified life. It's the night his share in our alienation from God, our estrangement from each other, our mental suffering and physical pain, our dying was turned for him into communion and joy and indestructible life. I've never forgotten my parish priest saying to me, after a Good Friday liturgy: 'How good to think he's out of pain now.' And tonight, at this Vigil, we can add: 'How good to think he's in joy now.' This is the night of this Passover, his Passover. But because Christ is he who he is, it's ours too. Ours too. Ours was the humanity he took from Mary. 'Ours were the sufferings he bore, ours the sorrows he carried', says Isaiah. 'He bore our sins [not his] in his body on the tree' [of the Cross] (1 Pt 2:24), says St Peter. 'He was put to death for our trespasses', says St Paul, 'and raised for our justification' (Rom 4:25). It was all 'for us', *pro nobis*. He is all 'for us'. And so tonight is our Passover, our passage. 'Let us pass over in the Passover of Christ', says St Augustine, 'lest we pass away with this passing world.'[1]

We've already, tonight, passed from outside to the inside, from a carpark to a church, from darkness to light, the light of the Paschal candle being passed to each of us. We've just passed—with all those readings!—from the

Old Testament to the New: from Genesis' 'in the beginning' to the new and greater beginning of an empty tomb. We've flicked through as it were our biblical family album: creation, Abraham and Isaac, Moses and the Exodus. We've listened to Isaiah, Ezekiel, and Baruch. We've watched the hope of Israel grow. Then came full light, the bells, the Gloria. We heard St Paul talking of baptism. We've sung our first Alleluia for forty days. We've seen the two Marys and Joanna,[2] the spice-bearers, discovering the tomb empty and Peter, baffled, confirming the fact. How much movement, momentum! How many suggestions of Passover, passage! 'Let us pass over in the Passover of Christ,' says St Augustine, 'lest we pass away with this passing world.'

Now, straight after this homily, there's a new, still more powerful, sequence beginning. Tonight, those being baptized and confirmed and receiving Communion for the first time are making their passage, our gallant quintet. Through the sacrament of baptism, they are dying and rising with Christ. They are passing from an old way of life to a new one: receiving the forgiveness of sins, being reborn as children of God. They are coming in from the cold and entering the family home of the Church. This is their passage. Then, after their baptism, all of us 'old-timers' have our moment. There's the renewal of baptismal promises. Our Lenten efforts come to their climax: we renounce Satan and sin once again, profess our faith again, and are sprinkled with newly blessed water. It's a recalling, renewing, confirming, progressing of our own passage. And then our candidate. She'll profess the Catholic faith, enter fully into the Church, receive the Gift of the Holy Spirit in Confirmation, together with the newly baptized, and make her first Holy Communion too.

Thus, we all converge, we all come together: together in the bond of faith, together in the bond of the sacraments, together in communion with the Church throughout the world, with the Holy Father, Successor of Peter and all the bishops in communion with him. 'You are a chosen race,' St Peter told his fellow Christians, 'a royal priesthood, a holy nation, God's own people, that you may declare the wonderful deeds of him who called you out of darkness into his marvellous light. Once you were no people but now you are God's people; once you had not received mercy but now you have received mercy' (1 Pet 2:9–10). This is our passage. And our passage is Christ's passage passing itself on to us. 'How good to think he's out of pain now, how good to think he's in joy now'—but not just in himself. If our hearts are right and our faith alive, he's out of pain in us, he's full of joy in us, here, now, tonight. St Joan of Arc put it famously: 'Christ and the Church, it's all one.' St Thomas Aquinas put it succinctly: Christ made his passage from death to life, he rose again, *ad informationem vitae fidelium*, 'to inform the life of the faithful'. He didn't mean Christ gives us some facts, some data, though in a real way he does. But he mainly meant that risen from the dead, Christ is the inner form, shape, pattern of who believers are. He's our template, our mould, our example. And more, he's our energy, our driving-force, the battery that powers and lights us.

And so we will pass to the Eucharist. Out of the womb of that Jerusalem tomb, Christ was born to the risen life. Out of the womb of the font, the Church is born to the life of faith, hope and love. And in the Eucharist, they kiss, they embrace, risen Bridegroom and washed and anointed Bride. We find ourselves at the wedding feast of the Lamb. The Eucharistic banquet, our Easter communion is the climax of all the journeys that converge this night and opens our passage to heaven, journey's end.

What a thing it is! How much to be grateful for! But the good news is, that's not the end. Christ's risen life passes to us and then on through us, on to others. Another Passover. Even when life is hard and we suffer, it is to radiate from us. Mary Magdalene and the other women took it to the disciples and the disciples passed it between themselves. He is risen! And then, men and women both, they began to pass it to the world. Here's what can carry on when we return to our carparks and homes. It's not some funny, overheated process. It's simple and natural. It's done, in the love of God, through our own human lives and loves, our natural relationships, to the people we know, neighbour to neighbour, between husband and wife, children and parents, friend to friend. It's done supporting, comforting, restoring, the good word, the kind gesture, the giving of time, through the daily bread of our human love.

Yes, tonight is too full not to explode. Christ passes from death to life, in himself, in us and out from us. He can't be stopped. 'Let us pass over in the Passover of Christ', says St Augustine, 'lest we pass away with this passing world.' Amen, may be it so! For those newly baptized and confirmed, for all of us. It already is so! Alleluia!

Notes

1. St Augustine, *In Johannis Evangelium* 55.1 (CCL 36, p. 464).
2. Cf Luke 24:12.

21

Easter Sunday

Christ is risen! He is truly risen!

In St Machar's Cathedral, Aberdeen, on 19 March, the Con Anima Chamber Choir gave a performance of Brahms' *German Requiem*. It was composed after the deaths of a close friend and of his much-loved mother. Brahms wanted to acknowledge all the grief of loss and yet offer consolation. He used texts from the Bible for this purpose. The result is a masterpiece.

There's a wonderful moment in the second movement which may help us 'realize' the Resurrection. Brahms takes well-known words from Isaiah 40: *For all flesh is like grass and all its beauty is like the flower of the field. The grass withers, the flower fades.* He sets them as a funeral march. It's solemn, stately, sad. It constantly builds. It returns after interludes. And it evokes, not just the passing of a friend or a close relative, but of all humanity—as if every life and all of history is a long procession to the grave. It's noble, but desolate. On and on it goes, until it can go no further. It ends. There's a pause. Silence falls. Then, loud and strong, the choir comes in. It comes in with the word *Aber / But*. There is this great 'but' thrown into the air, thrown to the audience. The rest of the text follows: *But the word of the Lord remains forever*—the word which promises eternal life, everlasting joy. And Brahms unfolds it as a victorious fugue.

If we want to 'realize' the Resurrection, perhaps that pause and that *But* and those words can help us. It may seem rather dark to think of life as one long procession to the grave. Certainly, beautiful things can happen on the way. But still… Or perhaps we can think of our life and the life of humanity throughout the centuries as one long wandering sentence, strung together by 'and' after 'and'. 'And then, and then, and then…' And all flesh *is* like grass in the end. Even, it seemed, the flesh of the Son of man. It withered and fell, and he was buried in a hurry on Friday night. Full stop / period. 'We had hoped,' say the two disciples on the way to Emmaus, 'that he was the one to free Israel.' 'We *had* hoped.' A pause, the Sabbath. The women rest, preparing spices, and, then the Sabbath over, they go to anoint the dead body. It's a loving thing to do, but it's only decorating the full stop. Enter the angelic choir: *Aber / But*. There was this unexpectedly empty tomb, the stone rolled away. A new sentence beginning. A message from angels. Bewilderment. Much rushing to and fro. The early morning run of Peter and John. Yes, the women are right. The stone has gone. The tomb is empty. The burial clothes are neatly folded. The Beloved Disciple got the implication immediately, Peter was slower. And then, later that day, to Mary Magdalene, to the other women, to the forlorn disciples en route to Emmaus, to Peter, to James; and finally, to all the lads gathered in the Upper Room, the Master showed himself. 'See it is I.' 'I am the first and the last, and the living one. I died, and behold I am alive for ever more, and I have the keys of death and the underworld.' 'The Word of the Lord remains forever.' The Word, who gives existence and form and purpose to the whole creation, the Word who had become flesh and died—because all flesh is like grass—this Word has risen from the dead and remains forever. 'Christ is risen! He is truly risen!' God has, as it were, interrupted our endless chatter, has drawn a line through our secret desperation.

He has opened a new sentence. A fugue of faith, hope and love has begun and, as it unfolds, voice after voice, instrument after instrument, individual after individual, generation after generation, can arise and enter it.

Peter is key to this morning. His perplexity, his conflicting emotions are so easy to relate to. But in the first reading, we hear him, some ten years after going into that empty tomb. He is proclaiming the Resurrection to a pagan household in Caesarea. First, the disciples had become part of the new sentence—then other Jews. Now Peter sees non-Jews too can join in, and do not have to become Jews to do so. More and more are drawn in; they add their names, their breath, their words, their lives to this new sentence: this sentence that begins with the risen Word risen. And we are invited also, to extend this new beginning. It's a sentence, it's a story that remains forever. It's a fugue which we're invited to take up, to add our voice too, following Peter. It's a new liturgy for humanity, St Paul says, that begins today, a liturgy of new life: 'Let us celebrate the feast, then, by getting rid of all the old yeast of evil and wickedness [these are grass, these are part of the funeral march] and eating only the unleavened bread of sincerity and truth.' And, this morning, in the city where Peter and Paul gave their lives for the risen Christ, Peter's living successor, Pope Francis, will proclaim the Resurrection—to the City and the world. 'Christ is risen! He is truly risen!'

Christ is this blessed *but* to our endless nonsense. He has launched this new sentence. He has intoned a new music. In a moment, renewing our baptismal promises, we will reject the old one and endorse the new: 'I do renounce Satan …'—his discords, his long walk to death. 'I believe.' The Creed tells a story, and when we say, 'I believe', we write ourselves into it. To be in the Church, in the community of faith, is to be in the music, to be part of the story. To remain forever.

'All flesh is like grass, and all its glory like the flower of the field ... but the word of the Lord remains forever.' That, as we know, is from Isaiah, from the Old Testament. But in his First Letter, which is part of the New Testament, St Peter quotes it. And he explains: this lasting word is the Gospel, the Good News that was preached to you—baptized Christians. And, for Peter, and the whole New Testament, that Good News is the proclamation: 'Christ is risen, He is truly risen!' So, the body of his letter begins: 'Blessed be God, the Father of our Lord Jesus Christ, who in his great mercy has given us new birth as his children, *by the resurrection of Jesus Christ from the dead*, so that we have a sure hope and the promise of an inheritance that can never be spoiled or soiled and never fade away ... You do not see him, but you love him.' His Letter begins from that empty tomb he discovered today.

Christ is risen! God's *But*. Let's write ourselves into the story and add our voice to the music. It's to be part of something that remains forever.

22

The Fifty Days of Easter

'Almighty and eternal God, who willed that the paschal mystery should be contained within a symbolic mystery of fifty days...' So begins the prayer for the First Vespers and Vigil Mass of the feast of Pentecost or Whitsun.

Easter's unique stature in the Christian year is made visible in many ways: by the Easter vigil, by the forty serious days of Lent, and, not least, by the fifty days of the Easter season. Do we appreciate these last sufficiently? They are more ancient even than Lent. They form its necessary complement. They have a unity, truth, goodness, and beauty all their own. The following is an attempt to highlight some of their significance.

Jesus our Lord, wrote St Paul, 'was put to death for our trespasses and raised for our justification' (Rom 4:25), and believers in turn, he says, have been 'buried with him by baptism into death, so that as Christ was raised from the dead by the glory of the Father, we too might walk in newness of life' (Rom 6:4). Both Jesus' death and resurrection are of significance for us, and it is in both that the Christian participates. And so, when, in the cycle of the year, the Church commemorates and relives the central moment of the story of Christ, his 'Passover' or 'paschal mystery', she doesn't do so one-sidedly but in a way that does justice to the whole. Just as at Christmas, the Church proclaims both the divinity and humanity of the Saviour, so at Faster she shows us both cross and resurrection: 'dying he destroyed our death, rising he restored our life.' If our knowing of Christ is to be full, it must be a knowing of the two sides of the single mystery. So, after the forty days of Lent, come the fifty days of Easter: forty days of preparation, fifty of appropriation; forty of toil, fifty of rest; forty of sowing, fifty of gathering in; forty (and its six Sundays) signifying the fragmentary and this-worldly, fifty (and its octave of Sundays) the eternal and complete. As Joseph Ratzinger has written, 'even through this temporal arrangement the Church has provided a profound psychological interpretation of what Easter means and of how we can and should celebrate it.'[1]

Why fifty days? As with forty the number is biblical. The span of time between Easter and Pentecost is the Christian transposition of the seven full weeks or fifty days (counting inclusively) between the Jewish Passover (Pesach) and the Feast of Weeks (Shavuot or Pentecost); more precisely between the first day after the Sabbath that falls in Passover Week to the same Sunday seven weeks or fifty days later (cf. Lev 23:15- 16). The Greek name, Pentecost (e.g., Tob 2:1; Acts 2:1), used for the Feast of Weeks, means 'the fiftieth day'. Yet the early Christians used the word not just for the last day of the Easter season, but for the whole fifty days. They would speak of 'the Pentecost', 'the season of Pentecost', 'the seven holy weeks of Pentecost', and to this day the Byzantine-rite service book for this period is called the 'Pentecostarion'. And what did it mean for them? Writing at the turn of the third century, the Christian apologist Tertullian challenged his readers: 'Call out the individual solemnities of the nations [i.e. the pagans], and set them in a row, they will not be able to make up a Pentecost.'[2] The point being made, if rather crudely, is that in the death and resurrection of

Christ, we have the ultimate feast or reason to celebrate, and that this is expressed in the extraordinary institution of a fifty-day celebration, 'an extremely joyful period'.[3] According to Eusebius of Caesarea, writing in the following century, 'when we have well and duly passed the Passage (celebrated the Easter Vigil), another, greater feast awaits us [the fifty days]. The children of the Hebrews call it by the name of Pentecost, and it bears the likeness of the kingdom of heaven'.[4] For St Athanasius, the light of Easter 'extends its beams, with unobscured grace, to all the seven weeks of the holy Pentecost', which is 'a symbol of the world to come', when light and joy will be had in their fullness'.[5] For St Basil, 'the entire season of Pentecost is [like Sunday] a reminder of the resurrection we expect in the age to come… During this time the ordinances of the Church instruct us to pray standing, and by this reminder our minds are made to focus on the future instead of the present'.[6] In the West, St Augustine says the same: 'these days after the Lord's resurrection form a period, not of hard work, but of peace and joy. That is why there is no fasting and we pray standing, which is a sign of resurrection … and the Alleluia is sung, to indicate that our future occupation is to be no other than the praise of God'.[7] And similarly, St Maximus of Turin:

> The Lord has so arranged it, that as we sorrow over his passion for forty days, so we should rejoice at his resurrection for fifty days. Therefore, we do not fast during the fifty days … A person cannot fast when he is being fed with the grace of the Saviour: for the companionship of Christ is, in a sense, the Christian's food. So, during these fifty days, we are fed by the Lord living with us.[8]

From quotations like these, from various contemporary re-statements, and most of all from the liturgy itself, a whole picture emerges. More precisely, a grace and the opportunity to receive and experience it, to realize, in every sense, what Christianity and who Christ is. 'Of all the seasons of the liturgical year, Eastertide,' wrote Dom Guéranger,

> is by far the richest in mystery. We might even say that Easter is the summit of the mystery of the sacred liturgy. The Christian who is happy enough to enter, with his whole mind and heart, into the knowledge and love of the Paschal Mystery, has reached the very centre of the supernatural life.[9]

The season of the fifty days, as another Benedictine, Patrick Regan, has written, 'is the time when the risen Lord continuously manifests himself in the Church as he repeatedly did to his disciples; it is the time when the Spirit is poured forth and received; it is the time when the hope of the Lord's coming, generated at his ascension, is fulfilled precisely through the gift of the Spirit who establishes the presence of the Risen One in the community of faith, and draws it into Jesus' transfigured humanity.'[10]

It is the time of 'mystagogy', when we join those sacramentally initiated at Easter in penetrating more deeply the meaning and place of the sacraments in our lives, especially Baptism, Penance and the Eucharist. 'They recognized him in the breaking of bread.'

It is the season of Alleluia, every Alleluia being, as St Augustine said so powerfully, a rehearsal for heaven and its praise.

It is a time for falling in love again with the beauty of the Christian life, which is not keeping of rules, a mere 'being' or 'doing' good, but a living of the life of the once crucified, now risen Christ.

It is a time when our interior, spiritual senses can be opened to the light and sound, touch, taste, and fragrance of things supernatural, and of the Lord himself; when prayer can become less a self-conscious act than a peaceful awareness of his presence and guidance, of his peace and joy; when the Scriptures, and our own lives, make sense in a new way.

It is a time when the Church, overwhelmed by the new wine that Christ has brought, reads nothing but the New Testament: the Gospel and Letters of John, the Acts of the Apostles, 1Peter, and Revelation, especially.

It is a time for being confirmed in our vocation, work, mission. And it is in the power of the risen Christ that we can take up our cross.

Everything that was given the first disciple between that first Easter Sunday and Pentecost is offered again, *mutatis mutandis*, to the Church, that is to us, during the fifty days. And in the simple beauty of the *Regina Caeli*, the Church remembers and shares the joy of Mary in her Son's resurrection.

The fifty days form a unity, a 'great Sunday' as St Athanasius said, and the liturgical books speak at the Sundays and weeks of Easter, not *after* Easter. The Paschal Mystery is viewed as a whole. At the same time, within the unity, there is a movement marked by Easter Sunday, the Ascension, Pentecost itself, following the order of events found in the writings of St Luke. There is a pattern to the readings of the season. The two approaches complement each other.

The kingdom of joy, Charles Péguy once said, is far less known, less travelled than the kingdom of suffering. The fifty days are a gentle invitation into this untravelled world, which is the one that will outlast everything else.

Notes

1. J. Ratzinger, *Seek That Which Is Above* (San Francisco: Ignatius 2007).
2. Tertullian, *On Idolatry* 14:7.
3. Tertullian, *On Baptism* 19.2.
4. Eusebius of Caesarea, *On the Paschal Solemnity* 5.
5. St Athanasius, *Festal Letters* 6,13; 1, 10.
6. St Basil, *On the Holy Spirit* 27, 66.
7. St Augustine, Letter 55.
8. St Maximus of Turin, Sermon 44.2.
9. P. Guéranger, *The Liturgical Year*, vol. VII, Book 2, ch.2 (Richmond: Loreto Publications 2013).
10. P. Regan, OSB, *Between Memory and Hope: Readings in the Liturgical Year*, ed. Maxwell E. Johnson (Collegeville, MN: Liturgical Press 2000), p. 226.

23

BEHOLD THE LAMB OF GOD

PART I

Introduction

One of the titles of our Lord prominent in Eastertide is that of 'the Lamb'. It occurs in three of the five Mass Prefaces we have at this time. It occurs in a hymn of Evening Prayer—quite a familiar hymn, I think, beginning in English: 'At the Lamb's high feast we sing.' We hear the phrase, from St Paul, 'Christ our Passover has been sacrificed' (1 Cor 5:7)—'Passover' here meaning the Passover Lamb, the Lamb sacrificed and eaten at the Jewish Passover. In other words, our Lamb is Christ.

For some reason, this title of Jesus has touched me. I have a hunch there is something here for us. There's something for us—in and beyond our current pandemic—something for our prayer and our life in the world in which we are, in this twenty-first century. I just want to try and 'suss out' what that may be. I doubt it can be captured in a single formula. As Tennyson once said of imagery in his own poetry: 'the thought within the image is more than any one interpretation.' This Lamb is large.

Scripture, surely, is the first place to seek him. 'It is remarkable how important a part is played in the Bible by the image of the lamb,' wrote Joseph Ratzinger, now Emeritus Pope Benedict.[1] Anyway, here I will follow the biblical trail.

There is art, though, too. Traditionally, and especially in Western Christianity, representations of Jesus as the Lamb are many. The image features in mosaics and frescoes, wax discs, statues, ivories, woodcuts, stained-glass, paintings—and in England at least on pub-signs too. I would recommend sight, especially, of the sixth century mosaic of the Lamb of God in the dome of the presbytery of San Vitale, Ravenna; of Francisco de Zurbaran's seventeenth century painting of 'The Bound Lamb' in the Prado of Madrid; and above all of Hubert and Jan van Eyck's wonderful fifteenth century altarpiece in St Bavo's Cathedral, Ghent, 'The Adoration of the Mystic Lamb', one of Europe's masterpieces—coveted, incidentally, by Adolf Hitler. Then there's music too, so many settings of the *Agnus Dei*. Think of the aria in Bach's B minor Mass, or the version in Beethoven's *Missa Solemnis* of 1824, 'a prayer for inner and outer peace'. The Gregorian repertoire is rich too, with the *Agnus Dei* from Mass settings 2, 4 and 11 especially fine.

To resume the thread: Lambs—defined as sheep up to one year of age—had a precarious life in the ancient world, and still do. Their life-prospects are not cheerful. Nowadays, they are sacrificed to the demands of the market, usually within four months of their birth. Anciently, they were one of the preferred animals for sacrifice to the gods, and were destined therefore not just for the table, but for a fire and an altar. Lambs and sheep have been easy fodder for the great crying human need to sacrifice to the gods, to make offerings to a divinity—all in an attempt to re-establish harmony between our struggling selves and the higher powers: to acknowledge them, propitiate them, win favours from them, be at peace with them.

This is in Scripture too, but at the same time Scripture moves beyond it. There is a path worth following here. As

I've tried to follow the thread of the Lamb, it does feel like hearing music. Not a theme and variations exactly; rather, a melody that is continually being enriched, incorporating new motifs, accruing new harmonies or being differently orchestrated. And it does all rise to a climax, as we shall see.

I want to look at Abel, Abraham, Moses, and the prophets, then at John the Baptist, John the Evangelist, John the Seer of the book of Revelation. And John the Baptist's line: Behold the Lamb of God can be a guide. It is a journey to prayer, I hope.

Abel

Let's begin. Life after the Fall begins with two brothers and two sacrifices: Cain with his fruit or cereal offering, mysteriously rejected, and the shepherd Abel's who 'brings some of the firstlings of his flock' (Gen 4:4), lambs in other words. 'And the Lord had regard for Abel and his offering' (Gen 4:4)—'regard' in English anyway—suggesting a look. We know the sequel. Out of envy, Cain kills his brother. The shepherd who offers lambs is accepted, but becomes a 'lamb for the slaughter' himself. Our Eucharistic Prayer no. 1, still prays over our own sacrificed Lamb: 'Be pleased to look upon these offerings with a serene and kindly countenance, and to accept them, as once you were pleased to accept the gifts of your servant Abel the just...' Connections already. The Eucharist constantly recurs.

Abraham

At the Easter Vigil, we read Genesis chapter 22: the heart-rending story of the test, the sacrifice of Abraham—commanded to do the unthinkable and offer his beloved son Isaac. 'And Abraham took the wood of the burnt offering and laid it on Isaac his son. And he took in his hand the fire and the knife. So they went both of them together. And Isaac said to his father Abraham, "My father!" And he said, "Here I am, my son." He said, "Behold, the fire and the wood, but where is the lamb for a burnt offering?" Abraham said, "God himself will provide the lamb for a burnt offering, my son." So they went both of them together' (Gen 22:6–8). As the story unfolds, the Lord prevents Abraham sacrificing his son. He sees a ram caught in a thicket, and it is offered instead. 'On the mountain God provides' (Gen 22:14), provides a lamb or a ram for sacrifice. But that ram is only a first fulfilment, as the paschal lamb is another. 'God himself will provide the lamb.' It has been said that the whole Old Testament history of Israel was a long waiting for that unconscious prophecy to be fulfilled. There will be a lamb provided by God, a lamb through whom God himself will put everything right, will put us and all creation at rights with him—on the mountain, the high place, of the Cross. 'God himself will provide', will provide 'for himself' some translations say. The Father himself will take on what he asked of Abraham, and the Son will take on the part of a willing Isaac. 'Thus'—it has been written—'the principle of self-sacrificing love belongs to the essence of the Godhead.'[2] 'God himself will provide the lamb.' There is, as it were, a Lamb-in-waiting, a Lamb-in-God. This is why St Peter, in his First Letter, links Christ with the paschal lamb and then says: 'he was destined before the foundation of the world but was made manifest at the end of the times for your sake' (1 Pet 1:20). This is why, beside the Jordan—perhaps at the moment when sheep and lambs were being herded towards Jerusalem for sacrifice—the Baptist identifies Jesus as 'the Lamb of God'. He is the Lamb provided by God himself, pre-existent in God, pre-destined by God to become flesh and take away the sins of the world. At the very least, there is a divine hinterland to the figure of the Lamb: 'God himself will provide...'

Moses and Passover

Let's pass now from Abraham to Moses, and hear the melody further elaborate. According to the Mosaic law, in Exodus and Numbers, two lambs were to be offered daily in the future Temple, one in the morning and one in the evening. This was certainly happening in Jesus' time. It was the core of Israel's daily worship, which was already seen as a means by which the world was kept in being. According to Leviticus, lambs could be offered by individuals who wanted to sacrifice to God for personal reasons. Most famously, most prophetically, there is the Passover Lamb of Exodus 12. 'Christ our Passover,' St Paul will say, 'has been sacrificed.' From the first reading on Maundy Thursday, we remember the rubrics. The setting is slavery in Egypt, but springtime too—'the first month of the year'. On the tenth day, as the moon is approaching its fullness, a lamb was to be selected. A lamb one year old, a male and 'without blemish', immaculate, in peak condition. On the evening of the fourteenth day, at full moon, the lamb was to be slaughtered, its blood put on the doorposts and lintels of the Israelites' houses, its flesh roasted and eaten. It was to be eaten, in each household, that very night, while the plague-bringing angel passed over the Egyptians, those at the meal, belted and spurred as it were, standing, ready to set out on the great expedition of the exodus, the journey to freedom. Again, this so anticipates the 'more' that is to come. 'God himself will provide.' 'Christ our Passover has been sacrificed', St Paul again; 'a lamb without blemish', says St Peter (1 Pet 1:19), picking up another element. In Jesus' time the slaughter of the Passover lambs took place in the Temple, and the rabbis by then understood this, not just as a practical piece of butchering, but as an atoning sacrifice. So, on the threshold of the exodus, of being set free from slavery, 'redeemed' (which is what that word means), a lamb is sacrificed, his blood sprinkled as a protection from harm and the flesh eaten as a viaticum, food for the journey. Again, we pick up the Christian resonances, especially the Eucharistic ones. The Eucharist fulfils the Jewish Passover.[3] It re-presents the sacrifice of the true Lamb, and gives us his flesh to eat, strength for the journey to God, and blood to drink, protection for the doorposts of the heart. No wonder we invoke the Agnus Dei / the Lamb of God as we approach. Connections again.

Prophets

Now, let's pass from Moses to the prophets, from the Passover lamb to the prophetic lamb. We are about to cross the bridge that leads from the Old Testament to the New.

In the Israelite world, it has been said, 'the sacrifice of a lamb was a common enough event to be used metaphorically for the suffering or death of an innocent on behalf of others.'[4] It is in the two great prophetic books, of Isaiah and Jeremiah, that this occurs.

Here is Jeremiah, suddenly aware of the evil intentions of his opponents: 'but I was like a gentle lamb led to the slaughter' (Jer 11:19). The passage is read, in reference to Christ, on Saturday of the fourth week of Lent.

Better known still is Isaiah 53:7:

> He was oppressed, and he was afflicted,
> yet he opened not his mouth;
> like a lamb that is led to the slaughter,
> and like a sheep that before its shearers is silent,
> so he opened not his mouth.

This verse, and the whole surrounding passage, Isaiah 52:13–53:12, describes a mysterious unnamed figure, God's servant, presumably a prophet, who endures rejection and apparently death and yet somehow vicariously saves his people. Looking back as Christians, we can hear the future coming. The whole passage is familiar to us as the 1st reading on Good Friday. Our particular verse, with its lamb, was being read by the Ethiopian eunuch, in chapter 8 of the Acts of the Apostles, when Philip meets him. It's 'beginning from this Scripture' that Philip expounds the 'good news of Jesus' (Acts 8:35).

There's plenty happening here. In both Jeremiah and Isaiah, the 'lamb' becomes a metaphor for a human being. This is a jump, a leap, a transposition. It's a humanisation. Both quotations use the phrase 'led to the slaughter'—a lamb's usual end. There's a strong suggestion, then, that these persons are headed for death. In both, the metaphor evokes the person's character or attitude.

Jeremiah the lamb is 'gentle'; the Isaian lamb is 'silent', 'opens not its mouth'. In the New Testament these become qualities of the suffering Christ; he eschews violence when arrested, and keeps his own counsel before the high priest and before Pilate. 'He committed no sin'—Peter will later write—'neither was deceit found in his mouth. When he was reviled, he did not revile in return; when he suffered, he did not threaten, but continued entrusting himself to him who judges justly' (1 Pet 2:22–23; cf. Is 53:9). Again, the figure of the Lamb is growing, the metaphor is continually being enriched. Most of all here, when the Isaian lamb becomes someone 'stricken for the transgression of his people' (v.8), who 'makes himself an offering for sin' (v.10), 'bore the sin of many, and made intercession for the transgressors' (v.12), making 'many to be accounted righteous' (v.11). As a devout Jew, steeped in his Scriptures, Jesus would have known this passage. There is no doubt it informed Jesus' own understanding of his destiny, as well as the early Church's understanding of him. And the figure of the lamb is there.

Part II

The Gospel of John

Now, we can come to the New Testament and the Gospel of John, and the witness therein of John the Baptist.

'The next day he [the Baptist] saw Jesus coming toward him, and said, "Behold, the Lamb of God, who takes away the sin of the world!"' (Jn 1:29). This is the first time Jesus appears in person, physically, in the Gospel of John. So the Baptist's description of God's Lamb is not a throwaway remark. It's a resounding opening chord. Christian imagination has pictured the Baptist using his finger to identify Jesus. I've already mentioned the sheep being led for slaughter milling around. In the Gospel of John, Jesus is the true Light, the true Bread, the true Vine, and so on. He gathers and perfects in himself so many elements of creation. John is saying here, he is the true Lamb too, the Lamb. The Lamb Abraham foretold. The Lamb prescribed by Moses. The One who exists before me, says the Baptist, and ranks above me (cf. Jn 1:30). The Lamb provided by God, in waiting from all eternity, consecrated, and sent by the Father to take away sins and fulfil the divine purposes. We have a sense of everything coming together. By describing Jesus in such terms, the Catechism says, John the Baptist 'reveals that Jesus is at the same time the suffering Servant who silently allows himself to be led to the slaughter and who bears the sin of the multitudes, and also the Paschal Lamb, the symbol of Israel's redemption at the first Passover'.[5] That is good exegesis!

The next day, John, 'standing with two of his disciples', sees Jesus again. He 'looks' at him, taking his own advice, and repeats the first part of this phrase, 'Behold, the Lamb of God' (Jn 1:35–36). What's striking this time is that the two disciples immediately 'followed Jesus'. Here's another strand. I remember an old farmer saying, 'Never trust a bull.' You wouldn't follow a bull, nor a lion, but a child might well run after a lamb. Jesus is not alarming, not frightening; he draws, he attracts, he is irresistible. He is, in that fine English word, winsome. He turns and sees the disciples following and, when they ask where he's staying, says 'Come and see.' 'Behold the Lamb of God.' And so the disciples begin their association with Jesus. In Revelation, this notion of 'following the Lamb' recurs. Another motif is entering the music.

Often, the Gospel of John mentions something at its beginning and returns to it at the end. And so with the Lamb. Though the phrase doesn't recur, the symbolism does. In John's Gospel, Jesus goes to his Passion carrying his own cross, as Isaac carried the wood in Genesis; he goes as the beloved Son, the Lamb God has at last provided. As already mentioned, Jesus is crucified while the paschal lambs were being slaughtered on Passover eve; he is the true Lamb. When his side is pierced by the soldier after death, blood comes out, as well as water: the blood of the Lamb. His bones are not broken, as was usual to shorten the agony of the crucified, and so another Scripture is fulfilled, 'Not a bone of him shall be broken' (Jn 19:36), a requirement of the Passover lamb (Ex 12:46). At the foot of the Cross, the disciple Jesus loved, probably one of the two who followed the Baptist's pointing finger at the very start, now in depth does what the Baptist says. He beholds the Lamb. 'Behold the Lamb of God.' 'He who saw it has borne witness' (Jn 19:35). 'They shall look on him whom they have pierced' (Jn 19:37).

The Book of Revelation

Now, with fear and trembling, we can, through the eye-glass of the Crucified, look further still. Let me quote Joseph Ratzinger again and a little more: 'It is remarkable how important a part is played in the Bible by the image of the lamb. We come across it in the very first pages, in the account of the sacrifice of Abel, the shepherd; and in the last book of Holy Scripture the Lamb is at the very centre of heaven and earth.'[6]

Let's turn to the book of Revelation.

'Behold the Lamb of God.' 'I, John'—yet another John—'saw' is a refrain that runs through the Apocalypse. And what does he see? Manifold things, in heaven and on earth, theatrical, cinematic, symbolical things, some beautiful, some bizarre, some terrifying: lampstands and thrones, angels with trumpets and bowls, armies and earthquakes, crowds waving palms and playing harps, falling stars and flying millstones, a dragon and two beasts, a woman clothed with the sun, a gaudy prostitute, precious gems and glass oceans, a city coming down from above. And most of all, a lamb—*the* Lamb. Our theme comes to its climax, its Alleluia chorus. Christ—the crucified, risen, and glorified Christ—is here called the Lamb 28 times, and he stands at the centre of heaven and earth. 'I, John, saw.'

The author of Revelation was (another) John, John the Seer we can call him. He was a Christian prophet. He was exiled on the island of Patmos for having preached the Gospel. He shared the visions he received so that his readers and listeners, then and now, might behold the Lamb of God. He 'wrote what he saw' (Rev 1:19) to encourage, empower, keep faithful fellow-Christians who, in a corner of the Roman Empire (the 'Province of Asia' in what's now Turkey), were under pressure: state persecution, apostasy and doctrinal confusion in their own ranks, and general political and economic insecurity. John wants them, and us, to see what he sees—above all, this Lamb and the God whose Lamb he is. It is an echo of the words of John the Baptist. Look at him: he is wounded, he has conquered. Keep looking and, however wounded you are, you will conquer too. This book celebrates the victory of the Lamb and ours in him.

So, who is the Lamb? Jesus, naturally. Jesus slain and risen. 'In the Apocalypse'—a scholar has written—'two ideas are represented [by the title of Lamb]: that of Christ as an offering, and that of the Messianic leader of men ... these two ideas are merged in the author's mind ... the Lamb who conquers is the Lamb who has given himself up as a willing sacrifice.'[7] The lamb led to slaughter has, precisely because of his willing sacrifice, now 'acquired majesty, dignity, honour, authority and power'. Both elements are his forever, and so he is the truest, strongest force in human history. He lives simultaneously, 'in the midst of the throne', that is, 'in the bosom of the Father', and in the midst of the Church, her communities, her faithful (cf. 1:13; 14:1). He is, however hiddenly here below, the centre of heaven and earth. His stage, his screen, is all creation. A fourteenth century English poem, *The Pearl*, goes further and speaks of the joy of the Lamb:

> The Lamb's delight let no one hope to imagine!
> Though he was hurt and had a wound,
> In his expression it was never seen
> His glances were so gloriously glad
> I beheld among his bright retinue
> How they superabounded with life.

Life and joy flow from this Lamb.

He it is who opens the scroll that contains God's purposes and so initiates their accomplishment. As 'king of kings and lord of lords' (17:14), he leads his followers to victory, His blood—that is, the power of his personal life, love, and sacrifice—transforms his followers; it cleanses them (7:14) and empowers them to live faithful Christian lives and to love, in turn, to the end (12:11). He draws his followers to himself, and they follow him wherever he goes (14:4). After the great prostitute has been judged and Babylon (Rome) has fallen (17–18), after the corporate strongholds of evil have collapsed from within (17:15ff), the 'marriage of the Lamb' (19:7) to his bride the Church can be celebrated with a joyful feast. Blessed indeed those who are invited to it (19:9)! And all creation worships him, as it worships the One upon the throne—the Adoration of the Lamb.

The Way of the Lamb

'Behold the Lamb!' See the Lamb who was slain and to whom past, present and future belong. John asks this of the Christian communities he is sustaining, harassed communities, experiencing their own lamb-like vulnerability He is also asking the whole world of his day, enslaved to totalitarian power and false ideologies (ch. 13), threatened by foreign invasion, war, food shortages, disease, and death (ch 6), and with economic collapse on the horizon (ch. 18), to turn in the same direction.

And when we do look at the Lamb, we see who God truly is. We learn that true power doesn't reside in the apparatus of the State or the thought police, or in any kind of violence. True power, true greatness belongs to the Lamb—John perhaps reinforces the paradox by using throughout a word that strictly means 'little lamb, lambkin'. His first vision of the Lamb is meant to 'throw' us. Who will open the scroll? All heaven is awaiting the answer. Is there anyone? Yes, says an elder: the Lion of the tribe of Judah, the Root of David—in other words, a figure of royal, leonine power. And who appears? 'A lamb that seems to have been slain.' Shock and bathos. (Cf 5:1–6). A slain Lamb is the medium of God's transforming power, and human fulfilment is to be found in inner connection to him, vulnerable and pierced (1:7) but the 'faithful and true witness' (3:14). Because he 'loves you' (1:5) and gave his lamb-life, he is 'the beginning of God's creation' (3:14). Having died and risen, he has the keys of death and hades (1:18) and is stronger than all the forces of destruction. This is the reversal of perspective John is calling for. It is a revisionist view of what really matters, of what determines the course of events, of what survives and outlasts the horrors of history and the trials of any life. It is the perspective of Dostoevsky's monk in The Brothers Karamazov: 'At some thoughts one stands perplexed, above all at the sight of human sin, and wonders whether to combat it by force or by humble love. Always decide 'I will combat it by humble love'. If you resolve on that once and for all, you can conquer the whole world. Loving humility is a terrible force: it is the strongest of all things, and there is nothing else like it.'[8]

This is the way of the Lamb. It is the way that personally and ecclesially—as the Church in this time and place—seems an apt ethic for now. We are called to be 'with' (14:1) the Lamb, his followers, his companions, and, like John the Seer of Patmos, to give witness to him and his Gospel (1:9). Those '*with him* are called and chosen and faithful' (17:14). To discern this way, one could usefully explore the pattern of Christian life envisaged by Revelation. It turns on the idea of 'testimony to Jesus' (12:17), witness, *martyria*, sometimes in the literal sense, but not always. It recognizes the fragility of Christians, not just in the sense that they are not protected from a violent death, but because they are the object of diabolical hostility (12:17) and testing (2:10) and can be deceived and conquered (cf. 13:7). Hence the frequent emphasis on 'patient endurance', on holding fast, on being faithful to the end. 'Toil' is mentioned (2:2) and there are calls to repentance (2:5 etc). The staples of 'love and faith and service' are required (2:19), and the keeping of the commandments (12:17). It requires chastity, abstention from any form of worship of false gods (14:4). It means constantly praying, 'Come, Lord Jesus' (22:17, 20). There are resemblances here to the 'signs of holiness in today's world', listed by Pope Francis in *Gaudete et Exsultate*, 'patience, perseverance and meekness', and the rest, and his call to 'spiritual combat, vigilance and discernment'.[9]

This way of the Lamb, in our own times, has surely been taken by the Dietrich Bonhoeffers and Alfred Delps, of the Maximilian Kolbes and Edith Steins; the way of the Hutu and Tutsi seminarians in Burundi who refused to separate when one side's gunmen came, and so died together as 'brothers'; the way indicated so lucidly by Bishop Pierre Claverie, OP, now beatified, not long before he and his Muslim driver were assassinated. The Church in Algeria, he said—a tiny Church in an Islamic ocean, in a country then racked by civil war—was with Mary and John at the foot of the Cross while Christ was being crucified by the surrounding violence. 'The Church deceives herself and deceives the world if she presents herself as one power among the others or as a purely humanitarian organization or as some spectacular evangelical movement.' The way is a love, for which 'Jesus has given us a taste and traced the way: "there is no greater love than to lay down one's life for one's friends."'[10] And this same way can be followed in less dramatic circumstances than those evoked. It can be lived unobtrusively in daily life and is—praise God—by countless people. In our own setting, we can live with the diminishing endorsement of culture and law or even of good reputation; we can live with our failures and do what we can to make amends; our mission is to offer a hope that attracts.

If we do 'behold the Lamb', surely something of his 'glorious gladness'[11] can flow into us, into a way of life which echoes his patience and gentleness and silence, his non-violence, his non-harming, and is permeated with a quiet alluring beauty; which has a sense of a prevailing divine providence and intention, privileges the gift of self and believes that it is loving humility which sustains and transfigures the world. John Saward has made connections with St Thérèse of Lisieux's way of spiritual childhood.

Let me quote Joseph Ratzinger one more time:

> According to the Book of Revelation, the Lamb is at the very centre of heaven and earth ... [and] the Lamb alone can open the seals of history. It is the Lamb, who appears as slain and yet lives, who receives the homage of all creatures in heaven and earth. The lamb which lets itself be killed without complaint is a symbol of meekness: Blessed are the meek for they shall inherit the earth. The Lamb with his mortal wound tells us that, in the end, it is not those who kill who will be the victors; on the contrary the world is sustained by those who sacrifice themselves. It is the sacrifice of him

who becomes the 'Lamb slain' that holds heaven and earth together. True victory lies in this sacrifice. It gives rise to that life which imparts a meaning to history, through all its atrocities, and which can finally turn them into a song of joy'[12]—the song of the Lamb.

Behold the Lamb of God! Let's go looking for him: on the Cross, in heaven, in the Eucharist—and in the company of those who follow his way.

Notes

1. J. Ratzinger, *Behold the Pierced One*, (San Francisco: Ignatius Press, 1986) p. 114.
2. R. H. Charles, *The Names of Jesus* (London: Macmillan 1953), p.117.
3. *CCC* 1340.
4. *Eerdman's Dictionary of the Bible*, ed. D. N. Freedman, A. C. Myers (Amsterdam: Amsterdam University Press 2000), s.v. 'Lamb'.
5. *CCC* 608.
6. Ratzinger, *Behold the Pierced One* (San Francisco: Ignatius Press 1986), p.114.
7. V. Taylor, *The Names of Jesus* 2nd ed. (London: Macmillan 1954), p.117.
8. F. Dostoevsky, *The Brothers Karamazov* (New York: Bantam Books 1970), bk. 6, chap. 3.
9. Pope Francis, *Gaudete et Exsultate* (2018), 4, 5.
10. Bishop Pierre Claverie, *Homily at Prouilhe*, 12 June 1996; author's translation.
11. Ratzinger, *Behold the Pierced* One, p.114.
12. *Ibid.*

24

The Seven Sundays of Easter

Second Sunday of Easter

Gospel: John 20: 19–31

This is the Sunday of St Thomas the Apostle. Eight days after Easter we hear, in the Gospel, first of Jesus appearing to the disciples on the evening of Easter Sunday, and then 'eight days later' appearing again. 'Peace be with you,' he says the first time, and then again the second time, 'Peace be with you.' Today is a second chance to receive the peace of Christ. And Thomas, who wasn't 'with the disciples' the first time, is the second, and receives 'peace in believing'. St Thomas found the whole thing difficult. His first instinct, on hearing of the Resurrection, was to shake his head and say, 'Na.' But today, the eighth day, he has his second chance. Golly, does he take it! 'My Lord and my God'—the most explicit and resounding act of faith in all the Gospels. 'God of everlasting mercy', goes today's Collect, 'who in the very recurrence of the paschal feast—this Second Easter—kindle the faith of the people you have made your own.' Today, 'eight days later', fire as it were comes out from the words of Christ and the wound in the side of Christ, and kindles the faith of St Thomas. 'And blessed are those who have not seen and yet believe.' Today is a second chance for us to believe.

This is Second Chance Sunday. At the time of his Passion, the disciples had all fled, but in his Resurrection,

Jesus came back to them. 'Peace be with you.' He didn't go off and look for others. 'Doubt no longer, but believe': that's St Thomas given a second chance. 'Simon, son of John, do you love me?': that's Peter given a second chance. This is the grace of Easter, straight from the 'God of everlasting mercy'.

In today's Gospel, Jesus comes back to his failed disciples. He breathes on them, like the Lord on Adam at the beginning, gives them the Holy Spirit and the power to forgive sins: to offer to the others the second chance they had received. Sins are forgiven in the Sacrament of baptism—the Church has the power to baptize—and baptism is like a second birth, a renewal, a regeneration, a second beginning for sinful man. And sins are forgiven in the Sacrament of Reconciliation—the Church has the power to absolve sins committed after baptism; the 'plank after shipwreck' in the ancient phrase. It's a second second chance. The Father can't stop giving his children yet another opportunity.

So, this Sunday is Easter come round again, the Second Easter an octave up, the Sunday of St Thomas, the Sunday of Divine Mercy, the 'second name of Easter': it is all one message, surely. It's the God of everlasting mercy, the God of fire and light, ever ready to re-kindle us, to re-light the grace of our baptism, to pick us up, dust us down and say, On you go! 'As the Father sends me so am I sending you.' At its level, even the pandemic fits in here: the Holy Father says again and again, this is a chance for a better world. Take it! Will we?

This is the Day the Lord has made, not just today, but every day in the new day that dawned in the Resurrection, the 'day that knows no setting'.

Third Sunday of Easter

Gospel: Luke 24:13–35

In Lent we talk a lot about changing—conversion, in the biblical word. We're reminded life is short, death is certain and after death comes judgement. Whether we really change for better during Lent is a moot point: am I less impatient, am I more generous? Well... But in the Easter stories, in Jesus' eight or so appearances told in the Gospels, we see it happening. It's as if the Lord decides to do what we have failed to do. The Easter Gospels are about transformation. Think of Mary Magdalen, weeping outside the tomb, turning, turning to someone she thinks is the gardener, turning again, in another sense, to recognize who he is, and then running, running to tell the others. Think of Thomas, grumpy stubborn Thomas, changing from unbelief to a blazing profession of faith: 'My Lord and my God.' Think of our two men today. At the beginning they are tramping along, shoulders slumped. At the end of the story, they literally turn round. They go back to Jerusalem, running surely. They turn round physically because they have been turned from disillusionment to recognition, because their hearts have burned and their eyes have opened. (One could footnote that: their disillusionment was actually an illusion. It can sound so adult to be disillusioned; but, beware, it might be very wrong). When they find the Eleven and their companions, they meet more change: 'Yes, it is true. The Lord has risen and has appeared to Simon.' Or again, think of Peter after that breakfast on the beach: 'Simon, son of John, do you love me?' What kind of man came out of that conversation?

'All changed, changed utterly. A terrible beauty is born.' Those are well-known lines from Yeats' poem, 'Easter 1916', about the Easter Rising in Dublin that year. It's a poem that shows ordinary, everyday people being changed by the desire to rise up and fight for the freedom of their country. Yeats describes, among others, a man whom he thought a 'drunken, vainglorious lout', who 'had done most bitter wrong' to a friend of Yeats in fact. But, like the others, even he, 'he too', is transfigured. 'He, too,' writes Yeats,

> has resigned his part
> In the casual comedy;
> He, too, has been changed in his turn,
> Transformed utterly:
> A terrible beauty is born.[1]

So it was. Neither these folk or Ireland were ever the same again. The Gospels recount, as it were, the first Easter Rising.

One by one, two by two, then as Eleven, the disciples are changed, in their turns. They resign their part 'in the casual comedy' of everyday life. For them, in any case, it had already ceased to be either comic or casual: 'they had him crucified, and we had hoped...' Then 'a terrible beauty' is born for them. It's born from the womb / tomb. It's born in them. It's beautiful because it's Christ; it's terrible because it utterly transforms. 'Did not our hearts burn within us, while he talked to us on the road?' Albeit in different ways, at different paces, this beauty does burn hearts and lives. There's a terrible beauty about having a purpose in life and sharing in the mission of Christ. And this Beauty destined to kindle and transfigure the world.

Fourth Sunday of Easter

Gospel: John 10:1–10, 11–18

Jesus presents himself first of all as the gate and then as the good shepherd. It's not clear where the first thought ends and the second begins. They run into each other, the imagery is compressed, and we can feel puzzled.

'I am the gate,' says Jesus. Here's a first thought: by saying it, he's actually allowing others to be shepherds— through him, with him, in him. He speaks of 'thieves and brigands', false shepherds, leaders who mislead. There is a context within his own ministry here. In chapter 9, the Pharisees were trying to rob the blind man of his miracle. But the Gospel also looks ahead—to the time of the Church. Jesus himself will pass from this world to the Father (Jn 13:1). To provide for that, he sends the apostles to carry on his work (Jn 20:21–23). 'I am the gate.' Peter and John, Philip and James and the rest, therefore, will enter the sheepfold through him, sent by him, and the sheep recognize their voice as his commissioned representatives, as true followers of the Lamb (Rev 14:4), 'shepherds in the one Shepherd',[2] shepherds moved by faith and love. 'Feed my lambs' (Jn 21:15), Peter is told. 'Tend the flock of God which is your charge' (1 Pet 5:2), Peter will write later to the presbyters of his day. The line continues. The apostles in turn appointed successors and helpers and so the ordained ministry of the Church has developed, with its bishops, priests and deacons. And the Church has always taken care to authenticate them. Bishops must be ordained within the succession of the apostles, and the ceremony of ordination begins with reading the letter of appointment from the Pope, St Peter's successor. Bishops in turn ordain and appoint parish priests to their charge. And so the flock knows it has authorized pastors sent to teach and celebrate the sacraments for them in the name of Christ. The human limitations are famous, of course, but there's something beyond them. 'Anyone who enters through me will be safe.' There is the blessed safety of being in Christ's sheepfold, part of Christ's flock.

Is there not great humility on Jesus' part, when he calls himself the gate? The Father, the 'kind shepherd' of today's Prayer after Communion, has shared his eternal shepherding of the human flock with his Son, ordaining him as our Shepherd and Teacher and Priest in the economy of salvation. Nor, in turn, does the Son monopolize the task of shepherding. He shares it. When he sees the hungry crowd in John ch. 6, he asks the disciples, 'How are we to buy bread for these people to eat?' (6:5) He was trying to enlist them, engage them, co-opt them. 'I am the gate.' By calling himself that, Jesus is calling out for shepherds. This is Vocations Sunday. '*You* give them something to eat' (Mt 14:16), he says. It's only when we assume responsibility for others that we grow up.

Now, let's widen the lens. Most of us are given shepherding to do in our lives. I know one father with four children to care for. It's a delight to watch him shepherding them; he's just so good at it. Teachers are shepherds, surely, parents, grandparents, doctors, nurses, social workers, politicians, civil servants, department heads. The list is endless, and you don't have to be at the top of the tree. It may be a full-time work or just happen occasionally, even by accident. But it is God's work, and when we do it we must pass through the gate of Jesus. 'Thieves and brigands', the false prophets, the wolves in sheep's clothing, the false shepherds, the other voices—God knows the air is thick with them. They have in common one thing. They 'rob'. They *take away* from the sheep. They subtract, they diminish, they reduce. They curtail our humanity. They make life and happiness consist in this or that: pleasure, money, power. We're told we're just here to get what we can out of life and should just focus on ourselves. And this life is the only life. But that's to rob us of what we are. Shepherding that passes through the gate of Christ wants the good of the other, not to milk the other of their good; not to 'fleece' them, as we say. 'The shepherds have fed themselves, and have not fed my sheep,' complains Ezekiel (34:8). True shepherding looks to the whole of our humanity in time and eternity, cares for body, soul and spirit, looks to each of us and all of us. 'I have come that they may have life and have it to the full.'

There it is. Each and all of us are sheep and each and all of us are shepherds. So, as sheep and shepherds, let's take care to pass through Christ's gate, turning a deaf ear to the voices that want to steal our humanity. Let's find true pasture. Let's take each other to pasture. It's there. In the end, it's what the Collect calls 'a share in the joys of heaven,' 'eternal pastures' says the Prayer after Communion. 'The sheep find their pasture,' says Pope Gregory, 'for everyone who follows him with a simple heart [will be] nourished on everlasting greenness ... the inner joys of paradise in flower. The pastureland of the elect is the face of God, seen in unclouded vision and feeding our humanity (*mens*) forever with the food of life.'[3] Let's be shepherded and shepherd one another: as an old monk once said, 'one beggar telling another beggar where bread is to be found'.

Fifth Sunday of Easter

Acts 14:21–27; Apocalypse 21:1–5; John 13:31–35

Reflecting on today's three readings, it struck me that the first is about faith, the second about hope, and the last (the Gospel), about charity / love.

As bishop, I often wonder: when the Lord looks at us, looks at our diocese, what does he see? What makes him smile? The answer is: faith, hope and charity in us. That's our beauty. And here today is this holy trio.

It's hope that drives us. And here is hope in the middle of our three readings. A French poet (Charles Péguy) once imagined Faith and Charity as two elder, rather stately sisters walking along, and in the middle, between them, tugging at their hands, is their little sister, Hope. She is jumping and skipping and hopping, pushing ahead. And it's she, the little one, who's really leading the other two.

> I, John, saw a new heaven and a new earth; the first heaven and the first earth had disappeared and there was no more sea. I saw the holy city, the new Jerusalem, coming down from God out of heaven, as beautiful as a bride all dressed for her husband.

Here's a first thought: how big our hope is. Often, we think of heaven too narrowly: heaven is where I'll be OK, I'll be happy, and see my friends again. But God's horizon is broader.

There will be 'a new heaven and a new earth'. The whole of creation, universe, nature will be transformed. We will have a whole new environment. 'There was no longer any sea.' That sounds strange. Many people love the sea. The language is symbolic, of course. In fact, the ancient Israelites, the Jews, generally didn't like the sea. It seemed to them huge, chaotic, destructive. Think of a tsunami. So, 'no more sea' means creation no longer at war with itself, no longer undermined or threatened by the enemy within, creation at peace. It's another version of Isaiah's vision of the lamb and the lion lying down together.

'I saw the holy city, the new Jerusalem.' Here's another dimension: a whole new way of living together, humanity at peace. I know a 13-month-old baby who smiles at everyone he meets. And sadly, you think, how long will that last? When will that be knocked out of him? We don't smile at everyone we meet. But in the heavenly city we will. We will because each of us will be a bringer of joy to everyone else. We will simply delight in each other.

And this city, this new human world, will be 'as beautiful as a bride all dressed for her husband'. We will correspond completely to God's hope for us. In the beginning, we were made in his image and likeness, reflecting him. We're always in his image, but not always in his likeness. We live in 'the land of unlikeness'. But in the new Jerusalem, the likeness will be restored to the image. Sin will be no more. God will delight in us and we will delight in him.

'He will wipe away all tears from their eyes.' That's what a mother does to her child often enough. Don't you think that behind the eyes of each of us, there's a kind of build-up of tears, a great sack of them? Isn't there, in the heart of each of us, a great bag of sorrow? Every one of us has lost something precious, every one of us has been disappointed and hurt. Every one of us is secretly grieving over something. Every one of us knows that the people we love are going to die, and we will too. And the picture in my mind is this: when we do die and meet Christ, this sack inside us will burst, and the tears, the accumulated tears, will all pour out. And God will wipe away every one of them. How I don't know. How the terrible evils of human history, of what we've done to each other over the centuries, how that's put right, I don't know. But the word is: 'He will wipe away every tear from their eyes.' God's tender touch can do even that. 'And death shall be no more, and there will be no more mourning or crying or pain—for the former things have passed away.'

That's our hope. This is why the little child in us still skips along, keeping our faith and love fresh. This is why the dog is straining at the leash.

Behold, I make all things new.

Sixth Sunday of Easter

Acts 10:25–26, 34–35, 44–48; Ps 97; 1 Jn 4:7–10; John 15:9–17

'While Peter was still speaking the Holy Spirit came down on all the listeners.' That's from the Acts of the Apostles, the book that tells the story of the first Christians and how the Church began. Often in the Acts of the Apostles, the Holy Spirit 'comes', 'comes down on', 'falls on', is 'poured out on', and 'fills' people. The story begins with the great public outpouring on the Apostles at Pentecost. But then there are others too—small-scale Pentecosts, as it were. The Holy Spirit is for everyone and all time. Forgive the comparison but think of a football that keeps bouncing across the field long after it was first kicked. In today's reading, the Holy Spirit comes on the pagan Cornelius and his household even before they are baptized. On two other occasions in Acts, he comes sometime after people have been baptized. He comes through the laying on of hands by an apostle, Peter, John or Paul. And our Sacrament of Confirmation picks up from this. We have been baptized, but then later (usually) we are confirmed. We are confirmed (usually) by a bishop—bishops are successors of the apostles. He prays over us and anoints us on the forehead with Chrism. And we are 'sealed with the Gift of the Holy Spirit'; we receive the Holy Spirit in his fullness with his seven gifts. This is why Pope St John Paul II called Confirmation 'a personal Pentecost for life'.

What a noisy place the world is! Not just physically. There are so many voices telling us what is good for us, for our health, for our life, for society, for the world. There's so much anger and pain. It's like the sound of an orchestra tuning up before a concert. It's cacophony. It's as though there are many songs all being sung at the same time, and we are being asked to join in. But they're not in harmony.

Then imagine that in the middle of that noise, another note is heard. It's quiet, but it's powerful. It's not easily heard, but while all the other noises come and go, this one persists. Think of a sonorous gong being gently struck again and again. This is Christ. He's the note struck by the Father, he's God's song entering into all this noise. The note of God's love and of true humanity is being sounded. It's good, true and beautiful, and it captures the heart that hears it. Christ brought it into the world when he was born of the Virgin Mary. He sang it out, so to say, in the beatitudes and the parables. He sang it most of all on the Cross, loving to the end. But the noise of the world crowded on top of it, muffled it, reduced it to silence in the tomb. Then God the Father, God the Composer, raised him from the dead, and that note sounded out again. It's a still small voice, like the one Elijah heard in the cave. But it's strong and resonant and it doesn't go away.

Faith is the opening of our inner ear to catch the note and hear the song. Faith recognizes its divine and human truth; its goodness and beauty. Faith hears the music that the Gospel of Christ is, and we are happy. But there's something more. We're not just asked to hear and believe. We're called to take the music in and then sing it out. 'Sing a new song to the Lord.' We're asked to join the choir, as it were, to add our own voice, to take up the song ourselves. We're asked to attune our whole lives to it—to make our lives a beautiful music for God. This is the grace of the Holy Spirit and his seven gifts. We are enrolled in the choir of the Church. We start to sing the music which is Christ. We become the song. We can recognize the false notes now, including our own. We have the music within us, and all the decisions and doings of our life, little or big, can be in harmony with God, and reverberate the beauty and truth of Christ.

Seventh Sunday of Easter

Acts 1:12–12; 1 Peter 4:13–16; John 17:1–11

I'd like to focus on today's first reading, and on one element of it. Today we see the apostles coming down the Mount of Olives, from where Jesus had ascended, re-entering the city and making their way to the Upper Room. They were staying there, says the reading. It was their 'pad', their base. There they engage in serious prayer, with the women, with Mary the mother of Jesus, and with Jesus' 'brethren'. Jesus, on parting, had told them to 'wait' in Jerusalem 'for the promise of the Father' (Acts 1:4), the Holy Spirit. They interpreted that 'waiting' as praying. And there they remain until the feast of Pentecost when the promise is fulfilled, and their prayers are answered.

The reading gives a vivid glimpse of these first disciples. This is 'the first Church', the first gathering of believers for prayer. They are our spiritual forefathers and mothers. They're the cell from which the body has grown.

And there is 'Mary, the mother of Jesus'. It can't be by chance that she's there and that she's mentioned. And I don't think she's there as an add-on, or an 'also ran'. In Eastern icons of the Ascension and of Pentecost, she is often set in the very middle of the apostles and the others, the central figure after Christ and the Holy Spirit. So, here is the first 'cell' of the Church, and at the nucleus of it is our Lady—'in the heart of the Church', 'in the midst of the assembly' (Ps 22:22).

What did her presence bring? I think the first thing would just have been joy. Our Lord's Ascension had conveyed that anyway (cf. Luke 24:52). Where there's sin, there's sadness, and in Mary's there's no sin. And therefore, there's joy. There's a transmission of joy. Regina caeli, laetare! 'He has risen as he said!' This comes to her and is passed on; we talk of 'infectious' joy. If you go to the great Marian shrines you can sense it, something positive in the atmosphere, light and uplifting. So it must have been in that Upper Room. So for us whenever we invite Mary into our own community.

Then, mustn't there have been something very reassuring about her presence? Salve radix, salve porta! 'Hail, Root; hail, Gate.' Mary was the gate through whom the Lord entered the world. She's the root—the daughter of Israel—from whom he sprang. And her presence must have rooted that early community. Mary went back to the beginning. She's the only person in the Gospels who's there at the beginning—her son's conception—and the end—his death, and now, after the Resurrection and Ascension. She's the one with the longest memory. She had had the treasure in her heart and been pondering more than thirty years. She knew her baby in a mother's way. She knew the growing boy. She knew every bend in the road of his life, as it were. She saw him go out on his mission. She'd witnessed the joyful beginning, water into wine. She had noticed everything, been baffled by many things, hurt by some, other times so full of pride and delight. And she'd been at the foot of the Cross. What she hadn't seen first-hand—she had had to stand back—she'd have garnered from Peter and the others. She wouldn't have a let a crumb of it fall on the ground. The Gospels have been called the 'memoirs of the apostles'. But before the written memoirs, there's memory, and her memory— full, deep, intimate. Her presence in that room was like an anchor for the others. In St Luke's mind, she is the first believer, the first disciple. And she's still there. And she's still the one—in the heart of the Church of heaven and earth, in the midst of the assembly—who has this whole memory, this insight, this love of her Son. After Pentecost, she would understand even better.

In the Church of all times and all places, Mary brings joy, Mary roots us in the memory of Jesus, Mary creates unity among believers. Now, in the heart of the Church, she waits for the promise of the Father, the coming of the Holy Spirit. She can teach us to wait now—hoping and praying and never despairing of mercy, waiting for the many, many things we all hope for, waiting for the Kingdom of God to come. With Mary, let's pray together for the coming of the Spirit of God.

Notes

1. W. B. Yeats, 'Easter 1916' in *Selected Poems* (London: Macmillan 1968).
2. St Augustine, *Sermo Guelferbytanus* 16, 2–3 (PLS 2, 580–81).
3. St Gregory the Great, *Homily 14 on the Gospels*.

25

THE ASCENSION OF THE LORD

*Acts 1:1–11; Ephesians 1:17–23, 10:19–23;
Luke 24:46–53*

According to the New Testament, Jesus withdrew from his disciples and was taken up into God on the Mount of Olives (cf. Acts 1:9; Lk 24:50). The small Chapel of the Ascension—also a mosque—marks the traditional spot. On the same hillside and hill, there are currently two Russian Orthodox monasteries of nuns. Sometime in the 1970s, an atheist Jewish teenager, from South Africa but living in Jerusalem, had developed an interest in Russian history. He heard that, in one of these convents, there was an elderly Russian nun who had had connections with the family of the last Czar. He gained permission to see her. She was paralysed and bed-ridden but received the boy and answered his enquiries. As he walked home down the Mount of Olives, he realized that this paralysed octogenarian nun—with everything against her, as it were—was the most joyful person he had ever met. So, he made another appointment. And he asked her, 'Why are you so joyful?' She smiled, and said, 'I am in love, you see.' And then something mysterious happened to him: he became aware of Jesus being there, quite unmistakably, quite undeniably. It would be twelve years before that Israeli boy would be baptized. That's another story. He is now a Jesuit, working in the Holy Land.

'Gladden us with holy joys, almighty God, and make us rejoice...' began today's Collect. Joy and the Ascension go together. When St Luke describes Jesus' Ascension at the end of his Gospel, he says that afterwards the disciples returned to Jerusalem 'with great joy' (Lk 24:52). You would not have expected it. The man who had filled their lives for three years and captivated their hearts had gone. The natural reaction would surely be to feel lost, bereaved, orphaned, scared, alone with their memories. Instead, though, they seemed to be echoing today's Psalm: 'God goes up with shouts of joy. All peoples clap your hands, cry to God with shouts of joy.'

It's worth exploring this. Why does Christ's Ascension unleash such joy? It is kept as a high feast. Even in my non-Catholic primary school, it was thought worth a half-holiday. In the monastery, the food is good today. Jesus had said, 'When the bridegroom is taken away from them, then they will fast' (Mk 2:20). But we don't. Why did such joy take hold of the disciples? Two 'men in white' appear in the first reading—a clue perhaps. Two angels, two messengers. Where there are angels, there are realizations, insights from above. *Gaudium de veritate*, Joy from the truth, is an old Latin tag. I think the disciples realized 'truth' and that gave them joy. They realized many things all at once perhaps, a complex realisation it would take the rest of their lives to unfold. What was it? I suppose the whole New Testament is one long answer to that, and indeed our Catholic faith. There's a sense in which the Christianity we know began with the Lord's Ascension.

Everything came together for them, I think. The whole story, from beginning to end. They saw that the One who had come down from heaven had now returned to his place of origin. They 'got' the plot. The One who had embraced our humanity in birth and work and the bother of daily life, who had gone on his mission, confronted evil and apparently been destroyed by it, who had suffered and died and been buried and had passed to the world of the dead, who had taken on the whole human experience, was now, in that same humanity, taken up into God. He was now returning our humanity to God, lodging it there, as it were, in his Father's safekeeping. Our flesh and blood and all the rest were now in the heart of the Trinity: consecrated in the Son, welcomed by the Father, transfigured by the Holy Spirit. And all of this 'for us'. 'I go to prepare a place for you' (Jn 14:3). We have a home at last, 'the promise of an inheritance that can never be spoilt or soiled and never fade away, because it is being kept for [us] in the heavens' (1 Pet 1:4)

This meant that the 'heavens', God's world, so inaccessible for so long, were now no longer closed. Our lockdown had been lifted. Centuries before, the patriarch Jacob had dreamed of a ladder reaching from earth to heaven, with angels going up and down (Gen 28:12). Now the dream was reality. Now the roadblocks were removed, and the traffic was flowing. It becomes possible to hope and to pray. There is a wide horizon and a new direction, life with a goal, and God always within hearing.

This isn't about astrophysics or Virgin Galactic. It's not a change of place for Jesus; it's the creation of a meta-space, another kind of space and place. It's about a new personal presence and closeness. At the Last Supper Jesus had said, 'I will not leave you orphans; I will come back to you ... On that day, you will understand that I am in my Father, and you in me, and I in you' (Jn 14:18, 20). Everything coming together.

One Greco-Russian name for this feast is 'salvation fulfilled'. That captures it. 'This same Jesus', the angels tell the disciples, 'will come back'. Early Christianity would realize that 'come back' did not simply mean 'at the end of time', but in any time, every day. St Paul speaks of the ascended Jesus lifted above everything, and made 'head of the Church, which is his body, the fullness of him who fills the whole creation.' And the final words in the Gospel of Matthew? 'I am with you always; yes, to the end of time.'

In his Ascension, Jesus transcends the world of time and space, and therefore can continually return to fill it. There are no forbidden places for him—good to remember when places are currently closed to us. The going was a coming, and the absence a presence. In ten days' time the coming of the Holy Spirit would confirm and seal all this. And the disciples realized this. 'Your joy no one will take from you,' Jesus had said (Jn 16:22).

I go back to that joy-filled Russian nun on the Mount of Olives. She would have lived through the Russian Revolution and seen terrible things. She was in exile in Jerusalem. She couldn't have returned to the Soviet Union at that time. She was living an enclosed life in a tense, sometimes war-torn city. She was old. She was paralysed—and the most joyful person that young man had ever met. That's what the Ascension enables. She knows this better now than any of us; now she is at home with Christ. 'I am in love, you see.'

26

Solemnity of Pentecost

On Pentecost day in Jerusalem, the sound of a wind filled the room where the disciples were, tongues of fire appeared above them and they were filled with the Holy Spirit. This is what we commemorate today. This is what we hope will be renewed today—not so much in its outward phenomena as in its inner meaning, in its grace. Today's Prayer is ambitious: 'you sanctify your whole Church in every people and nation ... pour out the gifts of the Holy Spirit across the face of the earth ... fill now the hearts of believers.'

Pentecost is a Jewish feast before it was a Christian one. It falls fifty days after Passover, and it marks the end of the grain harvest. Crops round the Mediterranean ripen far earlier than here. And here's a remarkable thing: according to the Old Testament on the Sunday after Passover, a sheaf of barley was taken to the Temple and presented to the Lord. That marked the beginning of the harvest. And it was on the Sunday after Passover that Jesus rose from the dead, the first-fruits of the Resurrection. Fifty days later, at Pentecost, two full loaves of freshly baked bread made from the new flour would be presented to the Lord, marking the end of the harvest. Ah! said the Fathers of the Church, those two loaves stand for us, for the harvest of believers, they stand for the Church. And why two? Because the Church is made up of, first, Jewish believers, like the apostles, and then Gentile believers, like us: two loaves. And Jesus' resurrection on the Sunday after Passover is completed in our resurrection to faith, hope and love, through the gift of the Holy Spirit given at Pentecost.

> They were all filled with the Holy Spirit.

Crammed together in a house in Jerusalem, fifty days after Jesus' Resurrection, there were the twelve apostles, and Mary, and the whole group of early disciples, 120 in all. They were there because Jesus before his Ascension ten days earlier had told them to wait in Jerusalem until they were clothed with power from on high. There they were, doing what he asked, praying and waiting. And there today, 'when Pentecost day came round', after hearing a sound 'like a powerful wind from heaven', after seeing 'what seemed like tongues of fire' resting on the head of each of them, 'they were all filled with the Holy Spirit.'

> They were all filled with the Holy Spirit.

This is what Jesus had promised. This is what John the Baptist had said, 'he will baptize you with the Spirit and fire.' This is what the ancient prophets had foretold: the outpouring of the Holy Spirit. The greatest Old Testament prophet was Isaiah. And in the very last chapter of the book of Isaiah, he says that the Lord 'will come in fire, and his chariots like the stormwind.' 'I am coming, says the Lord, to gather all nations and tongues; and they shall see my glory.' That's fulfilled today. It's fulfilled in the Church, born today, where the nations are gathered, and God's glory can be seen with the eyes of faith. It was fulfilled when after fire and stormwind had come, 'they were all filled with the Holy Spirit.'

Everything God the Father has to give, everything his Son has to give, is summed up and given in the gift of the

Holy Spirit. The Holy Spirit is the breath of God, the life of God, the love of God. He is all this in person. And he is given to us. On Easter Sunday, Jesus risen from the tomb, that first sheaf of barley, breathed on his disciples in the Upper Room, and said, 'Receive the Holy Spirit.' And they were filled with him. And we can be too. Even in our wandering minds and wavering wills and poor perspiring bodies, God can breathe. We can live with the life and love of God. And everything we do, outside what's deliberately wrong, can have the Spirit in it. He's God's yeast and we can be the wholesome loaves of God, the cereal offering, brought to the Lord and nourishing one another.

Jesus breathed on the disciples and said, 'Receive the Holy Spirit. Those whose sins you forgive they are forgiven; those whose sins you retain, they are retained.' A link is made: the Holy Spirit and the forgiveness of sins. The Holy Spirit and sin are enemies. Sin is something hard and stony; or knotted and lumpish; it's heavy. But the Holy Spirit is like flowing water, or wind, or fire, or green things growing. He's compared with things that live and move and breathe. So even in imagery, the Holy Spirit and sin are opposed. And when the Holy Spirit comes, when his influence starts to shape our lives, he disengages us from sin. He shows it up. He enlightens our conscience. Our excuses seem less convincing. He moves our hearts. Maybe we start to cry. We are being converted. We seek out the sacramental sources of forgiveness Christ has lodged in the Church: baptism if we've not been baptized, reconciliation for sins committed after baptism. We realize we have some forgiving to do ourselves, and some forgiveness to ask of others. The

Holy Spirit is in all this. It may happen suddenly. It may be a long process, with backward steps as well as forward steps; we may go round in circles for years. But this link: Holy Spirit-forgiveness is always there. It has been there since that first Easter and Pentecost. It's here now waiting to embrace us. The Holy Spirit moves us from the state of sin into the state of grace. The things St Paul mentions—'fornication, gross indecency, sexual irresponsibility; idolatry, sorcery; feuds and wrangling, jealousy, bad temper and quarrels, disagreements, factions, envy; drunkenness orgies and similar things', the whole soap-opera of fallen human existence—these things can be put behind. And that other litany—'love, joy, peace, patience, kindness, goodness, trustfulness, gentleness and self-control', the fruits of the Holy Spirit—can start to sing in us. Not only is the guilt of original sin and of our actual sins taken away. Something deeper is being shifted. The Holy Spirit gets to grips with our whole 'out of kilter-ness', our 'off-tune-ness', the sinfulness that lies behind our specific sins. It's a whole work of cleansing and purifying our heart that gets underway. Our re-creation in the image and likeness of God is being hammered out on the anvil of life. It will go on our whole life; after death if need be. Its upshot will be a final absolution, as it were, that will shine on us from the eyes of Christ when we see him face to face. 'My child, your sins are forgiven.'

The forgiveness of sin: Pentecost releases this into our lives. The path of holiness lies open.

'The Spirit gave them the gift of speech.' The apostles found their voice. They began to proclaim 'the marvels of God'. The Holy Spirit does this too: he enables Christianity to find its voice. It's the voice of praise (liturgy), the voice of communicating the faith among unbelievers (proclamation), the voice of charity and service (diakonia). This is the voice the Church has to find in so many different contexts. It's not a voice that will always be heard. It may struggle to find the right words or hit the right note. 'Yet their voice goes out through all the earth, and their words to the end of the world' (Ps 19:4). The Church, however stammeringly, does speak Christ to the world. The Holy Spirit gives her this power. He gives it to each of us in a different way. We find the way to voice Christ in our own time and place, in our life and actions and words. Yesterday in El Salvador, Archbishop Oscar Romero was declared 'blessed'. He was Archbishop of San Salvador from 1977 to 1980. He lived under an oppressive regime, and gradually he found his voice. He took courage. He began to speak out in defence of the poor, against the injustices and arbitrary arrests, imprisonments, torture, assassinations. He wasn't a politician; he was a pastor. He took his stand on the Gospel and the Ten Commandments. And it cost him his life. He was killed by a sniper on 24 March 1980, while celebrating Mass. His voice was silenced, it seemed. But it wasn't. His death became a word that gave hope, and still does. He is hugely loved in Latin America. And now his beatification sounds it out again.

'They began to speak.' We often say that we can hear the wind in the trees, but in reality we hear the trees, and their leaves, in the wind. It is the leaves which speak. In the wind of Pentecost, we leaves on the tree of the Church, we begin to speak. This is the grace of Pentecost, this is the grace of our Confirmation, that 'personal Pentecost for the whole of life'. The mission of the Church from Pentecost on, the mission of each of us anointed by the Holy Spirit, is to be speakers of hope. Saying Hope to ourselves and to others, in the small things and big things, in the daily things and the epic things, in the face of life's challenges and beyond death. We are called to be purveyors, conveyors, distributors, live-streamers, not of a false, illusory hope, not of any unworthy hope, but of the clear, upright, ennobling, great and beautiful hope released by the Resurrection. Don't we need it?

Yes, the Holy Spirit helps us Christians find our voice, despite all the attempts to silence us. He opens this path too: the path of the Church's mission through history, the path of our personal witness.

Let me end with the story of a saint. One cold snowy day in November 1831 in a Russian field, a layman, Nicholas Motovilov was talking to a monk, Seraphim of Sarov—now recognized as a saint. 'What's the goal of the Christian life?' asked the man. It's a good question: at the end of the day, what's the Christian life all about? This was a question that had bothered him from the age of 12. He'd asked it of many people. And he had been given many answers. It's about going to church, some said. It's about saying your prayers or keeping the commandments or doing good. But none of these answers quite satisfied. And so he put the question to Seraphim. And Seraphim, in so many words, said this: yes, these are all good things, and if we want to live a Christian, they're what we must do. They're indispensable. But they're not the end, the goal, they're the means. The goal is the *acquisition of the Holy Spirit.* The goal is to be filled with the Holy Spirit. And then St Seraphim took his friend by the shoulders, and said, 'look at me.' And Motovilov realized in the falling snow that Seraphim was ablaze with light, transfigured, shining with the Holy Spirit. And you are too, said Seraphim.

And they were all filled with the Holy Spirit.

This is it. 'Today we've reached the mountain-top of everything good.' Today the Spirit of the Lord has filled the whole world and wants to fill us. Today, I hope that everyone of us will go home filled with the Holy Spirit. So I end with today's solemn prayer: 'O God, who by the mystery of today's great feast sanctify your whole Church in every people and nation, pour out, we pray, the gifts of the Holy Spirit across the face of the earth and, with the divine grace that was at work when the Gospel was first proclaimed, fill now once more the hearts of believers. Through Christ our Lord.' Amen.

Let us indeed be 'led by the Spirit'!

27

SOLEMNITY OF THE HOLY TRINITY

*Exodus 34:4b–6, 8–9; 2 Corinthians 13:11–13;
John 3:16–18*

I would like to say something about the feast we keep this Sunday, the Solemnity of the Most Holy Trinity.

We have just passed through the whole cycle of Lent and Easter, ending on a high note with Pentecost last Sunday. Now it's 'Green Time', Ordinary Time, again and will be to the end of the liturgical year in late November.

But, as we know, Ordinary Time has its feasts as well, and in the time immediately after Pentecost three. There's the feast of the Trinity this Sunday, then next Sunday the feast of the Body and Blood of Christ, and then, the Friday after, the feast of the Sacred Heart. Three major feasts in less than two weeks, all solemnities.

They belong together. Liturgy has a history. It has built up over time. The Lent/ Easter cycle developed early. Then came Advent / Christmas. The Trinity, Corpus Christi and the Sacred Heart belong to a later stage. A feast of the Trinity appears from the ninth century, Corpus Christi from the thirteenth, the Sacred Heart from the seventeenth. They belong together at another level too. They all presuppose what has gone before, what has been celebrated in the Christmas cycle and especially the Easter cycle. They all look back on it; and they each draw from it one aspect and ask us to focus on it. In the case of the feast of the Trinity, that's clear. The whole Christmas, Easter, Pentecost story have the Father, Son and Holy Spirit as their source and content; they are the main actors. Then the Eucharist, because Christmas and Easter bring us Jesus and Jesus is wholly present in the Sacrament of his Body and Blood; it sums it all up and enables us to take and eat it. Then the Sacred Heart, because this is a love-story and Jesus' heart is the symbol and wellspring of his love.

Another comparison. At a concert, the performers return sometimes and give us an encore. It's as if from Advent to Pentecost we have been listening to a grand concerto. Then we are treated to these three encores. The conductor, the soloist, or whoever comes back on the stage, plays something again, and we can applaud and appreciate again. These are feasts of appreciation.

Another comparison. You know the pleasure of skimming stones across water and seeing how many times they bounce. And how if you throw well, you can get a good distance between each bounce on the water. Then the stone does just a few short ones, and sinks. Imagine, each liturgical year, God the Father on the shore of eternity. He throws the smooth stone of his Son into the water of the world. First bounce, Christmas; second bounce, Easter. It's a good throw, 50 days more, third bounce, Pentecost. And then, yes, it slows down, three short bounces in succession: the Trinity, Corpus Christi, and Sacred Heart. Does the stone then sink without trace? I hope not. I think it sinks into our hearts and becomes the foundation stone of a building, of the Temple of God that we are individually and collectively, the Church—but that's another story.

So, let's look at this feast.

The Entrance Antiphon goes: 'Blest be God the Father, and the only-begotten Son of God, and also the Holy Spirit, for he has shown us his merciful love.'

What we are doing on Trinity Sunday is looking back at the whole story from Advent on. We are, as it were, 'reviewing' it. And as we do, we realize that the chief actor is the triune (one in three) God. The Father has sent the Son (Christmas) and then, through the Son (dying and rising at Easter), the Holy Spirit (Pentecost). These events are the outward signs of God's inner being; as the theologians say, the missions in time reveal the processions of God's eternity, his inner life. God has drawn close to us as Father, Son and Holy Spirit. He has let us into the secret of his being. At the Last Supper, Jesus says, 'I call you friends because I have made known to you everything I have heard from my Father' (Jn 12:15). St Thomas Aquinas comments: 'the true mark of friendship is that a friend reveals to his friend the inmost secrets of his heart.'[1] This is what God has done. And St Thomas goes on: 'Since friends are one in heart and soul, when a friend reveals himself to his friend, he doesn't go outside himself.' So we can say that when God makes us his friends by disclosing himself, he is inviting us into himself, into his own house, as it were. Vatican II's Constitution *Dei Verbum*, on Divine Revelation, has a shot at summing things up: 'It has pleased God in his goodness and wisdom to reveal himself and to make known to us the hidden purpose of his will, by which through Christ, the Word made flesh, man might have access to the Father in the Holy Spirit and come to share in the divine nature. Through this revelation, the unseen God, out of the abundance of his love speaks to humans as his friends and lives among them, so that he might invite and take them into fellowship with himself.'[2] Another way of telling the same story.

St Irenaeus, an early Christian writer, uses a metaphor—it is only a metaphor—of the Son and the Spirit as the two hands of the Father. Through them the Father has created the universe, the world, human beings and through them he has drawn it back to himself in the process of redemption. Everything flowing from him and back to him, and we embraced.

For some forty years now, a Franciscan priest, Fr Raniero Cantalamessa, has been 'preacher to the papal household'. He has preached numerous sermons and published many books. One wee one is called *Contemplating the Trinity*. And what I really like is its subtitle: *the path to an abundant Christian life*.

Emotionally, psychologically, spiritually, this feast is all about abundance. The TRINITY is God's abundance and as we come to realize and relish the reality of it, so our life can abound.

So, the Entrance Antiphon blesses God the Father, the only-begotten Son and the Holy Spirit 'or he has shown us his love'. The Latin says, because he 'has done mercy with us': the great mercy of knowing and loving God as he really is, as he has shown himself to be.

In the Christian East, *Pentecost* is the feast of the Trinity. When the Holy Spirit comes, God's sharing of himself is complete. One of the Fathers says—I paraphrase—'God the Father has been revealed in the Old Testament, the Son of God in the New, and the Holy Spirit in the Church' (that is, from Pentecost on). Now, we stand back and 'see'. We should be gasping, feeling 'wowed'. This is fullness.

There's a famous antiphon from the Eastern liturgy often quoted here: 'We have seen the true light, we have received the Heavenly Spirit, we have found the true faith, and we worship the indivisible Trinity; for the Trinity has saved us.' It's the same idea as our liturgy.

So, the readings give us a sense of God's goodness to us. In the first from Exodus, the Lord passes before Moses and proclaims, 'Lord, Lord, a God of tenderness and compassion, slow to anger, rich in kindness and faithfulness.' In the second, St Paul ends his second letter to the Corinthians with a Trinitarian prayer-wish: 'the grace of our Lord Jesus, the love of God and the fellowship of the Holy Spirit be with you all.' It's that sense of embrace again. In the Gospel come Jesus' words: 'God loved the world so much that he gave his only Son, so that everyone who believes in him may not be lost but may have eternal life.' 'So much ...'

So, a sense is built up of us being gifted, of something rich, full, lavish, and all-encompassing coming to us, God with us in every dimension: a Father who is above and around us, a Son who is beside us, a Spirit who is within us and between us. A God 'From whom is everything, through whom is everything, in whom is everything.'[3]

Atheism is fashionable in some circles in our Anglo-Saxon world. Richard Dawkins is well-known with his books *The God Delusion* and now, *Outgrowing God*, and so forth. We could begin an interesting discussion here. But what I want to say is this: we might answer, No, I'm a theist. Fine. Or to make it clearer, I'm a monotheist. Fine again. But don't stop there. I think we often do. We stop there in our prayers even, maybe. Who do we pray to? 'God' perhaps. Fine. 'Jesus.' Fine. But have we grasped that we are not any kind of monotheist? We are Trinitarian monotheists. This feast first emerged in the eighth and ninth centuries, and the Christians of that time had a simple, touching phrase for their faith: 'the faith of the Holy Trinity / *fides sanctae Trinitatis*.' St Bede, the great Northumbrian monk and historian, used it often. It evoked all sorts of things for them. It was, in part, a response to early Islam. It captured for them the richness of God's gift and of the faith by which we open ourselves to it, the joy of believing in the Trinity, in a God who is one and three—without those two realities cancelling each other. What is the Trinity? The Trinity is not an extra, optional app in our Christian life. 'I believe in God.' So, I have downloaded the God programme into the computer of my life. And then up pops an advertisement, Get the Trinity app. I think, no, I won't, too complicated. I've got God. I've got Jesus. But the divine programme *is* Father, Son and Holy Spirit. The advert's a scam. God is Trinity. The Trinity's not an add-on. Nor for that matter, a theological Rubic cube: how can three be one? It's the path to an abundant Christian life.

Let me quote Cardinal Cantalamessa.

> Oh, how wonderful it is to have the Trinity as our God! When we discover the Trinity, we are no longer tempted to exchange Christian monotheism for any other monotheism. I would feel sorry for any God who had no one with whom to communicate and to share his joy with the profundity that is uniquely his. I think he would feel himself tremendously alone and unhappy! The proof of the Trinity's existence appears on the first page of the Bible: 'God created man in his own image', and precisely because we were to be in his image, he added, 'It is not good for man to be alone' (Gen 1:27; 2:18).[4]

Yes, there's a thought. We are individuals because God is one. We are social, we need and want others in our lives, because God is three. It's not that we have to 'explain' the Trinity—the Rubic cube. It's the Trinity that explains us.

The path to the abundant Christian life.

And we can say, the path to abundant Christian prayer as well. 'Our Father' and we his children. St Thérèse of Lisieux, saying the Lord's Prayer, sometimes couldn't get beyond those words—so beautiful do they seem to her. We are no longer orphans. 'Jesus, I trust you'; 'Lord Jesus Christ, Son of the living God, have mercy on me a sinner', 'Come, Lord Jesus': we pray to the Son. We pray through him, with him, in him. We have a brother, a companion. 'I will come to you,' he says. 'Come, Holy Spirit', too. *Veni, Sancte Spiritus, Veni Creator Spiritus*. 'He will be with you; he will be in you,' says Jesus (Jn 14:18). 'We do not know how to pray as we ought, but the Spirit himself intercedes for us with sighs too deep for words' (Rom 8:26). So, God prays in us. Christian prayer has this Trinitarian abundance to it.

The Father has unveiled his co-eternal Son and sent him among us. The Father and the Son then complete the gift and send us their Spirit. That is, as it were, Advent to Pentecost. '"I am the Alpha and the Omega", says the Lord God, who is and who was and who is to come, the Almighty' (Rev 1:8). Yes, the Trinity is the beginning and the end. We begin Mass, 'In the name of...', and end with, 'May almighty God bless you...' Our Christian life begins being baptized in the name of the Father, the Son and the Holy Spirit, and when we are dying, the prayer is said: 'Go forth, Christian soul, from this world, in the name of

God, the almighty Father, who created you; in the name of Jesus Christ, the Son of the living God, who suffered for you; in the name of the Holy Spirit who was poured out upon you...' We are encompassed.

On Trinity Sunday, we say 'Yes' to this abundance. We profess 'the faith of the Holy Trinity', Christian, Trinitarian monotheism. We don't need to work it all out during the Mass. We are just meant to rejoice in it, *gaudium de veritate*.

There's 'praise and worship' music, isn't there? Some like it, some don't. But, music aside, Trinity Sunday is for 'praise and worship'. This is our response to God the Father sending us the Word of truth and the Spirit of holiness. The first word of that Entrance Antiphon is 'blest' or 'blessed'. 'You are blest, Lord God of our Fathers', says the Responsorial Psalm. 'Glory be to the Father and to the Son and to the Holy Spirit', says the Gospel Acclamation. Both the Mass and the Divine Office for this day pile up words like acknowledge, confess, profess, thank, bless, adore, glorify, praise. This is the first fruit of Pentecost: praise. Praise takes us out of ourselves. Praise comes from love and gratitude. Praise anticipates heaven. The word praise links to our words 'prize' and 'precious' and 'appreciate'. We praise what we prize and appreciate, we praise what is precious. 'The faith of the Holy Trinity'. Trinity Sunday is a praise-day: of Trinity in Unity, and Unity in Trinity, 'praised by Angels and Archangels, Cherubim too and Seraphim', says the Preface. 'Holy, holy, holy'.

Notes

1. St Thomas Aquinas, *Commentary on the Gospel of John*, chap. 15, Lectio 3, sec. 3.
2. Second Vatican Council, *Dei Verbum* (1965), 2.
3. Lauds Antiphon for the Feast of the Holy Trinity.
4. Cardinal R. Cantalamessa, *Contemplating the Trinity: the path to an abundant Christian life* (Frederick, MD: Word Among Us Press 2007), 3.2.

28

SOLEMNITY OF CORPUS CHRISTI

Brothers and Sisters,

I would like to offer some catechesis on the feast we are keeping this coming Sunday. It was instituted for the whole Roman rite in 1264, by Pope Urban IV. Its proper day is Thursday—because of the echo of Maundy Thursday. And many countries keep it then. Many also, though, have moved it to the following Sunday, as in Scotland. This is done to bring more people together.

Feasts have a setting in the liturgical year; they have a history; they have a character, a feel; and they have their own language. Let's look at each in turn.

As mentioned in a previous catechesis, the setting of this feast is as part of a post-Pentecostal trio: Holy Trinity, Corpus Christi, and Sacred Heart. These feasts each look back on the Church's year so far, Advent to Pentecost, and try to burrow deep into it and bring out hidden treasure. The feast of Corpus Christi looks back at the institution of the Eucharist on Maundy Thursday, and so to speak holds it up for our contemplation. Tantum ergo Sacramentum. The Eucharist sums up, recapitulates, the whole 'economy' of Christ. The poet George Mackay Brown puts it well in a short story; a priest is speaking: 'This Bread that I will raise above your kneeling, It is entire Christ—Annunciation, Nativity, Transfiguration, Passion, Death, Resurrection, Ascension, Majesty, gathered up into one perfect offering.'[1] It's the whole Christ-Event, as the theologians say. Including the Parousia, the coming at the end of time. The Eucharist brings it all into our here and now, and makes it sacramentally live. It's not a picture on the mantelpiece. It's not something in the archives. Given this, and that Maundy Thursday falls in Holy Week, in a crowded time, it seemed good to allow the Eucharist a second space in the liturgical year and so allow us to feel its full force, and linger over it.

Another connection is to Pentecost. It's after Pentecost that the apostles began doing the Eucharist, breaking the Bread. The Eucharist belongs to the 'time of the Church'. It's a sign of the Holy Spirit at work in the Church through time, even on a rainy evening in Fochabers or a windy day on Fairisle. The Holy Spirit draws believers together, empowers priests to consecrate, transforms bread and wine into the Lord's Body and Blood and makes us 'one body and one spirit' in him.

The feast of the Trinity is echoed too: the Father gives the Son in the Eucharist by the power of the Holy Spirit, and Christ's Sacred blood-giving Heart is also revealed. So many connections here. Interestingly, a bishop is supposed to be in his cathedral on this day—as at Christmas, the Easter Triduum and Pentecost. It's a feast the Church holds high.

That's the setting.

Liturgy has a history too. And this feast very much so. Its origins are in the Low Countries of the thirteenth century. The leading and organizing of the liturgy can seem an exclusively male business, but there have been feminine influences too. The procession with candles of Candlemas was the initiative many centuries ago of a Palestinian abbess. The Second Sunday of Easter is called Divine Mercy—it's owed, as we know, to St Faustina

Kowalska. St Margaret Mary Alacoque is linked to the feast of the Sacred Heart. For its part, Corpus Christi is owed to a thirteenth century Béguine—not an enclosed nun, but a woman dedicated to a religious life. Her name was Juliana. She hailed from Liège in Belgium. In her prayer or a dream, she saw a full moon, lacking one part, with one dark spot. The moon was a symbol of the Church, its roundness of the liturgical year, and the dark in it the lack of a feast of the Eucharist. The Lord wanted the gap filled. The Dominicans, still in their early years, took this up. Then, by the strange workings of providence, a sympathetic diocesan priest of Liège became Pope, Urban IV, instituted the feast and charged the Dominican Thomas Aquinas to compose the liturgy for it—which is still essentially what we have today. Later, a procession would become part of the celebration.

Every feast has its setting; every feast has its history. Every feast also has its own feel, character, atmosphere. And Corpus Christi very much so, especially when linked with the first Holy Communions of children and outdoor processions. Summer in the northern hemisphere, a chance to take the faith outdoors, white garments, singing, flowers, a festal feel. Many strands come together here. Surely, a sense of the Eucharist as a great gift, the Giver completely given in the gift: 'this is my body, this is my blood', a real and self-giving presence of the Bridegroom to his Bride the Church. If there is a procession, we sense Christ walking with us through history. The spirituality, the piety which generated this feast was passionate for a real, felt, savoured, outer and inner connection with Christ, affecting our bodies and souls: 'take and eat'. That's there too.

Also conveyed is a sense of the Eucharist as a culmination of God's history with us, the climax to a story of drawing close. Many of the Old Testament types and figures, as we call them, are mentioned: the mysterious pagan priest Melchizedek with his offering of bread and wine, the paschal lamb, the covenant made in bulls' blood at Mt Sinai, the manna in the desert; there are phrases about the Lord feeding his people from the Psalms and we hear of the figure of Wisdom putting on a banquet for humanity. Jesus speaks of the real food he has to offer, multiplies bread for the crowds, makes himself known in the breaking of bread. In the letter by which he established the feast—really the first papal encyclical on the Eucharist, *Transiturus*—Pope Urban IV goes all the way back to Genesis and first, flawed eating of forbidden fruit. He sees the Eucharist undoing the story of sin, changing the human trajectory.

> It was through food man fell and through food he's lifted up again. Man fell by means of the food of the death-giving tree; man is raised up by the food of the life-giving tree. On the former hung the food of death; on the latter the nourishment of life. Eating of the former earned a wound; the taste of this latter restores health. Eating wounded us, and eating heals us ... About that [first] eating, it was said, 'On whatever day you eat it you shall die'; about this eating, he said, 'Whoever eats this bread shall live for ever.'[2]

Here the Eucharist reverses the dynamics, the direction of travel which selfishness promotes. The choice is between my self and Christ's Self, between taking to oneself and giving from oneself, between hoarding and sharing. The Eucharist is the centre of gravity for the Church and through her for everything; a place of convergence, not of divergence. It's true that not every person, not every believer, can at a given moment receive the Holy Eucharist—there are conditions of approach—but everyone is called in this direction. We walk a road of faith, conversion, belonging. The Eucharist is the place of reconciliation beyond our differences, an anticipation of the final communion at the marriage feast of the Lamb. The Eucharist is 'unity and peace' (Prayer over the Gifts). The Eucharist says every life matters, all life matters. This feast has a very generous feel to it. It's a cry to the whole world. It's the Gospel in bread and wine.

Every feast, too, has its own language, its own rhetoric. Here, unsurprisingly, it's of food and nourishment—but not any food. So, we hear of banquet, finest wheat, honey from the rock, hidden manna, bread from heaven, bread of angels, sweetness, savour, delight, joy. 'The hungry he has filled with good things, the rich he has sent empty away.' 'The poor will eat and be satisfied.' All this conveys a sense of fullness. This is the food, food that satisfies the emptiness of human hearts, the food of eternal life. A food for the poor in spirit and for all those life's usual satisfactions have bypassed. Edible beatitudes.

And this feast made a poet of St Thomas Aquinas, the theologian. We owe the Mass Sequence to him, *Lauda Sion Salvatorem*, and the three hymns of the Divine Office, which include the *Tantum ergo* and the *O salutaris Hostia*.

So, as with the feast of the Trinity if with a different focus, this is a feast to profess faith. Faith, first of all, in the reality of Jesus' presence under the appearance of bread and wine, the fruit of what the Germans expressively call die Wandlung, the divine act of transubstantiation. Faith that this bread is now his Body, the wine now his Blood. This is our thanksgiving, offered in his memory to the Father for the living and the dead, and given to us as 'real food', 'real drink'. We profess our Catholic faith with relish and gratitude, and distance ourselves from any reductions, any diminishments. And it's a feast to express that faith in adoration. It's festal and quiet all at once.

Now, we may say here, that's fine. But currently I am deprived of the Eucharist. Currently, the most I can do is keep this feast virtually.[3]

It's worth pausing over this. We have been living a Eucharistic fast, and it would be strange if that didn't hurt, if we didn't feel a lack. For many, it's a wound to the heart of their Christian life. As a priest I have continued to celebrate Mass privately, thank God, but I have felt the lack of a full, visible congregation, bodily present. For most lay people and many religious, it's the same in reverse, compounded by a still greater lack: no 'Body of Christ' to say 'Amen' to.

I'd like to address this and offer some alternative perspectives. I want to suggest that this time in a sacramental wilderness has been a time of grace.

So, let's try thinking differently. Let's think of ourselves not as deprived of the Eucharist, but as waiting for it. Waiting to return to it, waiting for It to return to us. Let's think of ourselves in a kind of Eucharistic Advent waiting for the Messiah to come in the flesh. Let's think of Christ waiting to return to us, think of Mary with Jesus in her womb, waiting to see him and touch him and hold him.

The Church in Portugal, just over a century ago, before the appearances of Mary at Fatima, went through a time of persecution. Churches were closed and the Mass proscribed. This sparked a thoughtful poem from Alice

Meynell, a Catholic. It is called In Portugal, 1912. It's a fine example of how good poetry can stand us on our heads and help us see things quite differently. It imagines the Eucharistic Christ in waiting:[4]

> And will they cast the altars down,
> Scatter the chalice, crush the bread?
> In field, in village, and in town
> He hides an unregarded head;
>
> Waits in the corn-lands far and near,
> Bright in His sun, dark in His frost,
> Sweet in the vine, ripe in the ear–
> Lonely unconsecrated Host.
>
> In ambush at the merry board
> The Victim lurks unsacrificed;
> The mill conceals the harvest's Lord,
> The wine-press holds the unbidden Christ.

We are not being persecuted, but this poem offers us light. 'Fruit of the earth and work of human hands', we say at the Offertory. The poet sees Christ waiting in the cornfields and the vines. Waiting in the mill that is grinding the corn and the winepress which is crushing the grapes. Lying in ambush in the bread and wine on our tables. In our parishes, children are waiting to make a delayed first Holy Communion. We tell them to use the extra time to prepare, for catechesis and prayer and so on. Perhaps we can do the same ourselves. Perhaps we can use the time to re-appreciate what this Sacrament is, Who it contains. St Paul, in his first letter to the Corinthians, was concerned by the Corinthians' flippancy regarding the Eucharist. So he said, 'Everyone is to examine himself and only then eat of the bread and drink of the cup' (cf1 Cor 11:28). Perhaps this fast has happened precisely for us to do this. We might think of our coming return to Communion—maybe by way of Confession—as a new first Communion, a new beginning. And think of Christ wanting to return to us, eager for us.

Here's another thought that might help. We are not the only ones who have had to wait. There were our forebears in the penal times who, because of persecution and scarcity of priests, would only rarely have received the Sacrament. There are many places in the world today where sacramental life is hindered. There are many people in Asia, Africa, South America to whom the Sacraments are only rarely available. In our waiting we are in solidarity with them. Perhaps we have forgotten how spoiled we are. Perhaps we have been taking too much for granted.

And now to the nub of it. What is the Eucharist? Three things. A mystery to be believed. A mystery to be celebrated. A mystery to be lived.[5] It's a mystery to be believed; the Church has a teaching here. A mystery to be celebrated, in the Mass. Most of all, a mystery to be lived. In the natural order, we eat and drink so as to live. In the supernatural order, likewise. Jesus says, 'As the living Father sent me, and I live because of the Father, so he who eats me will live because of me' (Jn 6:57).

Throughout our fasting Advent, we have still believed in the Eucharist. The Eucharist has still been celebrated, broadcast indeed, even if we have not been able to participate in it or only virtually. But the celebration of the Eucharist, even in a prison cell, quite alone, is an action of Christ and the Church. It keeps the gates of the world open to grace, and St Thomas Aquinas teaches that spiritual communion can be as grace-giving as sacramental communion. Most of all, though, we have lived the Eucharist. This has been happening, thank God, even when we haven't consciously 'clocked' it. And this is what counts: not how many times I have been to Mass or Communion, but how the Eucharist has changed my life, how we have been formed and shaped by it and, in St Augustine's phrase, become what we have received.

'I appeal to you, brothers and sisters, by the mercies of God, to present your bodies as a living sacrifice, holy and acceptable to God, which is your spiritual worship' (Rom 12:1). So says St Paul. Eucharistic living.

'Whether you eat or drink, or whatever you do, do all to the glory of God' (1 Cor 10:31). Eucharistic living.

'You are a chosen race, a royal priesthood, a holy nation, a people he claims for his own, to declare his wonderful deeds' (1 Pet 2:9). Eucharistic living.

'Be of a single mind, one in love, one in heart and one in mind. Nothing is to be done out of jealousy or vanity; instead, out of humility of mind, everyone should give preference to others, everyone pursuing not selfish interests but those of others. Make your own the mind of Christ Jesus' (Phil 2:2–5). Eucharistic living.

Faith, hope and charity: that is the Christian life. That is what we will be judged on. Not for a second, over these last three months, has it been impossible to believe or hope or love.

A common life in the body of Christ, which is the Church. Nothing need take that from us. We are always members of each other. 'Someone who lives in Rome,' says St John Chrysostom, 'knows that he is one body with believers in India.'[6] The extra effort that has been put in to keeping in touch with each other, weaving the coat of Christ; it's Eucharistic living.

I have been touched by people saying to me things like, 'faith seems to me stronger now'; 'I have never felt the closeness of God as I have during these weeks.' I have heard this kind of thing from people living alone, people in families. 'It has brought our family closer together.' Eucharistic living.

'Christ plays in ten thousand places,' said Gerard Manley Hopkins.[7]

Our last Holy Communion, someone has said, does not have an expiry date. Christ lives in our hearts. Apart from ourselves and our own sins, can anyone or anything take him away from there?

With thoughts like these, we can comfort one another and wait together for the return to our full sacramental life.

———✥———

Corpus Christi, it is the marriage feast of the Lamb. It looks forward to the final, unveiled, heavenly version. And this marriage goes on everywhere, and there is no end of it. I am echoing the Orcadian poet George Mackay Brown here. And it's brought home to us at every altar. The Bread that's lifted up is the entire Christ and Love itself, the 'Pelican of legend, Jesus, risen Lord'. And, 'not just we', but 'all creation rejoices in the marriage of Christ and His Church, animals, fish, plants, yes, the water, the wind, the earth, the fire, stars, the very smallest grains of dust that blow about' our streets.[8]

Blessed are those called to the supper of the Lamb.

Notes

1. G. M. Brown, 'A Treading of Grapes', in *A Time to Keep* (London: Hogarth Press 1969), p.75.
2. Establishment of the Feast of Corpus Christi throughout the Church, 11 August 1264 (author's translation).
3. As a result of the Covid lockdown from 2020 onwards.
4. A. Meynell, 'In Portugal, 1912' in *Poems* (London: OUP 1947).
5. Cf. the structure of Pope Benedict XVI's *Sacramentum Caritatis* 2007.
6. St John Chrysostom, *Homily on John* 65, 1 (PG 59.361).
7. G. M. Hopkins, 'As kingfishers catch fire' in *Collected Poems* (Oxford: OUP 1997).
8. Brown, 'A Treading of Grapes', p. 75.

29

SOLEMNITY OF THE SACRED HEART

Dear Brothers and Sisters,

I would like to offer a catechesis on the feast of the Sacred Heart that we keep this Friday. I do underline the word 'feast'. I am approaching this subject through the door of the liturgy.

This is the third of the three Solemnities of the Lord that follow on the feast of Pentecost: Trinity Sunday, Corpus Christi and the Sacred Heart. As I've said twice before these feasts inter-connect. And to assure you I am not making this up, here's Pope Benedict: 'Each of these liturgical events highlights a perspective which embraces the whole mystery of the Christian faith ... respectively the reality of the Triune God, the Sacrament of the Eucharist and the divine and human centre of the Person of Christ. These [each] ... in a certain sense sum up the whole itinerary of the revelation of Jesus, from his incarnation to his death and Resurrection and, finally, to his Ascension and the gift of the Holy Spirit.'[1]

Through all we have been celebrating from Advent to Pentecost, God has been drawing close to us. As somebody put it to me recently: in the feast of the Trinity, our focus is who has come close: Father, Son and Holy Spirit; at Corpus Christi, the focus is how the Lord is now close to us, the Eucharist; with the Sacred Heart, the focus is the why of it all. 'It was for love of you,' says Moses in the first reading. 'Love is his meaning,' says Julian of Norwich. For Bl. Columbia Marmion, the Irish Benedictine Abbot, this feast 'closes the annual cycle of the solemnities of the Saviour; it is as if, arrived at the term of the contemplation of her Bridegroom's mysteries, there is nothing left for [the Church] to do but to celebrate the very love that inspired them all.'[2]

It's as if we have been walking through a picture gallery, admiring each portrait or landscape or whatever one after another, this Sunday, that Sunday. Then suddenly, we stand back, and we notice the wall that holds the pictures, we notice the colour it has—a glowing red perhaps—which sets off and enhances every picture. Or maybe it's a red lighting that pervades the whole gallery—the glowing red of Christ's Heart.

What about the feast? The Dominicans have a claim to have originated it, at least remotely. From the late thirteenth century, on today's liturgical date, Friday after the Second Sunday after Pentecost, they commemorated the wound in the side of Christ—the wound that revealed his heart, and from which blood and water flowed. But usually, the honour of first celebrating the Sacred Heart of Jesus liturgically is given St John Eudes (1601–1680), a French priest of the seventeenth century, originally an Oratorian and later founder of two religious congregations. He is remembered as a great propagator of devotion to the hearts of Jesus and Mary, and first celebrated a Mass of the Sacred Heart on 20 October 1672, I think in Rennes, in Brittany. Just under two hundred years later, in 1856, the feast became universal in the Roman rite. In 1929, Pope Pius XI re-edited it, and with the help of a French Benedictine monk of Solesmes, Dom Henri Quentin (1872–1935), new texts, a new formulary as it is called, came in. After the Second Vatican Council, it was partially revised again, with an

Solemnity of the Sacred Heart

additional Collect, more Scripture (three sets of readings), a special Preface and a new Prayer after Communion.

I've mentioned before: Entrance Antiphons set the tone of a Mass. The one for this feast comes from Ps 32, vv. 11 and 19: 'the designs of his heart are from age to age, to rescue their souls from death and to keep them alive in famine'. It's a beautiful beginning, and the only time in the Psalter that the heart of God is mentioned. God's heart is the seat of his eternal plans, his designs, for the world and for us, and these designs are good: to rescue us from death, to feed us in a time of famine. God has a heart for us.

The Scripture of a feast is vital too. From the Old Testament, there is Deuteronomy: Moses, as the covenant is renewed, reminding the people of Israel, how the Lord set his heart on them, not because they were many or mighty, but from a free, gratuitous love. In Years B and C, we hear from the prophets Hosea and Ezekiel. Here the Lord is shown as the one who rescues Israel after its going astray: a wandering child, errant sheep. This unfurls as it were the depths of God's merciful love. 'I am the Holy One in your midst and have no wish to destroy'. This is a love that recalls and rebuilds. There's the First Letter of John, predictably, inviting us to recognize and replicate the love of God. There's St Paul in Years B and C, and in the Divine Office, straining language in his attempt to have us grasp 'the breadth and the length, the height and the depth' of it all, wanting us to know the love of Christ 'which is beyond all knowledge'. Then there are the Gospels, which I'll come back to at the end.

What is this feast about? I remember visiting a Benedictine convent of nuns, which had been founded by a bishop in the nineteenth century. In their cloister was a jar, and in the jar was the preserved heart of the bishop. This was rather disconcerting. And I don't think it would provide a helpful approach to our feast. For a start, Jesus is alive.

So, let's ask the question, who and what are we celebrating in this feast? What's brought before us? The Sacred Heart indeed. But let's go a bit deeper.

This is called a 'solemnity of the Lord'. The focus is Jesus himself, in person. It celebrates Him, God and man in one, our crucified and risen Saviour, present among us. It celebrates him as the One who has loved us, from the beginning, who has shown that love, not least on the Cross, and who loves us still. 'To him who loves us,' says the Book of Revelation, 'and has freed us from our sins by his blood and has made us a kingdom, priest to his God and Father, to him be glory and dominion for ever and ever. Amen' (Rev 1:5–6). That's the spirit of this feast.

Most feasts celebrate *events* in our Lord's life: he is born, he is shown to the wise men, he is presented in the Temple, he is baptized, and so forth. These are happenings in Christ's life. He undergoes and / or does something in history, even though we know it goes beyond a moment in the past and has present relevance. In the case of our feast, he is the object of attention once again, but differently: not in relation to a specific or one-off event, but to something more pervasive, underlying. We are highlighting not so much some special thing he *did* (ascend into heaven, for example) but something he *has*: a heart, a heart full of love for us, for each of us, a heart 'containing, in the Spirit, an infinite divine-human love for the Father and for his brothers and sisters.'[3] We are marking what he *has*, what he *has* as the very core and centre of his being, at the heart of who he is: divine-human (theandric) love for his Father and for us. We are celebrating Jesus having a heart for us, having us at heart.

This is something to celebrate!

There's a fine little poem by Francis Thompson, *Arab Love-Song*.[4] The man is inviting his beloved to come secretly to his tent at night, and he ends:

> And thou—what needest with thy tribe's black tents
> Who hast the red pavilion of my heart?

That could be Christ speaking to us, calling his Church to 'the red pavilion' of his heart.

Before exploring that further, one more thought about who and what. Everything Christian liturgy gives thanks for comes first of all from the Father and is related back to him. Liturgical prayers are almost always directed to God the Father. So we are giving thanks for the gift the Father has made us in the opened heart of his Son. The Son's love conveys the Father's. 'God's love for us was revealed when God sent into the world his only Son so that we could have life through him.' That's St John in the first reading of Year A. The reading in the Divine Office is from Romans 8: 'Who will separate us from the love of God made manifest in Christ Jesus' (Rom 8:39). The divine deeds of creation, of the choice of Israel—'the Lord set his heart on you'—of the forgiveness and rescue of his people from disloyalty and exile, culminate in the Father's gift of his Son in the Incarnation. And so we feast the Father too. 'I thank you, Father, Lord of heaven and earth, for revealing these things to mere children,' says Jesus in the Gospel this year. Our feast shares in his thanking of the Father. And if we are feasting the Father and the Son, then of course the Holy Spirit too, divine love in person.

Personally, this feast has grown on me over the years. St Jerome wrote once, 'Plato makes the chief human element the intellect; Christ puts it in the heart.' Isn't an underlying question in every life, Am I loved? After his Resurrection, Jesus asked Simon Peter, 'Do you love me?' And when we turn to Christ, to God, it's the same question that torments us. It is a point of Catholic doctrine that none of us knows now whether he or she will be finally saved, but we do know that we are from eternity definitively loved. To know this is healing, redemptive, life-giving—and not at all easy to absorb. It isn't something inevitable, something we can just read off the world or our own experience. It isn't easy for us fallen humans—for all our bravado—to recognize that we are loved. And this, with a love beyond all knowing. In the conversation between the serpent and the woman beside the garden tree, the serpent subtly insinuates the idea that God does not want the good of human beings, but rather to defend his own prerogatives. And this lie we swallowed, and it is now well-digested in our 'system', as it were: God as enemy. In its contemporary, secularized form, it says, faith is not good for you. It cripples you or fanaticizes you, or meshes you into self-serving structures. It's the source of most of the troubles in the world. This feast undermines this lie. It is not saying that God's love simply delivers comfortable endorsements of our personal projects or cultural fixations. This love is a refashioning fire, and no individual and no culture that gives it space will emerge unscathed. But it's also the only ultimate ground on which we can stand and flourish and come together as human beings. It is the treasure hidden in the field of faith and for sharing everywhere. This is the love that makes missionaries. This is the love with which Dante ends his Divine Comedy, 'the love that moves the sun and the other stars', that turns tragedy into the best of all comedies and, most astonishingly of all, like a Holy Communion, has its whole heart to give to each least one of us, as the smallest flower feels the full force of the sun. 'For each, the entire monopoly of day; for each, the whole of the devoted sun.'[5]

In recent years, this feast has been associated with the practice of praying for priests, for our holiness. Such prayers would be gratefully received: prayers that we who are ordained may be, like David, shepherds after God's heart.

> This Heart, it has been written, calls to our hearts. It invites us to step forth out of the futile attempt at self-preservation and, by joining the task of love, by handing ourselves over to him and with him, to discover the fullness of love which alone is eternity and which alone sustains the world.[6]

There are many prayers we might pray to the Sacred Heart. There are many beautiful prayers, like the Litany of the Sacred Heart. But we can just simply ask to realize we are loved, or just say, Thank you.

The Christians of the Middle Ages would be surprised how little our liturgy uses the Song of Songs—a few allusions in the reading from St Bonaventure in the Divine Office. But they would feel at home with references to John Ch. 19, the final scene on Calvary, the piercing of Jesus' side, the issue of blood and water and the quotation from the prophet Zechariah: 'they will look on the one whom they have pierced.' The Gospel of Year A is Christ's appeal to come to him, gentle and humble of heart. The Gospel of Year C is the parable of the shepherd seeking the lost sheep. But the Gospel of Year B is John's. The Preface holds up the same scene. A Communion Antiphon re-echoes it. This is, as it were, the icon of this feast.

As Mary stood by the Cross, with the beloved disciple, the faithful witness, so does the Church. Through the aperture of the visible wound, she sees far into the invisible wound of God's love for us, the divine vulnerability. Julian of Norwich, standing in the same place, as it were, found her understanding led by Christ through the wound and beyond.

> And there he showed a beautiful and delightful place, large enough for all mankind that will be saved to rest there in peace and love ... And in this sweet beholding he showed his blessed heart, cloven in two...and he revealed to my understanding ... the endless love that is without beginning and is and ever shall be. And with this our good Lord said most blessedly, 'See how I love you', as if he had said, 'My darling, behold and see your Lord, your God, who is your maker and your endless joy. See your own brother, your saviour. My child, behold and see what love and what joy I have in your salvation ... See how I love you.'[7]

Let me go back to Francis Thompson's *Arab Love Song*:

> Leave thy father, leave thy mother
> And thy brother;
> Leave the black tents of thy tribe apart!
> Am I not thy father and thy brother,
> And thy mother?
> And thou—what needest with thy tribe's black tents
> Who hast the red pavilion of my heart?

Notes

1. Pope Benedict XVI, *Angelus address*, 7 June 2009.
2. Bl. Columba Marmion, *Christ in His Mysteries* (London: Sands & Co. 1919), p.365.
3. *Directory on Popular Piety and the Liturgy*, (Vatican City) 166.
4. F. Thompson, 'Arab Love Song' in *Works* vol. 1 (London: Burns & Oates 1913).
5. A. Meynell, 'A General Communion' in *Poems* (London: OUP 1947).
6. J. Ratzinger, *Behold the Pierced One*, p. 69.
7. Julian of Norwich, *Revelations of Divine Love*, trans. Barry Windeatt (Oxford: Oxford University Classics 2015), chap. 24.

30

Solemnity of St John the Baptist

Two familiar things can be said on this feast day of John the Baptist. The first is that as Jesus' birthday falls just after the winter solstice when the days begin to lengthen, so John the Baptist's falls just after midsummer's day, when they begin to shorten. Christ is the rising sun. John is the man who said, 'He must increase, I must decrease' (Jn 3:30).

The second is that, of all the saints, it is only his and the Virgin Mary's natural birthdays that are kept. The feasts of other saints often fall on the day of their death or martyrdom, the day of their heavenly birthday, not their earthly one. But Mary and John were different. They had a pre-natal holiness. Mary was conceived immaculate. John was conceived by a woman who was infertile and past the age and he was 'filled with the Holy Spirit' (Lk 1:15) in the womb when he leaped at the sound of Mary's voice. So, his birth, like Mary's, is part of the history of redemption and grace. It was a moment of joy for Elizabeth and Zechariah and their friends and relations. It was talked about 'through all the hill country of Judaea' (Lk 1:65). So, in those eager circles of Palestinian Judaism his birth was a sign that God was still alive. And the Liturgy, which is all about re-enactment, prays in the Collect that we in turn may experience 'the grace of spiritual joys', and sense that God is alive among us.

It's perhaps asking too much that we should feel that specifically about John's *birth*. But taking him as a whole is different. He is one of these biblical characters who really 'speak'. He is a type, a figure, a model, a pattern. He's representative. He's someone in whom some of the great biblical themes and ideas converge; they take on a name, face and voice; and then they re-echo. John's a mirror for seeing ourselves. He really is the last and greatest of the prophets, and he's still a carrier of the word of God.

One striking thing is surely this: just how, from his mother's womb, he is completely turned towards Christ. His own birth anticipated Christ's, and so did his death. His whole life's work, with the silent preparatory years in the desert, was 'to make ready a nation fit for Christ the Lord'. He was the new Elijah sent to prepare for his coming. He's Christ's Forerunner. He's his herald. He's the last in the line of Israelite prophets, the one where hope for the messiah becomes most explicit. He could point with his finger at the Lamb of God. And the climax of his mission was to baptize Jesus and so reveal him to Israel and beyond as the Son and Servant of God. He called himself, beautifully, the friend of the Bridegroom (Jn 3:29). He was completely Christ-focused. And this was not just by his own choice—that came second—but by vocation, predestiny, grace. And so he shines. He's all prophet, nothing but prophecy. He embodies all that Israel was ultimately about: the coming of the Christ. And more than that: he gives off the meaning of what it is to be human. Christ is the shining Sun or Centre of the universe and of human history. And we are all planets and stars to him. And when we realize that we have found where we belong. For all the unfinished business, we have found the essential meaning of our life. And the famous joy can quietly enter in. Christ is the Goal, the End, the Omega, not just of John's life, but of every life. This is the great truth John brings every generation. Turn to Christ, look at him. 'Behold' him! We've just had the feast of Corpus Christi. How eloquent that as the priest holds up the Host and Chalice before Communion, it's John's words he uses: 'Behold the Lamb of God, behold him who takes away the sins of the world'! When Herod beheaded John, he thought he had silenced that inconvenient voice for ever. But two thousand years later, it is ringing out around the world in every Mass of the Roman rite.

So, here's light—for ourselves, ourselves as Christians, as the Church. John's mission was to prepare for the first coming of Christ. The Church's mission and ours is to prepare for the second coming—for Christ's any and every coming in fact. This is why hermits and monks and contemplatives, waiting for God in the wilderness, have always cherished John the Forerunner. But we can all be Johannine. 'I was thinking, "I have toiled in vain, I have exhausted myself for nothing"; and all the while my cause was with the Lord, my reward with my God' (Is 49:4). To be Johannine is not to lose hope. It's to hold the Gospel and Eucharist at the centre of our lives. It's to live, like John's finger, pointing to someone greater than ourselves. It's to be happy to decrease, to feel poor, to be imprisoned metaphorically or even really, as long as Christ can increase and enrich and act freely around us. It's to be a voice that only wants to speak what's true, good, kind, a passing voice at the service of the eternal Word.

Blessed are we if there is even one drop, one echo, one brushstroke of compatibility between John and us!

31

Solemnity of Saints Peter and Paul

Today we remember two great figures of Christianity, known well beyond its borders. Two lampstands burning before the Lord; two olive trees; two founding fathers of our faith. Two foremost knights of the Round Table of which Christ is King Arthur; the Prime Minister and Foreign Secretary, as it were, of Christ's United Kingdom.

They are what they are by the Father's will and the choice of Jesus and the grace of the Holy Spirit. The golden eagle of the Trinity, so to speak, swept down and picked them up in its talons, like Sam and Frodo at the end of the Lord of the Rings. They were chosen men. One, a fisherman, caught by Christ by the Sea of Galilee. The other, a learned rabbi, brought to the ground by him outside Damascus. Of Peter, we have two letters, the first a gem. But most of all we have his story, his character, his professions of faith and love of Christ, and Christ's for him. Of Paul, we have 13 letters, so rich that Christian thinking is still digesting them, saints still being inspired by them—universities have chairs of Pauline theology. But here again we have a story, a personality, a lover of Christ. These two have marked history and geography. When we hear of Galilee, Capernaum, Caesarea Philippi, Jerusalem, Tarsus, Damascus, Antioch, Corinth, Ephesus, Philippi, and Rome, who comes to mind? 'We are not talking here,' as St Augustine said, 'of some obscure martyrs.'[1] And today, on the day that marks their martyrdoms, they are lifted up by the liturgy for us to recall and honour, pray to and give thanks for.

What can we learn from them? First of all, surely, the hold that Christ can have on the human person. Yes, Christ can impact, impress, enchant, entrance, rescue, transform and relaunch us. Take Christ out of Peter and Paul and we're left with Simon and Saul, the first, a poor fisherman, destined for oblivion, the second perhaps to a footnote in studies of Second Temple Judaism. Take Christ out of Peter and Paul and, forgive the analogies, but what's left but an empty cigarette packet or a bag with all its crisps eaten? Glittering roadside litter at best. 'Lord, to whom we do we go? You have the words of eternal life. Lord, you know all things, you know that I love you … Although you have not seen him, you love him; and even though you do not see him now, you believe in him and rejoice with an indescribable and glorious joy' (Jn 21:17; 1 Pet 1:8). Those are all from Peter, and you can parallel them from Paul. These were men, believers, disciples, who had fallen in love with Christ, come under the sway of his magic. And everything they experienced, everything they did—little things and great things, crazy things and sensible things, their living and their dying—all of it was under his spell. Thanks to them we know it can happen, and we can long for it to happen to us. May Christ be—even a little bit—as real to us!

A second thing: like the other apostles, they were founders of the first churches, the first Christian communities. Peter and Paul worked, separately, in a great arc from Jerusalem northwards, through modern Syria, Lebanon, Turkey and Greece and into Italy, all the way to Rome. Essentially, they have bequeathed us the Church with a capital C—what we call in our Creed the 'one, holy, catholic and apostolic Church': our spiritual mother and home, the sheepfold, the body to which we belong, the family of God, the house built on rock, the true Jerusalem. Thinking of Peter and Paul, we think especially of Rome and of the Pope, the successor of Peter, who under Christ is the visible source and foundation of unity. Just like a personal relationship with Christ, so membership of the Church too is part of our Christianity.

And this flows into one last thing. The apostles are the first priests, the first to exercise the pastoral ministry in the name of Christ, the service of leadership. 'Feed my sheep.' All authority in the Church, authority to teach and to shepherd, to bind and to loose, goes back to them. From them it extends through history all the way to now and on until the end of time. It's one way Jesus' word is fulfilled: 'Behold, I am with you always even to the end of the world.' It's part of what we mean when we call the Church 'apostolic'. Jesus appointed the apostles, the apostles appointed successors, bishops. Priests, whom bishops ordain, are their co-workers, and deacons, whom they also ordain, are their assistants. There is a coherence here, with the bishops in communion with one another and the Successor of Peter, the faithful in communion with their bishops and priests, and all of us together, laity and clergy, in communion with Christ and the Father in the unity of the Holy Spirit in the one Church, to which all humanity is called. Today is the sixty-sixth anniversary of the priestly ordination of Mgr Robert MacDonald. The day before yesterday, Fr Peter Macdonald, only two years a priest, passed away. Next Friday, with God's help, two new priests will be ordained for the diocese and one permanent deacon. Death and life mysteriously intertwined. But the story goes on. Christianity has not been swallowed up by the centuries or run into the sand. The gates of hell have not prevailed. The energy of the Holy Spirit keeps the show on the road. (Think of those plays or musicals, like the Mousetrap or Mamma Mia, which are always running!). It's us now. Each of us and all of us, each with our own vocations. And among them the priestly ministry. Is there anybody there?

Christ, the Church, the priesthood: Peter and Paul connect to all three. May we too have the same connections.

Notes

1. St Augustine, Sermon 295 *on SS Peter & Paul* (PL 38), in *The Divine Office*, vol. 3 (HarperCollins: Dublin, 2006), 83.

32

THE FEAST OF ST MARY MAGDALENE

Song of Songs, 3:1–4b; John 20: 1–2, 11–18

But Mary stood outside the tomb weeping (Jn 20:11)

John's account of Jesus' appearance to Mary Magdalene is unforgettable. Surely, she would never forget it. We're not told in the Gospels how she first met Jesus, or how he drove the 'seven demons' (Mk 16:9) out of her. We find her first as one of his companions in Galilee, then a spectator of the crucifixion, then a witness to the burial. Of all the female companions of Jesus' last hours, she is the most mentioned. In the accounts of the events of Easter Sunday, she has priority too, and not least here in John's. She has come to the tomb, 'while it was still dark' (20:1), she finds the stone removed, runs back to tell Peter and the other disciple, and—we are left to assume—comes back to the tomb in their wake. They verify the emptiness and go home. But Mary stays outside. In George Mackay Brown's imagining, Adam the gardener goes out into his garden, and is surprised:

> Over by the fountain a woman sat. It was early in the morning, the last star was in the sky, the sun was beginning to brighten the mountains eastward. As the light grew, I could see that the woman was weeping. Tears glittered here and there on her face. On any other morning I would have sent such an intruder about her business.[1]

'And as she wept she stooped to look into the tomb.' 'Why she did so I don't know,' says St Augustine, and wonders, was it *divino instinctu*? In any case, this begins the transformation. First, an encounter with angels; then turning to see one she thinks the gardener; again her refrain, 'they have taken him away' (three times it comes: vv. 2, 13, 15); then the naming; her turning again, the cry 'Rabbuni'; his reply, 'Do not hold ... but go ... say ... I am ascending.' And last, her obedience: she goes, she tells.

In these few moments, Mary moves from misery to mission. From misery to mission via a meeting and a message, that is the story. And though we hear no more of her, except in legend, we know that these few moments shaped the whole of her life and all her eternity.

Mary is more than herself. In chapter 20 of the Gospel of John, she's the second of three individuals, each of whom embodies the movement to faith in the Risen One. She is a type of the believer. She is *philochristos*, says St Cyril. She prefigures, says St Augustine, those who'll believe in Christ after his ascension, the Church drawn from the Gentiles. Yes, 'Mary, type of the Church, looked into the sepulchre,' says St Ephrem.[2] She is, says St Gregory the Great, the Bride. 'Who are you looking for? Whom do you seek?' is the question Christ asks at the very centre of the story. Surely that strikes the monastic heart! It called up the *Song of Songs* for Gregory:

> Upon my bed during the night I sought him whom my soul loves; I sought him and did not find him. I will rise and go about the city, through its squares and streets; I will seek him whom my soul loves (Song 3:1–2).[3]

Mary, for him, is an icon of love desiring, questing, and keeping on, an icon of perseverance, of authentic holy desire only increased by delay. For 'Mary loved who turned a second time to see the sepulchre she had already looked into.' And to the Canticle he adds Isaiah: 'My soul has longed for you during the night, my spirit too, deep within me; from early morning I will keep watch for you' (Is 26.9), and the Psalmist too: 'God, my God, for you as soon as it is light I keep watch, my soul is athirst for you' (Ps 62:2). Mary, then, is the type of the Church as bride, of the Church as seeking. 'Experience with Mary,' says Guerric of Igny to his brethren.[4]

Respect and affection are what the Church has always given her, and rightly. And yet this is a story of conversion. Twice, says St. John, she turns, and between the beginning and the end she is totally turned, from misery to mission. It's worth dwelling a while on the misery. 'Woman, why are you weeping ... Woman, why are you weeping?' Let's try to enter her mind. Mary goes to the tomb and discovers it empty. There we have a datum of experience, a fact. Then she runs to Peter and says, 'They have taken the Lord out of the tomb, and we do not know where they have laid him.' There we have an interpretation of experience, of the fact: 'The body has been stolen.' 'Not only has he had to suffer all he suffered in the Passion, but now *they* (notice that!) have stolen the body.' It's the 'rational', 'realistic' interpretation based on the kind of thing people do—graves are robbed, bodies stolen. And it's that interpretation which makes her miserable. It's rooted in forgetfulness. She has forgotten whatever hints of resurrection there had been, or more than hints, in Jesus' life and words. And progressively it takes her over; it obsesses her. She repeats it, as I've said, three times.

It's never said before, in any of the Gospels, that Mary cried. But now she does. This is the last straw, this is the unkindest cut of all—as if what has happened hadn't been ghastly enough, now there's this final indignity. Strong as she is, she all but breaks. She breaks into tears, anyway; emotion wins out. She's reduced to misery. And she is wrong. She is completely wrong (a blessed experience, incidentally). She has misread the situation. She has seen in it only human nastiness. She has been blinded, numbed by her own interpretation of the facts, by the rain of her tears. She thinks she's in dialogue with reality, in fact she's prisoner of her mind. She is, in classic monastic terms, the victim of *logismoi*, thoughts. Is not the whole warfare of the monk precisely here, and so often with thoughts like these? Either I rule them or they rule me, it is so simple! And is not our misery usually less in the external circumstances, in 'them', in the brethren, in the system, but in our interpretation, our reading, our reacting, our thoughts? Is it even possible that we are, with all our rationality, all our realism, simply wrong? 'Woman, why are you weeping?' ask the angels, asks the Lord. Bl. Guerric identifies the appearing Jesus with Wisdom. The implication is that he's rescuing from folly. 'O foolish men and slow of heart!' And would it not be folly to spend our whole monastic life irritated, aggrieved, with circumstances, with others ('them'), with our own interpretation of the empty tomb of our lives, while all the time the Risen One is standing behind us, the other side of our thoughts, in the garden? Mary thought the situation should be changed, the body recovered. She didn't see that God had changed it already.

'Whom do you seek?' the figure asks her. She could only repeat her grief. If she'd said 'Jesus', everything would have become clear; prayer has that effect, the holy Name clarifies. So, 'Jesus said to her, "Mary". The Good Shepherd calls her by name, 'and in that direct personal address,' says B. F. Westcott, 'awakens the true self.'[5] One thinks of the prodigal son, 'he came to himself', and in coming to himself returned to the Father. So with Mary. She recognized him who recognized her. This is why she turns a second time, even though she'd already turned. She'd only turned so far to her second misconception, the gardener. Now she was turning to the truth. And so the misery is dissolved by a meeting. 'Jesus said to her, "Mary". She cries, 'Rabbuni', and clasps him, clasps his feet ...

'Do not hold me, for I have not yet ascended to the Father; but go to my brethren and say to them, I am ascending to my Father and your Father, to my God and your God.' This verse is the climax of the whole pericope. The meeting becomes a message, and the message confers a mission.

'Do not hold me, do not cling to me, for I have not yet ascended to my Father.' Mary is still not quite there. She still misunderstands. She imagines a return to the way it used to be, the intimate, comforting times. The Fathers of the Church—preoccupied with Arianism and other heresies—will say she hadn't yet grasped his equality with the Father. The Cistercian Fathers, marked by 'the turn to the subject', will say she wasn't yet living simply by faith, her spiritual life was still at the psychic, emotional level, too dependent on experiences. She needed to ascend with the ascending Christ, to let him go and go with him.[6]

> Become beautiful and then touch me; live by faith and you are beautiful. In your beauty you will touch my beauty all the more worthily, with greater felicity. You will touch me with the hand of faith, the finger of desire, the embrace of love; you will touch me with the mind's eye.[7]

'I have not yet ascended ... I am ascending.' The surprise is the emphasis upon Ascension, just when we'd expect festivity around the Resurrection. But isn't it completely Johannine? 'I am ascending to *the Father*.' This is the Gospel of the One who comes from the Father and goes to the Father. Resurrection, of itself, looks back. It looks back to a *terminus a quo*; it is 'resurrection *from the dead*' (cf 20:9). More important, though, is the *terminus ad quem*, the goal of the movement, and it's that the concept of Ascension proposes. It proposes the Father. As of the Passion, so of the Resurrection, the deepest meaning is, 'I am going to the Father.' But still there's more. What Jesus is conveying here is not simply information about himself, about his personal journey. It is, beyond that, a promise of all that will follow his Ascension. So, he says, 'I am ascending to my Father and your Father, to my God and your God', the disciples now 'my (that is, his) brethren'. With his Ascension there begins a new epoch, there opens a new world, of relationships. All that was said in the Last Discourse is about to be fulfilled:

> I will not leave you desolate; I will come to you. Yet a little while and the world will see me no more, but you will see me; because I live, you will live also. In that day you will know that I am in my Father, and you in me, and I in you' ... Judas (not Iscariot) said to him, 'Lord how is it that you will manifest yourself to us, and not to the world?' Jesus answered him, 'If a man loves me, he will keep my word, and my Father will love him, and we will come to him and make our home with him ... I tell you the truth: it is to your advantage that I go away, for if I do not go away, the Counsellor will not come to you; but if I go, I will send him to you ... When the Spirit of truth comes, he will guide

you into all the truth ... He will glorify me, for he will take what is mine and declare it to you ... Truly, truly I say to you, if you ask anything of the Father, he will give it to you in my name. Hitherto you have asked nothing in my name; ask, and you will receive, that your joy may be full' (Jn 14:18–20, 22–3; 16:7, 13, 14, 23–24).

It is through his Ascension that all this glory will be opened to the disciples, and they be able to enter into it, 'that the love with which you have loved me may be in them, and I in them' It is through his Ascension that all the glories that a Catholic theology of grace stutters to articulate will be conveyed. It is through his Ascension that the Church, in its most essential reality, as a brotherhood in Christ, will come into being. It is through his Ascension, the Spirit will come and prayer in Christ begin.

Irresistible here are the words Newman puts on Our Lord's lips, in his Anglican *Lectures on Justification*:

> Thou hast seen Me, Mary, but couldst not hold Me; thou hast approached Me, but only to embrace My feet, or to be touched by My hand; and thou sayest, 'O that I knew where I might find Him, that I might come even to His seat! O that I might hold Him and not let Him go!' Henceforth this shall be; when I am ascended, thou shalt see nothing, thou shalt have everything. Thou shalt 'sit down under My shadow with great delight, and My fruit shall be sweet to thy taste.' Thou shalt have Me whole and entire. I will be near thee, I will be in thee; I will come into thy heart a whole Saviour, a whole Christ,—in all my fullness as God and man,—in that awful virtue of that Body and Blood, which has been taken into the Divine Person of the Word, and is indivisible from it, and has atoned for the sins of the world,—not by external contact, not by

partial possession, not by momentary approaches, not by a barren manifestation, but inward in presence, and intimate in fruition, a principle of life and a seed of immortality, that thou mayest 'bring forth fruit unto God.'[8]

So we come back to Mary and her mission. She is not sent into the whole world, or to the whole creation. She is sent to Christ's brethren. She is sent to the Church. There are two simultaneous movements in play: Jesus' to the Father and Mary's to his brethren, and they are not in conflict. As he goes to the Father and she to the brethren, he also goes with her to them, and she with him to the Father. It is all one. It is a world of impossibles reconciled, of spiritual bilocation. And she is sent to the Church, to her fellow disciples, to announce, to be the angel (*angelousa*, says the Greek) of the imminent new realm of grace, of holiness, of the Spirit, of relationship with the Father and with one another in Jesus. She is to proclaim its advent and by implication its beauty. In her we're called to enter the Church ever more deeply, so as to be the Church, and show forth the beauty of Christian being, Christian brotherhood, Christian life, Christian prayer, of all that Christ's Ascension has brought to mankind.

From misery to mission, then; from misery to mission via a meeting and a message. It's not a movement we make once for all; we make it daily, every day, in the garden of the Resurrection. Every day, we need to be turned from living in our minds, from subjective assessments, from interpretations not of God, from meaningless miseries. Every day, we need to be turned back to our mission, to the priority of seeking holiness, in daily work, daily prayer, in the heart of the Church. And every day it can happen, because, as Guerric says again, what he did corporally on Easter day 'he does not cease to do spiritually day by day'.[9] Every day, he says my name, and calls me back to my true self, away from *logismoi*. Every day, he comes with a word and himself (the Liturgy of the Word, of the Eucharist; *lectio*, prayer). Every day he says, 'Go to my brethren'; every day, 'I am ascending to my Father and to your Father, to my God and to your God.'

Notes

1. G. M. Brown, *The Rose Tree* (York: Celtic Cross Press 2001), 7.
2. St Ephrem the Syrian, 'Hymn on the Nativity', in *Hymns*, trans. K. E. McVey (New York: Paulist Press 1989), 201.
3. St Gregory the Great, *Homilies on the Gospels*, 25.
4. Bl. Guerric of Igny, Sermon 3 *for Easter*, 2.
5. B. F. Westcott, *Commentary on John, XX*, 16 (London: John Murray 1894), p.292.
6. See Duccio di Buoninsegna, Painting *Appearance of Jesus to Mary Magdalene*, 1311.
7. St Bernard, *On the Song of Songs*, vol. 2 (Collegeville, MN: Cistercian Publications 1971), 28:10.
8. St John Henry Newman, *Lectures on Justification* (San Francisco: Ignatius Press 1997) IX, 8.
9. Bl. Guerric, Sermon 3 *for Easter*, 3, 3.

33

THE TRANSFIGURATION OF THE LORD

And they went into the cloud ... and a voice came from the cloud saying, 'This is my Son.'

Today is a great feast, the Transfiguration of the Lord. Today, a great gift is given—in the persons of Peter and John and James—to the Church: the gift of the knowledge of the Trinity: not book-knowledge, but knowledge like the knowledge a man has of his wife and a woman of her husband, a knowledge of faith and love, a knowledge had in prayer, knowledge of the Father, the Son and Holy Spirit.

Today the Church—the visible Church founded on the Apostles—receives the grace of prayer; she is taught to contemplate.

> In the shining cloud the Spirit is seen; from it the voice of the Father is heard: This is my Son, my beloved, in whom is all my delight. Listen to him.

Mary had received the grace of this knowledge at the annunciation; John the Baptist received it by the river Jordan, baptizing Jesus. And now Peter and John and James, too, go into the cloud and hear the Father's voice and receive—indelibly—this same knowledge.

They receive it so indelibly that even their own failure at the time of the Passion—Peter's failure especially—cannot stop them from turning back to the one they failed and running to the tomb on Easter morning. 'Lord, you know that I love you.' That knowledge is in these men as the character of baptism is in us. And when the Holy Spirit, not in the form of a cloud but in tongues of fire, comes down on the whole Church at Pentecost, it is Peter, standing up with the Eleven, who proclaims the Trinity and baptizes the crowds into the knowledge of Father, Son and Holy Spirit, with faith and prayer.

And the gift is not recalled. The signs of this are all around us. The other day, someone told me he had become a Catholic because he saw that Catholics prayed.

The three Evangelists who tell this story all mention that Moses and Elijah appeared with Jesus. But only Luke goes on and says: 'and they were speaking of his passing which he was to accomplish in Jerusalem.' Now, the word 'passing' translates the Greek word for 'exodus'. Moses (who stands for the Law) and Elijah (who stands for the prophets) were talking with Jesus about his *exodus*. 'Exodus' is a loaded word. It is a key to what we are doing through Lent and Easter, to what our Lord accomplished in Jerusalem, and to our own lives. So let's explore this word a little.

It refers in the first place to the series of events that took place some 1300 years before Christ. *The* Exodus was the liberation of a group of Hebrew slaves from the grip of the most powerful empire in the ancient world, located in the valley of the Nile. It launched them on a journey over the Red Sea, through the desert and on towards the Promised Land. It brought them into a new relationship, a covenant, with God, sealed at the foot of Mt Sinai. It made them into a people, bound to God and one another by a God-given Law. It grounded a new liturgy, Passover, and a new place of worship, the Tent of Meeting. It was all at once historical fact, epic story, a book in the Bible, and an extraordinary revelation of the name (the nature) and the power of God. Suddenly, the God of Abraham, Isaac and Jacob remembers their descendants. He hears their cry. The Supreme Power intervenes in history in defence of the powerless, turning the world upside down. And over time this Hebrew, Israelite, Jewish 'thing' has become something that belongs, even unconsciously, to everyone. It's still with us. It has shaped our mentalities and our history. Why is Palestine so fraught a place? Why is freedom the great ideal? Why do we demand justice for the oppressed? Why so much history of revolutions and movements of liberation and calls for emancipation? Many reasons no doubt, but first of all because the story of the Exodus is part of our collective memory, because once upon a time God freed his people from Egypt. To put it another way, no Exodus, no Israel, no Jews. No Jews, no Jesus. No Jesus, no Church. Without the Exodus, we wouldn't be here and this cathedral wouldn't be here. There's an unbroken chain.

And, at the Transfiguration, Moses and Elijah were speaking with Jesus about the 'exodus' he was to accomplish in Jerusalem. Clearly there is more than one Exodus. One might suggest there are four.

Let me share a fancy of mine. It may be quite wrong. But if, as the current thinking is, humanity began to be in Africa, in East Africa specifically; if the geography was not utterly different from now: then when the first human beings migrated north, into the Middle East and Europe and Asia, they presumably anticipated more or less the route of the later Exodus—from the mouths of the River Nile round into the Levant. There would have been this *first*, prehistoric exodus. And it would have marked a major moment in human history. Perhaps ...

Secondly, with no 'perhaps', there is Israel's Exodus, commemorated every year at Passover. This was something more than a mere migration. It was liberation from slavery into a new relationship with God. It was the birth of Israel's vocation.

Now, much biblical history, often far from happy, followed. There was exile, and there were new forms of oppression. The prophets spoke of a new exodus. And the thoughtful Jews of Jesus' time shared such a hope. They were looking for social and political freedom, from Rome immediately, but for more too. They sensed that a closer, purer, less compromised relationship with God was called for. They had a feeling that their deepest need was freedom from the slavery of sin. And Moses and Elijah, great symbolic figures of Israel's past, were talking with Jesus about the exodus he would accomplish in Jerusalem. They were speaking about the *third* exodus. This was the final and definitive one, the true and lasting one, completing what had gone before. On Maundy Thursday, we hear the Gospel of John: 'It was before the festival of the Passover, and Jesus knew that the hour had come to pass from this world to the Father.' This is his Passover, his exodus, the one we commemorate in our Paschal Triduum and our Paschal Vigil. This is the exodus that went through the Red Sea of death, into the desert of the tomb, and then out into the sunlit Land of Resurrection. A passage from this world to the Father. An exodus from the 'Egypt' of sin and death to the Land where God is known and immortality reigns.

Already Israel's Exodus was an exodus made by one people on behalf of everyone else. Jesus' exodus, Jesus' Passover, was one man's, the God-man's, made for all of us. It made possible the *fourth* exodus: ours joined to his. Life is full of little exoduses, surely. Each of us, as we grow up, leaves the garden of innocence, and learns the sad knowledge of good and evil. Then, 'a man leaves his father and mother and cleaves to his wife.' Parents have children and children change their parents' lives. We pass from place to place, situation to situation, even country to country. And in the end we leave this life. Exodus is part of being human. But all these little exoduses cry out for another—the exodus our heart most longs for. An exodus away from everything that weighs on us into freedom of spirit, an exodus from meaninglessness into meaning, from a chaos of desires into purity of heart, forgiveness and peace. And if we link our lives to Christ's, this becomes our exodus. Our changing life is joined to his. We needn't pass away with this passing world. Instead, we pass over with him from this world to the Father and find the world again transfigured by him. We begin this exodus here below. We begin it in two ways: by sharing in the sacramental life of the Church, crossing the Red Sea of baptism, and eating the fruit of the Promised Land, the Eucharist, and by living lives of faith, hope and love, acknowledging our sins, taking up our cross and following him. We have a horizon now of a radiant Face and shining clothes, a glorified Body. And, please God, when the exodus of death is upon us, our faith will be speaking in our hearts of the exodus of Jesus, accomplished in Jerusalem, working out in us. And the Church will be praying beside us:

> Go forth, Christian soul, from this world in the name of God the almighty Father, who created you,

in the name of Jesus Christ, Son of the living God,
who suffered for you,
in the name of the Holy Spirit who was poured out
upon you.
Go forth, faithful Christian.

And then if we want a sign, here and now, of the power of the Transfiguration, a sign of how deeply knowledge of the Trinity is in the Church and brought to us, isn't it in the Mass? The Mass is the mountain, and the Holy Spirit comes on the gifts and changes them into the Body and Blood of the Son, the Chosen and Beloved One. It is as if we go into the cloud, and the gift of the Transfiguration is renewed in us, and we can pray, as sons and daughters, to the Father.

So let us pray with the Church: 'Lord, by the Transfiguration of your Son, make our gifts holy, and by his radiant glory free us from our sins ... May the food we receive from heaven change us into his image. Amen.'[1]

Notes

1. Prayer over the Offerings; Prayer after Communion.

34

SOLEMNITY OF THE ASSUMPTION

Aberdeen is a rather sombre place at present: locked-down again, football-less and most of all grieving at what happened on the railway line near Stonehaven, with three lives lost.[1]

So, all the more reason to allow the feast of Mary's Assumption to cast its radiance over us. It is the patronal feast of our cathedral in Aberdeen, and of our diocese of Aberdeen. It is also the chief patronal feast of Pluscarden Abbey. It is good to be under such protection.

I'd like to offer here some reflective catechesis on the liturgy before us.

Firstly, this is indeed a major feast, a solemnity. In the ninth century, Pope Nicholas I even declared that it should be ranked with Christmas, Easter and Pentecost—that's as high as it gets. I would certainly suggest that it is the principal feast between the solemnities of Pentecost and Corpus Christi on the one hand and of All Saints and Christ the Universal King on the other, that is, between May / June and November. At Pentecost, the Holy Spirit came on Mary as wind and fire. In her life as a member of the early Christian community, she would have taken part in the Breaking of Bread and received sacramentally the Body of her risen Son. The Holy Spirit and the Eucharist are the two great gifts of the glorified Lord to his people, gifts for our bodies and souls, and we can say that Mary's Assumption body and soul into heavenly glory at the end of her life is the working out of those gifts of in her life. It is the Spirit who will raise our mortal bodies, says St Paul, and he who eats the bread that I shall give will live for ever, says Jesus. At the same time, too her Assumption presages the Church's completion in holiness which we celebrate at All Saints and anticipates the coming of Christ the King to transfigure the universe at the end of time. Such are the 'mighty deeds' of God that cluster around our Solemnity.

This is, too, a feast with a long history and a broad geography. There is evidence from fifth century Jerusalem of a Marian feast—probably originating earlier—on 15 August. It focused first on her motherhood, but grew to encompass her passing as well. It was taken up into what we now call the Orthodox world, and into that of the Oriental Orthodox, and it passed to the Latin West as well. It is a feast of the Christian *oikumene*; it has an ecumenical character. Over the centuries, it has acquired several names. It has been called her birthday, her *natale*, that is, her birth into heaven. It has been called her falling-asleep or dormition, her *koimesis* in Greek, the presupposition of her Assumption. In the West, it's that last title that has prevailed. 'Assumption' means being 'taken up' and 'taken to'. It's the repercussion of the Lord's Resurrection and Ascension in her. In fact, the Acts of the Apostles speaks of the Lord being 'assumed into heaven' (Acts 1:11). The German word for the feast means 'journey to heaven'. The Polish word means a 'taking up into heaven'. An Irish name for is 'the Feast of Mary in Harvest-time'. 'Easter in August' is another description. We're familiar with that formidable complex of buildings in Moscow, the Kremlin. Among much else, it includes four Cathedrals, of which one is the Uspensky Cathedral. It dates to the fifteenth century and was the work of an Italian architect. It is the church where Czars were crowned, and patriarchs are enthroned. Uspensky comes from the old Russian word *uspenie*, meaning Dormition.

So, in our terms, it's the Cathedral of the Assumption, and is held to be the mother Church of all the churches of Russia. It's the patronal feast of all women called Mary and all churches dedicated, without further specification, Simply to 'St Mary'. In Armenia, there's an old tradition: if you're called Mary, you have to throw a party today!

Liturgies Eastern and Western abound for this feast. Different traditions with a variety of biblical readings and allusions, many prayers, much imagery. There's a poetic and Scriptural fullness here, attempts to evoke the many splendours of the Queen now seated at the King's right hand. To honour the twelve stars that crown her in the Apocalypse, let me call out twelve themes from the repertoire of tradition, prefacing each with the evocative liturgical word 'today'. So:

> *Today*, Mary is envisaged as falling asleep in the Lord and being wakened to glory.
> *Today*, the one conceived without sin at the beginning of her life and a virgin throughout it is taken beyond bodily decay at the end of her life, and so shares fully in her Son's victory over our double enemy of sin and death.
> *Today*, the one who gave birth to the Lord in this life is now born into his risen and ascended life in heaven.
> *Today*, say some of the old texts, she 'migrates' from the Egypt of this world to the Promised Land of the world to come.
> As the precious Old Testament Ark of the Covenant held the word of God, the tablets of the Law, so she as Virgin Mother carried the Word of God made flesh, and as the Ark was carried up in

procession to rest in the Holy of Holies of the Temple, so *today* Mary is taken up by the angels and finds rest in the Temple of the Trinity. 'Go up, Lord, to the place of your rest; you and the ark of your strength.'

Today, like the beloved in the Song of Songs, she's taken into the chamber of her Lover and Lord.

In our Gospel, she rises and goes in haste to the hill country; it's a small pointer to her going up to *today*, not to Zechariah's house, but to the house of Father, there to sing her definitive Magnificat.

Today, like Mary of Bethany who was happy to sit at the Lord's feet and listen to him, so she now, the first disciple, finds rest in the presence of her Son.

Today, she's brought to the fullness of life in Christ, and her resurrected Son full of love and gratitude towards his mother raises her from the dead.

Today, an old prayer says, though she underwent death in time, she couldn't be held down by the bonds, ties, fetters of death, by our biological liability to it; she could not be locked down or as the Mass Preface says allowed 'to see the corruption of the tomb'. It's a day of liberation.

Today, at the end of her earthy life, she is taken up body and soul into heavenly glory. 'And a great sign appeared in heaven appears in heaven, a woman adorned with the sun, standing on the moon and crowned with twelve stars', 'a sign of sure hope and comfort to God's pilgrim people.'[2]

Today, she enters fully into her mission as our companion and sister, mother and friend, and is close to us now, in every place and each generation, in all our entanglements and confusions and hopes and joys.

Does this over-egg the pudding? No, actually. Mary was indeed once just a slip of a girl, as we say, a 'wee quine' from Nazareth. She is just a single human being, one leaf on the tree of life. She sings of her 'nothingness' in the Magnificat. But the Lord has done great things for her and all generations will call her blessed. So, why shouldn't we? She's a small window, if you like, but on a great hope.

Because Mary's Assumption was defined by Pope Pius XII as a dogma of faith only on 1 November 1950, we might think this belief a mere decorative add-on, an optional extra, Catholic icing on the core Christian cake. No. It's a key, a door, a window on the whole mystery of divine revelation.

Let me try to say why. We inhabit a culture which emphasizes our autonomy, our capacity for self-determination, the desirability of individual initiative. Maturity means shedding dependence and becoming the agent or protagonist of our own life. Indeed. But for this to be kept wholesome, on the right side, as it were, of solipsism and egoism, there's a need for a complementary truth: the sense of life as essentially response. The great realities precede us. We waken to them. We don't invent them; we discover them. And living wisely and well means responding wisely and well to what is given us. This dialectic begins with our mother and widens to the rest of our family. It widens to the world, the natural world, the countries we belong to, the schools we go to, the studies we undertake, the people we get to know, the profession, the business, the craft I engage in. They are all there first, and I respond to them. Historical events, political and social, convulsions, wars, viruses; good things, bad things, difficult things, painful things. My spouse, my children, my job. I am always responding. The quality of these things and the quality of my response determine the quality of my life. My life is my response. Suppose I am a football enthusiast. I discover this sport; it's there; it's all over the world. I become involved. It becomes part of my life—even more! Or take music. It does something for me, let's say. I 'get into' it. It takes me over. It might become my career, my life.

There's a structure here: a given and a response. And it's in responding that I live. Children reflect this so clearly—in their spontaneous responding to what comes their way.

Our faith has the same structure. The first half of our faith, as it were, is that God has shown himself, presented himself, come to us and made himself known, addressed us, given himself. Through the whole history of salvation, in the person of Jesus, in the community of the Church, in the promise of more to come, God gives himself to us. The 'mystery of faith' is all a given and at some point—through our parents or however—It's given to us; it comes home to me. God presents himself. And we / I respond. This is the second half, as it were. This is what the Church is: the Bride of Christ, an answer, the corporate response of humanity to the living God. That's what faith, hope and charity are for each one of us. They name the response which makes our Christian life. The Bible speaks of covenants, two-party agreements. It speaks of a marriage. There's the repeated refrain in the Bible: 'They shall be my people and I will be their God.' Faith means mutuality, reciprocity. Christianity is gift and acceptance. The Fathers of the Church say: God has become man so that man can become God. Thus, the pattern that makes our life is replicated here, but at a higher intensity, and all to the good if we respond well. A saint, I suppose, is precisely someone who responds wholeheartedly, with a full heart and mind and soul, to the presentation God has made of himself. And that is their life. And the more the Lord imparts himself and the more wholeheartedly we respond, the more life we have. The more we feel the life-giving Spirit in ourselves.

If this is how it is and if we then 'read' Mary's life in this light, is not she the great responder? A young Jewish woman, and God's messenger comes her way: you will be the mother of the Messiah. She responds with her acceptance. Or take today's Gospel. Mary 'sets out', responding to the need of her cousin; the child in Elizabeth responds to the child in Mary, and Elizabeth recognizes Mary's own response to the message that came to her from the Lord: 'Blessed is she who believed.' So, Mary responds to God's gift with her Magnificat. And so her whole life unfolds: she responds as a mother to her divine child. She responds to the shepherds and Simeon and to the drama of losing and finding her Son. She keeps what comes to her in her heart, reflecting on it. She responds to the suffering and death of her Son just by being there, by suffering with him. She responds to her Son's promise of the Holy Spirit by joining in prayer with the other disciples waiting for his coming. St Paul says of himself, 'For me to live is Christ, and to die is gain.' He means, my life is spent in responding to the gift of Christ, and if I die it will only mean more Christ and therefore more life. As Mary came to the end of her life, she could have said the same. The pattern of her life—gift and response—is now coming to its climax. She died of love, says St Francis of Sales. She must have become so simple and light, so unweighed down, so ready to go. Christ comes to her now, in the fullness of his risen reality. He comes with the offer of a full share In his Resurrection. And there were no tangles or entanglements in her to impede a wholehearted response, a final Fiat. She was open to transformation, unresisting, easily taken; so free of sin that she could not help but be taken beyond death, even bodily. So, the gift that awaits us at the end of time, God's final 'great thing', great deed, can be realized already in her.

I think Mary helps us grasp and enter into this understanding of life. She takes us out of any locked-in, self-referential 'take' on things. She helps us become simple, generous responders to the gifts of God and the gift of God himself.

Allow me a final coda. Mary isn't just Mary. Mary is more than herself. She is the great *sign*, clothed with the sun, the moon under her feet and crowned with stars. The imagery means that she brings the whole universe with her. She brings womanhood. She brings the whole is the Church in person. Her 'body and soul' recapitulate all creation. She is all that isn't God and in her Assumption she is raised to meet him. A poet once asked, 'O earth, what is your intent, what is your task, if not transformation?'[3] In Mary, glorified in body and soul, 'earth' is transformed, and the hope of transformation is given every living being. Now, beside the new Man stands the new Woman; beside the King a Queen. Heaven and earth have met. Christ and the Church have embraced. There is Giver and Receiver, Revealer and Believer, Speaker and

Listener, Teacher and Disciple. We feel drawn in. We have a great sense of homecoming, of all being ultimately well, of nothing good being lost, only evil falling away: Today, we see Mary as the sign of hope and comfort for the pilgrim people of God, our companion and sister, mother and friend.

May she pray for our cathedral and its parish, for our diocese, for everyone, for the three who died in the train and those who mourn them.

Notes

1. See https://en.wikipedia.org/wiki/Stonehaven_derailment.
2. Preface for the Solemnity of the Assumption.
3. R. M. Rilke, *Dueno Elegies* 9 (author's translation).

35

Nativity of the Blessed Virgin Mary

Today we celebrate, with the whole Church, the birth of Mary, the mother of Jesus. Feast days like this don't just fall from heaven. They come to be because at a certain place at a certain time certain people begin to celebrate them.

In the first Christian centuries a tradition grew up that Christ's grandparents lived in Jerusalem, in a house by the pool of Bethesda, where Jesus later healed the paralyzed man.[1] In that house, it was believed, Mary herself was born. So, in the late fifth century, by the Sheep Gate, over some ponds identified as the pool, a basilica in honour of Mary was built. And the respectable theory for the origin of this feast is that 8 September was the date of the church's dedication and was thereafter kept annually as the feast of Mary's birth.

Liturgies celebrated in Jerusalem tended to spread throughout Christendom. In the sixth century, St Benedict's time, under the Emperor Justinian, the feast was taken up in Constantinople and so spread to all the churches of the East, becoming one of the twelve great feasts of the Byzantine liturgical year. A century later, the feast was adopted in Rome, prayers were composed for it (for example, the Collect which we still use), and in time it spread throughout the West. It became very popular in the Middle Ages. In many monasteries of the period, it would have been one of the fifteen occasions in the year when the Prior or Abbot was expected to give a full sermon to his community in the chapter house. In fact, it only ceased to be a holy day of obligation with the Code of Canon Law of 1918.

The tradition that Jesus's grandparents lived in Jerusalem and that Mary was born there can hardly be proved and may be false. But that is not the point. The point is that in a certain place at a certain time certain people began to celebrate this feast—and certain others followed them—and thanks to their initiative something good and lasting has entered the Church's life.

In Jerusalem, there's a fifth century church where this feast was first kept, now known as St Anne's. It's worth recalling this church's history. In 614 the Persians captured Jerusalem, destroying many churches; in 638 the Arabs took the city and kept it. The church, though, survived both onslaughts and continued in use. In Charlemagne's time there were nuns attached to it. When the Crusaders took the city in the late eleventh century, it was still there. It was then rebuilt, beautifully, in Romanesque style, and a community of Benedictine nuns was established there, one of whose abbesses rejoiced in the name of Sybil. When, in 1187, the Muslims reconquered the city, the famous Saladin turned the church into a school of Islamic theology, a madrassa. In the nineteenth century, when the Western powers were in the ascendant and the Ottoman Empire in decline, the property was given to the French. The church was restored and is now in the hands of the Missionaries of Africa, the White Fathers. What a strange and typically turbulent history! Here, says tradition, Mary was born. Here, as the centuries passed, were heard Greek liturgies, the prayer of nuns, Latin liturgies, the chanting of the Koran and now again, amid Israeli–Arab tension, Christian prayer. And what will happen next?

And so to another piece of history, the Gospel we just heard. How much has been written about St Matthew's genealogy of Jesus, his book of the genesis of Jesus. At one level, it is so serene and orderly, Providence moving undisturbed to its goal. Abraham, David, the deportation to Babylon; three sets of fourteen generations. At another level, how full of anomalies. Saints and heroes, yes, others otherwise unknown, the few and invariably unorthodox women who feature, other people, like Ahaz or Manasseh, one wouldn't dream of going on vacation with.

Why, though, do we celebrate Mary's birth? Because it points us to another birth, the birth of her Son. Today is the birth of a certain girl who, as she grows up, will at a certain place and in a certain time, say yes to the word of God and be the means by which the Word became flesh and dwelt among us, by which the Father will beget his Son in a new way, as God with us.

And so today's Gospel is about how Jesus Christ came to be born. The passage from Paul's letter to the Romans is about how we're conformed to Christ, or, if you like, how he is born in us. And Mary born today is the one whom, centuries before, Micah called the *parturiens*, the *Virgo paritura* as she is venerated at Chartres, the one the meaning of whose life would be to give birth to the Son of God.

The three readings read at Great Vespers of this feast in the Byzantine rite are Genesis 28:10–17, which ends, 'How awesome is this place! This is none other than the house of God and this is the gate of heaven'; Ezekiel 43:27–44:4, ending 'And I looked and behold, the glory of the Lord filled the temple of the Lord, and I fell upon my face'; and Proverbs 9:1–11, beginning, 'Wisdom has built her house, she has set up her seven pillars.'

Today is the birth of Mary, the house of God which, at the Incarnation, the glory of the Lord will fill, which Wisdom will enter so as to eat with us.

And today is the birthday of St Mary's Monastery, Petersham, Massachusetts. What is a monastery? The readings, and the stories that are part of this feast, suggest an answer. A monastery is something more than the baffling mix of saints and sinners, the collection of unlikely characters, the strange, anomalous, uneven history, it will usually be made up of. It is a Mary. It's a certain place where, by the power of the Holy Spirit, Christ is conceived and born and grows, where the Incarnation is prolonged—in and among the monks themselves, to begin with, but we hope not only there, but also, however mysteriously, in others too. It is a place where God is with us. In a certain place, this town, at a certain time, on this day, certain men took an initiative. A monastery was born. And in and through that monastery, here and now, sustained by Mary's motherhood, we pray that Christ continues to be born.

Notes

1. Bethesda is a Hebrew name composed of two words, "beth" meaning "house", and "hesda" or "kindness, charity" or the "House of the merciful waters."

36

Exaltation of the Cross

Today is the feast of the Exaltation or Triumph of the Holy Cross. It's a feast with complex origins and multiple associations. It has connections with what was thought to be the discovery of the Cross on which Christ died by the Empress Helena around 327, with the dedication of the basilica erected at the supposed location of Calvary in Jerusalem, the Martyrium, in 335, with the act of the lifting-up of the relic of the Cross in that church for the veneration of the faithful, which would take place on 14 September, and with the recovery of that relic from the Persians by the Emperor Heraclius in 630. These things, however, merely occasioned the feast and its spread; they are not its object. From the historical point of view, this feast incorporates into the liturgy the ancient devotion to the Cross and later Crucifix which is so central to the symbolic world of Christianity. It is an early parallel to the way in which the liturgy has incorporated in the feast of the Holy Trinity the early medieval devotion to the Mystery of the Three in One, or in the feast of Corpus Christi the high medieval delight in appreciation of the sacramental presence of Christ and the Eucharist, or in the feast of the Sacred Heart the seventeenth-century appreciation of the unfathomable depth of love pierced by the soldier's spear. But, at the deeper level of the mystery being celebrated, it is simplest perhaps to think of today's feast as Good Friday in autumn. Here we were just prior to the autumn equinox celebrating the same mystery of redemption that was celebrated just after the spring equinox. The approach, the 'theme', the 'spirituality' is the same. At the ritual level, the primary 'lifting up' of the Cross, its 'showing' in view of adoration, actually takes place in the liturgy of Good Friday. What we are remembering today, then, is the redemption won for us by Christ on and through the Cross, by way of the Cross. And the grace we are asking is its completion in heaven.

If we are practical people and want something to do, then it is a good day for what Roland Walls called brushing the dust off our signs of the Cross, for banishing the senseless squiggle from our lives.

Another reflection occurs to me. I'm always fascinated by how, looking at reality of any kind, even, I think, material reality, one finds this structure of 'the whole in the part'. I suppose a human cell, with its DNA, is a good example at the level of biology. But the pattern seems at its strongest when we look at the mysteries of the faith, especially as expressed in the liturgy. What we are celebrating always is God's great work of our redemption, our being set free and given a life which outlives death and is even a share in the life of God. And in each 'part' of, for example, the liturgical year, in each 'particular', the whole is present. Each 'part' turns out to be a symbol, something which throws together, gathers the scattered into one. And so, in a real sense, the whole of redemption is in the Cross, and therefore on Good Friday and today's feast. In another sense, it is wholly in the empty tomb or rather in the Resurrection, and therefore 'available' on Easter Sunday and in Eastertide. In another way, it is completely present in the Eucharist. In another way again in the Incarnation as manifested at Christmas and Epiphany. In another way, in the gift of the Spirit—the forgiveness of sins in person—renewed at Pentecost. In another way, in the pierced Heart and so on. One or other of these symbols may have particular eloquence for us as individuals, or for Christians en masse at a particular period of history. Sometimes, saints are shaped and 'made' by one or other of these parts, but it is always by a part because, in that part, is the whole. This is not a phenomenon unique to Western Christianity either. Think of how the Transfiguration 'transfixed' Athonite monks of the fourteenth/fifteenth centuries. The healthy thing about a spiritual life centred on the liturgy and rhythmed by the liturgical year is that it's fed by all the symbols, by the whole in each of its parts. It is guaranteed a balanced diet. Today, then, we are reminded that the whole is in and from the Cross.

This is the feast of the *triumph* of the Cross, its lifting-up, exalting, glorification; the Cross as a boast à la St Paul. Yes, life is a battle and we're meant to win. We must never forget that. Victory is what we're after: the victory, precisely, of the Cross, that is, to say, of Christ's humble love. This is what we find it so hard to accept. Even as Christians, we so easily misconstrue the victory. The Church, as a whole, and each community within it, and each member of it, is signed with the sign of the Cross. And NO OTHER victory is promised us, this side of the End, than the victory of cruciform love. The victory of Good Friday: 'Father, into your hands, I commend my spirit.' 'Father, forgive them, for they know not what they do.' The vertical and the horizontal. Prayer and forgiveness. No other victory than the victory of Good Friday; and the victory of Good Friday a light that can never be put out, the tree of life that can never be hewn down.

What the Cross teaches us is to look beyond appearances. I suppose we all of us have visions of victory, and not just for ourselves, but for the Church and for Christ. It may be Parliament outlawing abortion or fearless bishops thundering against immorality or Muslims by the million begging for baptism or overflowing seminaries or Carmels being established in every village in Scotland, so many are thirsting for the contemplative life. Of course, such things can happen and if they do, can have the grace of God within them, be signs of the Resurrection at work in history. I think many a seed must have been sown in the Jubilee year, to sprout in the decades hence: even in the Western world or in the Muslim world. The seventeenth century saw a more thorough Christianization of European society than the fifteenth. The nineteenth century was one of the great centuries of Christian history and there was far more Christianity slopping around in the 1870s than in the 1770s. Couldn't the twenty-first century see yet another revival.

But, in the end, all those things are in God's hands, and the victory of the Cross is something always and everywhere present, not dependent on the vicissitudes of history. It is always hidden, and always there. And who can say, in a sense, where it is? 'The Kingdom of God does not admit of observation.' A convent of nuns, which has run its course and done its work, and 'dies', may in its dying be closer to Christ than it ever was in its living. The contemplative life, in particular, has to be something hidden and fragile and suffering. And if in the West, now, that often takes the form of ageing and diminishing, maybe that is the very truest expression of cruciform love, of standing with the Marys and John. One of the great nineteenth century political commentators, maybe de Tocqueville, famously said of Russia: 'when it is strong it is never as strong as it looks and when it is weak it is never as weak as it looks'. This seems, to me, even truer of the Church. If there is the humble love of the crucified Christ in the strong new and bursting movements, it's *that* is to be hailed. And if there is patience and prayer in a weak and dying community, there is no need for tears if it dies, because it is dying in God and life will come from it. 'When I am weak, then I am strong.'

May the Cross of Christ deliver us from all false expectations and all rash judgements, 'We have this treasure in clay jars, so that it may be made clear that this extraordinary power belongs to God and does not come from us.' St Paul, if anyone, grasped and lived the paradox of the Cross.

So, 'loving humility is a terrible force; there's nothing on earth that can resist it.'[1] So said Dostoevsky. It is the one true victory, God's, and there's no point bothering about any other or, to be honest, by all the evil in the world. It has been defeated. May we live under the sign of the Cross!

Notes

1. F. Dostoevsky, *The Brothers Karamazov*, bk. 6, ch. 3.

37

Saints Michael, Gabriel and Raphael

The Roman Calendar devotes this day to the three archangels known from Scripture, Michael, Gabriel and Raphael. The Benedictine Calendar is more global. It entitles the feast, St Michael and All Angels. It invites us, therefore—and its Collect too—to consider the angelic world as a whole, and its interaction with the world we think of as our own.

That angels are is an article of faith. Bodiless persons, pure spirits, invisible beings; powerful, numerous, 'ministering spirits sent forth to serve' (Heb 1:14); presences in the physical world, influences on human history, key figures in the story of salvation; our helpers, our enlighteners, guides towards the joy of heaven: such are the things Scripture and Tradition tell us. Yes, but peripheral, some would say, and dispensable: part of the background clutter our faith would travel lighter and further without. But are background and periphery really dispensable? What would an artist say? The Lord, the Father, the Spirit, the Church, the Eucharist, the Sacraments, life in Christ: these are the centre and hold the foreground, certainly. But believe in the angels, and you will not find yourself distracted from these things, but rather find those things more centred in yourself. 'The angels keep their ancient places'[1] is a familiar line from Francis Thompson, and a true one. But they keep other things as well. They, and only they, I think, keep some vital things alive in our hearts, for lack of which we will be less alive. A person who believes in angels—I mean really, sensitively, intelligently—can be more of a person than one who doesn't. It makes a difference.

Three things in particular one might mention that the angels keep alive in us: our need for help, possibilities of insight, and the reality of joy.

First, our need for help, or better, the presence of help. In his Rule (1:4), St Benedict uses the lovely phrase *multorum solacium*: the help, support, solace of many. It's the comfort of the cenobite. 'Brother helping brother is a strong defence,' says Proverbs. What monk or anyone, hasn't experienced this? But we have angelic brothers, too, brethren in the Mystical Body. We entangle ourselves, we imperil ourselves, and, when all is said and done, our world is a threatening place. We can't possibly go it alone. But 'the Lord rescues the souls of his servants and those who hide in him will not be condemned,' says the Psalm (33:23). And he rescues them through their brothers, through the angels, 'God defends his chosen ones in the Church, in troubled times he is himself their shield, and through the watchful care of angels he protects them. He presents the angels to his own as servants ... to further their salvation, to report their needs...' said Richard of St Victor. The Bible says it again and again. An angel rescued Lot. An angel stopped Abraham sacrificing Isaac. An angel led Israel through the desert. An angel helped Elijah on the way to Horeb. An angel protected Shadrach, Mishach and Abednego. An angel took Habakkuk by the hair and brought Daniel dinner. An angel strengthened Judas Maccabeus. An angel counselled Joseph when the Child's life was under threat. Angels ministered to the Lord in the desert. An angel took Peter out of prison. In every case, help was needed, consciously or not. And help was given. But mediated help, angelic help. Creation was sent to rescue creation, servants sent to fellow-servants. Belief in the angels will keep our awareness of these things alive, will keep us in the truth. 'Over all the doings of men,' wrote Max Picard, 'there is mercy beforehand, a great pre-forgiving. How many dreadful things pass through man's soul, through his mind, between 6 o'clock in the morning when he awakens and 10 o'clock in the evening when he falls asleep! But man is not able to do all these dreadful things, he is protected against himself. We *are rescued—more than we know*.' Yes, 'the Lord rescues the souls of his servants', and the angels are the symbols and agents of this. We have 'the solace of many'.

Then, possibilities of insight: of the sight of what's within, of the inscape of things. And isn't this precisely what the monastic tradition, since Evagrius, calls 'the contemplation of created realities'? And who, in that same tradition, are the symbols, guardians, instruments of such a contemplation, such an insight? The angels. 'If you pray in all truth,' wrote Evagrius, 'you will come upon a deep sense of confidence. Then the angels will walk with you and enlighten you concerning the meaning of created things.'[2] That is, they will show you the 'inscape' of things, persons, events and situations. 'What will it be to be God's side, even of such a little thing?' asked Alice Meynell in a poem on a daisy.[3] And isn't that where the angels lead us? To see the soul in the eyes or an empty tomb as the place of resurrection? St Thomas and his followers say the same. Angelic guardianship 'aims at enlightenment ... as to its final, chief effect'.[4] Indeed, wrote Anscar Vonier, 'according to St Thomas, it is not too much to say that the human race is kept in mental equilibrium through the unceasing watchfulness of the good spirits.'[5] Beyond their natural knowledge, they enjoy another, one that is the source of their supernatural happiness, the knowledge 'by which they see the Word and things in the Word'.[6] And this they can share with us, as they shared it with Mary, with the shepherds, with the women at the tomb, with the disciples gazing after the ascending Christ. They lead us to the contemplation of the Mystery as it unfolds in the heart of the world and of men. Their presence is our possibility of insight.

Lastly, the reality of joy. Angels abound, says the Tradition. 'Turn but a stone and start a wing.'[7] They fill churches and holy places. 'May your holy angels dwell here and keep us in peace', we pray in the evening. Can't we imagine our house filling up with them at that moment? Or there is the invariable mention of them at the climax of the Preface of the Eucharistic Prayer. Mightn't that be their cue? Suddenly the sanctuary is thick with them: concelebrating angels, as the Church is bold enough to call them. And what of the physical world? What of the woods, for example? Who doesn't think of woods as somehow full? Full of what? Full of fairies and leprechauns? Or, more soberly, full of the spirits of their ancient human inhabitants? Or can't we say, full of angels? Newman goes further: 'Every breath of air and ray of light and heat, every beautiful prospect, is, as it were, the skirts of their garments, the waving of the robes of those whose faces see God in heaven.'[8] And that, if we think it through, means joy. Angels see God. Angels are in joy. And the world is full of angels. Therefore, full of joy. 'Reality is joy,' said Paul Couturier. But by the ministry of angels. We cannot, usually, 'see' this physically, nor appropriate it emotionally or psychologically. We cannot, at those levels of our being, as yet 'enter into' joy. But the angels are a pledge that the joy is there and waiting to be entered. If we allow the angels to 'keep their ancient places', keep them in our hearts, then we are keeping joy in our hearts. And we will have experience not only of help, not only of illumination, but of having 'the roads to Sion' in our hearts, walking 'with ever growing strength' till 'we see the God of gods in Sion' (Ps 83:6, 8) and enter into Joy among the angels.

May this feast, then, revive our faith, and the indwelling Spirit assure us 'companionship with angels'.[9]

Notes

1. F. Thompson, 'In No Strange Land'.
2. Evagrius, *Chapters on Prayer* 80.
3. A. Meynall, 'To a Daisy'.
4. St Thomas Aquinas, *Summa Theologiae* I, q. 113, a. 5, ad 2.
5. Dom A. Vonier, *The Angels*, 2nd ed. (Newark, NJ: Assumption Press 2013), pp 48–49.
6. Aquinas, *Summa Theologiae* I, q. 57, a. 5.
7. F. Thompson, 'In no strange land'.
8. St John Henry Newman, 'The Powers of Nature', *Parochial and Plain Sermons* (San Francisco: Ignatius Press 1997), II, XXIX.
9. St Basil the Great, *On the Holy Spirit* 23.

38

The Guardian Angels

On 29 September the Church keeps the feast of the Archangels Michael, Gabriel and Raphael; on 2 October, she remembers the Guardian Angels. This, then, is an appropriate moment for thinking about the Angels.

No doubt, there are many ways of doing this, and each of us can follow his own preference. My own way is to turn to this one angel to whom I have been entrusted and think simply about him.

It has for long been the conviction of the Church that each of us has such a guardian angel. The Jews of our Lord's time believed this, and our Lord confirmed that belief when He said 'See that you never despise any of these little ones—that is children, but also metaphorically, believers—for I tell you that their angels in heaven are continually in the presence of my Father in heaven.' 'No one mindful of these words of the Lord,' says St Basil, 'can deny that an angel is present to each person, as a kind of pedagogue and shepherd, guiding his living.'[1] And if an angel is present to each person, an angel is present to me. And I can turn my mind to him.

And my first thought, simply, is, what a remarkable being he must be. He is a pure spirit, which is why I cannot see him with my two eyes. He does not have a body. He is not a part of the material world. And if he is a spirit, he's a person. He's not an impersonal force. He's an individual being of a rational nature. He has a mind and a will of his own. He is not an automaton. He's an independent centre, free. He thinks; he makes decisions; he acts. He has a character of his own. He is also greatly more powerful than I am, in terms of spiritual power. He knows more. The range of his mind is far greater than mine; its operation far faster. He can penetrate into any matter so thoroughly and rapidly, that he never has to reverse a decision. He's also superior to me in point of time. It is true he has a beginning; he is not eternal, but it also seems that he has existed at least as long as our universe. He existed when the 'Big Bang' happened, if it did. He existed when the first signs of life appeared; when the first men appeared. He has existed through all the centuries of human history. The only qualification to be made here is that an angel's experience of time is quite different from a man's. It is not measured by days and nights, weeks, years, centuries even. An angel lives in angelic time, which Cardinal Newman describes as 'measured by the living thought alone'[2]—a difficult idea to grasp and one which need not detain us.

My second thought is that this remarkable being, this spirit-friend of mine, is above all a servant of God. He is among the 'thousand thousands ... the ten thousand times ten thousand' whom Daniel saw standing before the Ancient of Days and 'serving' Him. He is there, of course, by the mercy of God, but he is also there by choice. He has been 'tested' and found 'worthy'. The story of the human race opens with a test and so does the story of the angelic race. We do not know precisely what form this testing of the angels took. St Thomas Aquinas says that the testing of the angels was the revelation of the supernatural. By the supernatural, he means God's free and gracious plan 'to unite everything in Christ, things in heaven and things on earth', to raise both angels and men above their natural capacities and make them 'partakers of the divine nature'. The angels were offered this, called to it. Their vocation was shown to them. They were called not to rest in whatever excellence belongs to them by nature. They were called out of their own sphere into a higher one, which was at the same time more universal, involving community with lower spirits, with man. They were called at one and the same time to a greater glory and a new humility. They were faced with the sovereign freedom of Almighty God, the 'ever-greater'.

Perhaps they were shown human nature joined to the Second Person of the Trinity and lifted far above them; perhaps they were shown Mary, a merely human being but one day destined to be their Queen and nearer God than they were. We don't know. We only know that, somehow, they were called; love and obedience were asked of them. And at that moment, the great split in the angelic world took place. Lucifer and his angels cried out 'I shall not serve' and went into rebellion, into active opposition to God's plan of redemption, into hell. Michael and his angels cried out: 'Who is like God?' and chose to serve. Among them was my angel. My angel chose God. He chose to serve.

The choice was for ever. It opened heaven to him, the vision of God and torrential joy. He became 'a ministering'—literally, liturgical—spirit, waiting to be 'sent forth to serve, for the sake of those who are to obtain salvation'.

And so he became, in the fullness of time, an agent of God's redemptive providence towards the human race. He co-operated willingly in the evolution of planet earth, knowing it was destined to be the home of creatures dear to God. He went about unknown missions in the long centuries between the first sin of those creatures and the call of Abraham. He watched over the Chosen People. He was with them when they came out of Egypt; he was one of the angels mediating the law to Moses; he strengthened the hands of those who fought their way into the promised Land. He rejoiced at the immaculate conception of a Jewish girl called Mary, knowing that this was the dawn of salvation, and when that girl, in time, conceived by the Holy Spirit and the Son of God entered the human race, my angel heard God say: 'Worship Him!' and he did. Perhaps he was among the 'multitude of the heavenly host' on the first Christmas night singing 'Glory to God in the highest and peace among men on earth.' Perhaps he was among the angels who ministered to Christ in the desert after his fast of forty days. Certainly, now, after the Ascension, he stands among the 'many angels, numbering myriads of myriads and thousands of thousands, saying with a loud voice "Worthy is the Lamb who was slain, to receive power ... and honour and glory and blessing!"' Certainly, again, he will be among the angels who, at the end of this world's time, will come with Christ in the glory of the Father, and 'gather his elect from the four winds, from one end of heaven to the other' (Mt 24:31).

And so I come back to where I began. This remarkable being, this faithful servant of God, is also my friend. Extraordinary though it may sound, it is his joy to serve me, to be a 'fellow servant' with me. It is his joy to be to me an angel of peace, and of penitence, and of prayer, protecting me from trouble, urging me back to God when I sin, taking my prayers to God and God's answer to me. He does all this. He does all unobtrusively, uninterruptedly. There is a constant flow from him to me, a constant friendship. He is always beside me. He is with me now, and I hope is pleased that for once I have not forgotten him.

Notes

1. St Basil the Great, *Adversus Eunomium* 3:1 (PG 29.656B).
2. St John Henry Newman, *The Dream of Gerontius* (Oxford: Family Publications 2001), p. 42.

39

All Saints

I must confess that this is one of my favourite feasts. In the Monastic Divine Office it is one of the most beautiful, in its texts and music. At Vespers especially, in the dark of a November, Pluscarden evening, it's supernaturally luminous.

This feast has us too standing before the Throne, amazed at the expansive creativity of God, how his white Trinitarian light refracts in the many colours of the Saints, with tale upon tale of tears wiped away, wounds now shining, evil turned to good. The Aberdeen philosopher, David Braine, who often worshipped in this Cathedral, used to say that this life is like the orchestra tuning up before the concert begins. Today perhaps we catch a strain of the heavenly symphony. However humanly obscure they were, everyone who has said Yes to God, and become all Yes, is a music-maker now. 'All I could never be / all man ignored in me / this I [am] worth to God', says a poem.[1]

Surely, says St John Henry Newman,

> not even the world itself could contain the records of his love, the history of those many saints, that 'cloud of witnesses', whom we today celebrate, His purchased possession in every age! We crowd these all up in one day; we mingle together ... all the choicest deeds, the holiest lives, the noblest labours, the most precious sufferings, which the sun ever saw.[2]

In Eastern Christianity, this feast—kept on the Sunday after Pentecost—commemorates, I quote, 'all the saints, all the righteous, the prophets, apostles, martyrs, confessors, pastors, teachers and holy monks and nuns, men and women alike, known and unknown, [all] who have been added to the choirs of the saints and shall be added, from the time of Adam until the end of the world, [all] who have been perfected in piety and have glorified God by their holy lives.' The comfort is that this cloud of witnesses, as Pope Francis says, 'may include our own mothers, grandmothers, or other loved ones. Their lives may not always have been perfect, yet even amid their faults and failings they kept moving forward and proved pleasing to the Lord.' 'The saints next door.'[3] There's a half-amusing tale of a Byzantine Emperor who had a great respect for the holiness of his wife. When she died before him, he wanted a church dedicated to her. He was told that her holiness had not been recognized. So he changed the dedication to All Saints, and so he could honour her freely. If you don't have a saint's name, today is your Name Day.

There is a sense of amplitude today. The Collect asks for *abundance* of reconciliation. Come to me, says the Lord, *all* you who labour and are overburdened—think of them through history. Think of the lives abbreviated by sudden violence, think of miscarriages, of lives taken in the womb or lost in childbirth. All Saints gives us hope these are not forgotten. Think of the poor in spirit, the gentle, the mourning, those hungering for what is right, the persecuted. Even we know they're not few. The Preface speaks of 'the great array of our brothers and sisters', all children of the heavenly Jerusalem our mother. Today is God's harvest festival.

We know from the New Testament and other early Christian records what a strong sense the first Christians had of being connected to, surrounded, accompanied, befriended, helped and awaited by believers who had gone before and 'rest in the sleep of peace'. Over time this blossomed into the veneration of the saints that we know, devotional, liturgical and so on. This is part of our inheritance. We share it with the Eastern and Oriental Orthodox. It seems to be growing again among our Protestant friends. It's a great treasure. It's one of our Catholic assets. It enriches our Christian life no end. 'By their way of life you offer us an example, by communion with them you give us companionship, by their intercession sure support', says one prayer. Who knows the unseen help we earthlings receive from our heavenly brothers and sisters? One theologian has written this: 'Those who have died in Christ are invoked by the Church to exert their powers of intercession on behalf of the living. Centuries after their death, saints are believed to retain an actively beneficent relationship with the human race and its historical struggles. Like the risen Christ, they may well achieve more on behalf of the human family after their deaths than before them; like the risen Christ, their lives may have been judged as failures by purely human standards.'[4] But now they are, as it were, 'full on'.

Let me take one step further. In his Paradiso, Dante ends by invoking 'the love that moves the suns and the other stars'. T. S. Eliot spoke of 'the drawing of this love and the voice of this calling'.[5] There is this divine fire of love at the heart of creation. The saints are those who feel it most. They are at rest, certainly, held in the everlasting arms. But they are also intensely alive. The Force is with them to the highest degree. They are dynamized and energized; moved and drawn. As another Christian poet has it, the saints are 'the gathered glories of his wounded love'.[6] And because they are 'moved' and drawn and called and gathered, they too move and draw, call and gather—the whole created universe. That's what's happening even when they answer our prayers. Each of us, each of the saints, is one and individual, one leaf on the tree, but the tree is the tree of all creation. Each of us connects to everything and everyone, chemically, biologically, historically. Each of us carries within us at least the times and the places and the people we have lived with. And Christ, standing before the Father, carries the saints and us in himself, and in him we hold and carry each other and all else. In the Holy Spirit he draws us, presents us to the Father, takes us into the heart of the fire, connects us to the overflowing life of God, and so brings creation to its goal: the Kingdom of heaven. Our own lives are snakes and ladders, circles and reverses, stops and starts, but underneath, and despite the counter currents of history, there is this other gravity, another energy, taking us not back into nothingness, but into God. 'I am entering into life,' said St Thérèse.

Glory to God. Amen.

Notes

1. R. Browning, 'Rabbi Ben Ezra', in *Poetical Works* (London: OUP 1940), p.441.
2. St John Henry Newman, *Parochial and Plain Sermons* II, 32, p.477.
3. Pope Francis, *Gaudete et Exsultate* (2018), 3, 6.
4. J. J. Navone, SJ, *Triumph through Failure* (Eugene, OR: Wipf and Stock 1984), p49.
5. T. S. Eliot, 'Little Gidding' in *The Four Quartets* (London: Faber 1959).
6. M. Guite, 'All Saints' in *Sounding the Seasons* (Norwich: Canterbury Press 2012).

40

COMMEMORATION OF ALL SOULS

Why has God given us faith? Certainly, we may feel it's wobbly at times. But let's forget that for a moment. We do have faith. And faith is a gift of God.

So why has God given us faith?

He's given it to us for own sake, certainly—to help us through life and open the door of heaven to us.

But, surely, it's not just for that. It's also for others. Thanks to faith, we're members of the Body of Christ. We're part of Christ, instruments of Christ, extensions of Christ. We can be sharers in his ongoing work of redemption. St Paul famously said, 'In my flesh I complete what is lacking in Christ's afflictions for the sake of his body, the Church' (Col 1:24)—and not just for the Church, but with the Church for everyone. And what was true for Paul is true, at its level, for each of us.

God has given us the gift of faith for others. But how does that work out in practice? One way—not the least way—is prayer.

We believe in God's mercy. We believe he wills all to be saved. And we pray, 'Thy will be done.' And this prayer is heard. In ways known only to him, he gives everyone the possibility of sharing in Christ's Passover from death to life.

In his Encyclical on the Joy of the Gospel, *Evangelii Gaudium*, Pope Francis mentions 'the missionary power of intercessory prayer'. And he writes this:

> The great men and women of God were great intercessors. Intercession is like a 'leaven' in the heart of the Trinity. It is a way of penetrating the Father's heart and discovering new dimensions ... We can say that God's heart is touched by our intercession, yet in reality he is always there first. What our intercession achieves is that his power, his love and his faithfulness are shown ever more clearly in the midst of the people.[1]

Now, surely, these 'people' include the deceased. Here we are on All Souls Day. Here we are in the month of November. And the Church shines the torch of her prayer beyond this life: into the great world of the dead, into the twilight we call Purgatory. Humankind is one, and this oneness embraces the dead. They're like a great, hidden continent, and the light of Christ is meant for them as well as for the continents of this world.

We are still in the centenary year of World War I. It has been calculated that in the twentieth century overall some one hundred and seventy million people died violent deaths. And it's remarkable that, through that same time, the Church has been quietly raising the status of today, of this Commemoration of All the Faithful Departed. It's only since 1969, for example, that it has been possible to celebrate the Mass of All Souls on a Sunday, when all of us are gathered. If we put our ear to history, is it sheer fantasy to hear a great cry, coming up from all the cemeteries of the world, from the mass graves, from the unknown graves, from the depths of the sea, from all the pain of the bereaved? And faith has the ears to hear this and the Church the gift of turning it to prayer. 'Blessed are the peacemakers', we heard yesterday. Isn't prayer for the dead one way we, the living faithful, can make peace? We want to be instruments of reconciliation. Isn't this a dimension of that? Doesn't the soil stained by all this violence call out for the purifying of prayer?

We're given faith to pray for others. And the Church is the mother and teacher of prayer. In every Eucharistic Prayer, she and we pray for the dead: 'Grant them, O Lord, we pray, and all who sleep in Christ a place of refreshment, light and peace' (EP I). 'Remember also those who have died in the peace of your Christ and all the dead whose faith you alone have known' (EP IV). Open a Missal and you find a section of Masses for the dead: for the departed in general and in particular. There are Mass formulas for deceased parents, for deceased couples, for a young person, for someone who has died after a long illness, for someone who has died suddenly, and so on. These are real things, and the Church's prayer is there—leaven in the heart of the Trinity and the heart of life. And we are part of this praying Church.

How good our customs are here! Let's keep the departed in our prayers this month, let's ask for Masses to be said for our loved ones, let's visit cemeteries and pray there. Let's teach our children to pray for the dead.

And what about today's Gospel? It's so, so familiar. 'Come to me, all you who labour and are over-burdened, and I will give you rest.' We always think of those words as directed to us. We imagine our Lord standing arms open, speaking to a crowd in front of him, and we in it, and him saying this to us. Fair enough. But, by faith, we are members of Christ. We're part of him. So, we can imagine ourselves standing beside him and echoing his great cry. Still more: through our prayer, we're his actual voice. We can call out with him—through the medium of his Body, as it were. We add our voice to his. We call to the great crowd of the dead: 'yes, come to him and find rest.'

And so we pray, 'Eternal rest grant unto them, O Lord, and let perpetual light shine upon them.' Amen.

Notes

1. Pope Francis, *Evangelii Gaudium* (2013), 283.

41

The Solemnity of St Andrew

Romans 10: 9–18; Matthew 4: 18–22

Who was he

A first century Jew, a Galilean, born in Bethsaida, son of a certain John or Jonas, brother of Simon Peter. Like him he was a fisherman by profession who, at the time the story opens, was living and working in partnership with him in the lakeside town of Capernaum.

And so it might have remained.

But this young man was sensitive to the plight of his people. He shared their sorrow and, like others, he looked for 'the consolation of Israel' (Lk 2:25). He was on a quest and so became a disciple of John the Baptist.

And through John the Baptist, by the River Jordan, he met Jesus. 'Behold, the Lamb of God', said John. And Andrew and another disciple followed the pointing finger. 'What are you looking for?' asked Jesus. 'Rabbi, where are you staying?' 'Come and see.' So, John chapter 1, verses 35 to 39. A little later, back in Galilee, Jesus walked past the two brothers casting their nets, and called them to follow him. They did immediately. 'I will make you fishers of men.' So, Matthew chapter 4, verses 18 to 19. Andrew, then, is one of the first disciples. He is sometimes called the 'protoclete', Greek for 'the first called'. In time he was appointed one of the twelve (cf. Mk 3:13ff.). Among them he seems to be one of the inner circle. In the four New Testament lists of the Twelve, he is always named second or fourth, one of the four closest disciples of Jesus. He was among the four who were privy to Jesus' discourse on the destruction of Jerusalem and the end of the world (Mk 13).

There's another strand too, noted especially by the Gospel of John. Andrew had the gift of bringing, introducing people to Jesus. He does not seem to have done this by great speeches or sermons, as a first century tele-evangelist, so to speak. He did it simply, one to one or one with a few. After his meeting with Jesus, he tells his brother, 'We have found the Messiah' (Jn 1:41) and brings him to Jesus. And in that meeting, Simon becomes Cephas, the rock on which the Church is to be built. The rest is history. Later, in John chapter 6, St Andrew points out the boy with five loaves and two fish. By the power of Christ, this would feed a multitude. It presages the Eucharist. Later again, in John chapter 12, there were the Greeks who wanted 'to see Jesus' at Passover time. They approached Philip, a Greek-speaker. Philip told Andrew, and Andrew and Philip together tell Jesus. Again, he would lead them to Jesus who would see in them the future harvest of his death. Bringing his brother to Jesus, he was the first 'home-missionary' (Jn 1). Bringing the Greeks, he was the first 'foreign missionary' (Jn 12). It's striking with what foundational events he connects: the call of Peter, the Eucharist, the conversion of the Gentiles.

Like the others, he must have run away at the time of Jesus' arrest (cf. Mk 14:50). But like the others too, Judas aside, he was in the Upper Room that Easter Sunday evening (cf. Lk 24:36) and, with the others again, was filled with the Holy Spirit at Pentecost (cf. Acts 2:1ff).

As to his life after Pentecost, his missionary course, there are many traditions. The one accorded most credence is that he evangelized in northern Greece and in what was then 'Scythia', now, among other places, the north-eastern Balkans and Ukraine, and was finally martyred in Patras, Achaea, on the western seaboard of Greece. A great Cathedral there honours his memory. Traditionally, he was martyred on a saltire cross. The Collect for the feast sums up these years in two words: praedicator, i.e. proclaimer, preacher, and rector, literally ruler, effectively pastor. In other words, he did what we presume all the apostles and early Christian missionaries did: gather and establish communities by preaching, creating small islands of faith in the Lord. The reading from Romans 10 refers to this too.

Who is he now?

A transfigured man fully alive with the glory of the risen Christ. In this context, the Collect calls him intercessor, continuing in another mode his work of bringing people to Jesus. The life of the Church triumphant and of the Church militant interpenetrate, and St Andrew, though unseen, is not inactive. Through what we experience as time, he fulfils and 'grows' his mission: a fittingly universal, missionary, ecumenical, unifying one. He is still the man with the net.

He lives on in the four Gospels. Brief though the mentions of him be, they can still inspire. He 'teaches us to follow Jesus with promptness, to speak enthusiastically about him to those we meet and, especially, to cultivate a relationship of true familiarity with him, acutely aware that in [Christ] alone can we find the ultimate meaning of our life and death.'[1]

St Andrew lives in the Liturgy, being remembered for centuries and universally on 30 November. With that date, he is often the first saint and apostle to be kept in Advent, as the liturgical year begins—fittingly for the 'protoclete'. In the Anglican Communion, there is talk of Andrewtide and there are special prayers for the missionary work of the Church around his feast.

He is a heavenly patron—of Scotland, of course, from the eighth century—but prominently too of Orthodox countries: Greece, Russia, Ukraine, Romania, Georgia. Since the sixth century he has been claimed as the founder of the see and patriarchate of Constantinople, which has proved ecumenically suggestive. The 'sister churches' of Rome and Constantinople have two apostolic brothers as their respective patrons, and delegates from the one attend the feast days of the other—on 29 June and 30 November. And so St Andrew's prayers are asked to bring the Catholic and Orthodox confessions together into full union with Christ. This is echoed in the hymn for Lauds of the Roman Office. As a gesture towards union, in 1964 St Paul VI returned the Vatican's relics of St Andrew to the Greek Orthodox community in Patras.

His continuing presence is felt again wherever his relics are venerated: in Patras, in Amalfi and Sarzana in Italy, in the church of St Andrew and St Albert in Warsaw and in St Mary's Cathedral, Edinburgh.

And who is he for us?

So we come back to ourselves, here in Scotland. The historians tell of how the association began and distinguish legend and credible fact. The ruins of his great Cathedral remain, with Mass celebrated there now and then. The city and University remain, and their beauty.

Let's end, though, with a beautiful imagining by George Mackay Brown. In his Hymn for St Andrew's Day, before any relics of St Andrew come to Scotland, Andrew comes himself. The poet traces the journey north:[2]

> The world is wide, to cast nets in.
> The Holy Spirit
> Fills his coat like a sail.
> He speaks to fishermen on the Alpine lakes,
> He lingers by Belgian rivers,
> They listen, rough Breton fishermen,
> Minglings of sea-wit, laughter, gull-talk.'
> But still further north he goes:
> 'Where are you taking me, Spiritus Sanctus?'
> ...
>
> 'Where are we bound, ruthless dove?'
> He lands in Scotland.
> 'Well, I am content. This place will do
> With sinners, saints, mostly
> Gray minglings, like fish in a barrow.
> Alba, Pictland, Scotia,
> The beach strewn with curraghs and sea-gear.

'Well, I am content.' Let us be content too with being here and, inspired by St Andrew, cast the nets for Christ.

Notes

1. Pope Benedict XVI, *Discourse at General Audience*, 14 June 2006.
2. G. M. Brown, 'Song for St Andrew's Day', in *Collected Poems*, ed. A. Bevan and B. Murray (London: John Murray 2005), 386.

42

CHRIST THE UNIVERSAL KING

When the angel visited Mary, she heard that the Lord would give her son 'the throne of his father David' and that 'he will reign over the house of Jacob forever; and of his kingdom there will be no end.' She was to be the mother of a king.

When Jesus stood on trial before Pontius Pilate, he was asked, 'Are you a king?' and he replied that he was—with a difference.

When Christ was raised from the dead, he was 'given all authority in heaven and on earth'. He was seated at the right hand of his Father, 'far above all rule and authority and power and dominion' (Eph 2:21). He was given 'the name above every name, so that at the name of Jesus every knee should bow, in heaven and on earth and under the earth and every tongue confess that Jesus Christ is Lord, to the glory of God the Father' (Phil 2:9–11).

It is this kingship of Jesus that our liturgy is acclaiming today. It is the kingship of a son of man who is the Son of God. It's a kingship of someone who laid down his life to redeem us: kingship from the Cross. It's the kingship of Christ, raised and glorified, the One who will come again in glory.

Here's a question for a Catholic quiz: whose was the first photographed martyrdom? Bl. Miguel Pro. What were his final words? *Viva Cristo Rey!* When? 23 November 1927. And when was this feast of Christ the King established? 1925. There's a connection.

Pius XI was a far-seeing man. He established this feast just seven years after World War I had ended, at a time when dictatorships were being born: new kinds of 'kings' coming to power who claimed absolute control over every aspect of life. We know the names: Mussolini, Hitler, Stalin. And we know what happened: twenty million died in World War I, fifty-five million in World War II. Nor has it stopped there: Stalin, who lived into the 1950s, was responsible for more deaths than Hitler. Chairman Mao, who lived into the 1970s, was responsible for more deaths than Stalin. These and others, and others today, are the anti-kings, the anti-Christs, who lead their people to death. This is a topical feast. Who do I want as king?

In another way, it's a very ancient feast. It takes us back to the first Christians. Christians were called Christians after Christ. What does Christ mean? Anointed One, that is, the Messiah. And who is the Messiah? The expected King of Israel. So to be Christian is to acknowledge Jesus as my King. Again, in the early Church, the simple profession of faith at baptism, was 'Jesus is Lord.' That meant too—in the context of the time—that Christ was the one really in charge, and not the Lord Caesar, not the Roman Emperor or Empire, not the State.

And these professions of faith meant freedom. For the early Christians, it meant entering into a new and better 'space'. That Christ was the king, the real authority, the real power, was good news. Here was a king who didn't conscript people into wars of conquest but accepted death on their behalf. A king who makes his subjects kings. A king who is gentle and humble in heart. A king who washes our feet, forgives our sins, feeds us with his Body and Blood. A shepherd king, a servant king, bringing 'a kingdom of truth and life, a kingdom of holiness and grace, a kingdom of justice, love and truth' (Preface). A king whose only weapon is the truth, and that truth is that we are greater than we think. We're not just the random products of a blind evolutionary process. We are willed and wanted by God, created in his image and likeness, called to be the sons and daughters of the heavenly Father. We're beings with immortal souls, promised resurrection from the dead and life everlasting. We're not just citizens of a state or Scottish or Nigerian or taxpayers or on benefits or workers or students or diagnosed with cancer or divorced or miserable or happy or old or young. We may be those things: some of them fine, some not. But most of all we're children of God. We're 'a line of kings, priests to serve [our] God and Father'. We belong to a kingdom that will have no end.

Viva Cristo Rey!

I was walking back to Old Aberdeen one evening just when the football had ended and the crowds were streaming down King Street, sporting the red and white scarf: happy after a victory. Well, we support Team Christ. When we're baptized, we buy the t-shirt. We learn the songs. In many ways, that's what the early Christians meant by 'faith': allegiance to Christ, loyalty. Faith is like putting all your money on one horse. But a horse who has already won. Or it's enrolling in an army whose General has already defeated the ultimate enemies: sin and death, and is now sharing out the spoils, the loot with us—the Holy Spirit and the Eucharist. There are all sorts of powers, good and evil, legitimate and illegitimate, wise and stupid; they shape our lives. But, sooner or later, willingly or unwillingly, they all have to bend the knee to the God-man on the Cross.

Brothers and sisters, deep down we all know the real rival kingdom. It's the kingdom of 'me'. The kingdom of my own self-will, of my needs and my wants. It's a kingdom supported by a culture that privileges autonomy, that promotes my choice, my body, my end of life, my truth—half-truths that have gone wild. Brothers and sisters, there is someone who knows who I really am far better than I do, who cares for me far more than I do, who knows what my well-being really consists in. Let's choose him as king. '*Viva Cristo Rey!*'

www.ingramcontent.com/pod-product-compliance
Lightning Source LLC
Chambersburg PA
CBHW020942230426
43666CB00005B/131